AP 15 - Hand in Bib. cards

Pg 197

WRITING
Process and Purpose

ELLEN ANDREWS KNODT
The Pennsylvania State University
Ogontz Campus

Macmillan Publishing Company
New York

> *To the memory of*
> JACK DUNLAP ANDREWS
> *and the courage of*
> BETTY ANDREWS LOCKE

Macmillan Publishing Company
866 Third Avenue, New York, New York 10022

Library of Congress Cataloging in Publication Data

Knodt, Ellen Andrews.
    Writing : process and purpose.

    Includes index.
    1. English language—Rhetoric. I. Title.
PE1408.K6885 1986   808′.042   85-24135
ISBN 0-02-365340-X

Printing: 1 2 3 4 5 6 7 8   Year: 6 7 8 9 0 1 2 3 4 5

Acknowledgments: pp. 174–175, Alma Bagu, "On the Rim of Belonging," *The Center Forum,* Center for Urban Education. Reprinted by permission; pp. 59–60, Lloyd Byers, "Into the Wild Blue Yonder," February 28, 1979, Op-Ed. Copyright © 1979 by The New York Times Company. Reprinted by permission; pp. 11–12, Rachel Carson, from *Silent Spring* by Rachel Carson. Copyright © 1962 by Rachel L. Carson. Reprinted by permission of Houghton Mifflin Company; pp. 148–149, "The Death Penalty Is Right," Editorial, May 23, 1979. Copyright © 1979 by The Miami Herald. Reprinted by permission; pp. 100–102, Joan Didion, "The Santa Ana." Excerpt from "Los Angeles Notebook" in *Slouching Towards Bethlehem* by Joan Didion. Copyright © 1967, 1968 by Joan Didion. Reprinted by permission of Farrar, Straus & Giroux Inc.; pp. 106–107, René Dubos, excerpted from "Choosing Altruism" in *Beast or Angel?* Copyright © 1974 René Dubos. Reprinted with the permission of Charles Scribner's Sons; pp. 117–120, Fact File, Freshman Attitudes, 1981. Copyright 1982, The Chronicle of Higher Education. Reprinted with permission; pp. 127–129, "Frozen Breakfasts." Copyright 1980 by Consumers Union of United States, Inc., Mount Vernon, NY 10553.

(continued on p. x)

ISBN 0-02-365340-X

Preface

Writing: Process and Purpose was written with students' needs clearly in mind. First of all, students need to have some knowledge of the writing process *before* they begin to write, and they need to practice such writing techniques as getting started, finding a focus, and revising their writing before they will feel confident enough to write an essay. Chapter 1 of *Writing: Process and Purpose* introduces the writing process and provides practice in key principles before any major writing assignments are made. In this chapter students are introduced to the important issues of purpose and audience, which indeed become key points of discussions later in the text as well. Although the process is presented step-by-step, the text acknowledges the recursive nature of the writing process; to emphasize the nonlinear nature of composing, several exercises refer students back to earlier steps. In Chapter 1, students are asked to write a short paragraph both as practice and as a basis for implementing other principles, such as revising.

In addition to understanding the writing process, students need to become acquainted with major developmental and organizational strategies used to fulfill any writing assignment, whether for composition or another academic discipline. In Chapter 2, students are introduced to the strategies (or modes) used to develop an essay and to ways of organizing their writing.

They learn through exercises to see how other student writers combine strategies to accomplish purposes, and, at the end of this chapter, they write a short essay to practice the principles learned in Chapters 1 and 2.

Students also need to be able to adapt what they learn in the composition classroom to the requirements of other writing situations. This goal is more easily accomplished if it is understood that writing in college generally fulfills one of four purposes: explaining, substantiating, evaluating, and recommending. Part II (Chapters 3 to 6) examines each of these purposes with the help of student and professional essays that are approximately the length of the papers students will be writing. Discussion questions on each essay direct attention to the writers' techniques. Writing assignments for each purpose are progressively more complex so that students will grow in ability and confidence as they move through the text. To give students an even better chance to apply what they learn in composition to writing in other academic areas, several assignments are similar to those used in disciplines other than English. At the end of each major purpose, students are offered topics for writing Mastery Assignments, which permit them to demonstrate what they have learned and to increase their confidence in writing. The number of assignments and topic options for the assignments provide flexibility for instructors using the text.

Finally, many students (but not all) may need to learn to write research assignments. *Writing: Process and Purpose* presents the research assignment in an appendix, which may be used or not as individual course requirements dictate. This discussion follows the same format as Chapter 1, thereby moving the student from the beginning stages of a research assignment to the end. A full student research paper is included in this appendix.

A brief guide to usage also appears as a second appendix. Although this material should prove useful as a reminder of basic grammatical and structural principles, it is not intended to substitute for a handbook, if a handbook is normally used in a course.

Writing: Process and Purpose has been class-tested for over two years and has been evaluated by instructors and students as an effective text for improving writing ability and writing confidence.

ACKNOWLEDGMENTS

This text owes its beginnings to Richard Young at Carnegie-Mellon University, who explained the notion of structuring the text cyclically, beginning with the entire writing process and then applying it in subsequent chapters, increasing in difficulty as the book progressed. Linda Flower, Beekman Cottrell, and Robert Slack, also of Carnegie-Mellon, contributed their expertise and insight to the development of the text. My colleagues and students at Pennsylvania State University's Ogontz Campus helped me refine and test the text under actual classroom circumstances. Of these, I would particularly like to thank Ellen Furman and Leonard Mustazza for their advice. Margaret Taylor typed several drafts of the manuscript with patience and good humor. Reviewers from many institutions helped me shape the text to meet the needs of their students. I would like to thank H. Mark Reynolds, Jefferson Davis Junior College; Fay Chandler, Pasadena City College; Robert Cosgrove, Saddleback College; Sam Dragga, Texas A&M University; C. Jeriel Howard, Northeastern Illinois University; Celest A. Martin, University of Rhode Island; and Gail M. Morrison, South Carolina Commission on Higher Education.

Finally, I owe a debt I can never repay to my husband Kenneth for his love, advice, and willingness to help in so many ways.

Ellen Andrews Knodt

Contents

ACKNOWLEDGMENTS *(continued from p. ii)*

Reprinted by permission from *Consumer Reports,* October 1980; pp. 103–104, Sheldon L. Glashow, "Science Education and U.S. Technology." Reprinted with permission from *Physics Today,* Vol. 36, No. 4, pp. 9 and 81 (1983). © 1983 American Institute of Physics; pp. 16 and 17, Jane Jacobs, from *The Death and Life of Great American Cities,* by Jane Jacobs. Copyright © 1961 by Jane Jacobs. Reprinted by permissions of Random House, Inc.; pp. 130–133, Martin Luther King, Jr., "I Have a Dream." Reprinted by permission of Joan Daves. Copyright © 1963 by Martin Luther King, Jr.; pp. 61–64, Alan Lightman, "If Birds Can Fly, Why Can't I?" Reprinted by permission of *Science 83* magazine, © 1983 by the American Association for the Advancement of Science; pp. 41–42, pp. 42–44, pp. 44–46, and pp. 46–47, reprinted with permission from *Penn Statements,* Vol. 1, No. 2 (Spring 1980); pp. 97–98, Albert K. Schaaf, "Whatever Happened to Always?" *Philadelphia* magazine, November 1981, p. 234. Reprinted by permission of Albert K. Schaaf; pp. 65–67, Gail Sheehy, from *Passages,* copyright © 1974, 1976 by Gail Sheehy. Reprinted by permission of the publisher, E. P. Dutton, Inc.; pp. 140–142, Adam Smith, "The Japanese Model." Reprinted with permission from *Esquire* (October 1980). Copyright © 1980 by Esquire Associates; pp. 136–138, John Steinbeck, from *The Grapes of Wrath* by John Steinbeck. Copyright 1939, renewed © 1967 by John Steinbeck. Reprinted by permission of Viking Penguin Inc.; pp. 167–168, Gloria Steinem, "The Time Factor," from *Outrageous Acts and Everyday Rebellions* by Gloria Steinem. Copyright © 1983 by East Toledo Productions, Inc. Reprinted by permission of Holt, Rinehart & Winston, Publishers; pp. 69–70, Potter Stewart, "Inside the Supreme Court," October 1, 1979, Op-Ed. Copyright © 1979 by The New York Times Company. Reprinted by permission; pp. 170–173, Lewis Thomas, "The Technology of Medicine," from *The Lives of a Cell* by Lewis Thomas. Copyright © 1971 by Lewis Thomas. Originally appeared in the *New England Journal of Medicine.* Reprinted by permission of Viking Penguin Inc.; pp. 56–58, Barbara Tuchman, "The Black Death," from *A Distant Mirror: The Calamitous Fourteenth Century,* by Barbara W. Tuchman. Copyright © 1978 by Barbara W. Tuchman. Reprinted by permission of Alfred A. Knopf, Inc.; pp. 159–161, James W. Wickenden, "How the S.A.T.'s Are Used and Sometimes Abused." Copyright 1980 by The Chronicle of Higher Education. Reprinted by permission; pp. 94–95, Tom Wicker, "Exploding a Myth," May 10, 1983. Copyright © 1983 by The New York Times Company. Reprinted by permission; p. 50, "Who Gets the Chair?" Editorial of May 23, 1979. Copyright © 1979 by The New York Times Company. Reprinted by permission; pp. 134–135, "Outrider" by Garry Wills, copyright 1983 Universal Press Syndicate. Reprinted with permission, all rights reserved.

PART I
The Writing Process

Before we begin talking about the writing process, we need to know that some ideas we may have about writing are false.

How many of these do you believe?

1. You need to be inspired to write. You have to have a "real gift" for writing.

   False. If these first ideas were true, very few of us could write, especially on Monday mornings! Most people, teachers and professional writers included, say that good writing comes from hard work; it does not spring fully finished from the mind. There are strategies, however, that can help people to get *and* communicate ideas effectively.

   Second, the truth is that anyone can learn to write clearly—no special creative talent is necessary. Some people write better and more easily than others just as some play sports better than others, but all can benefit from lessons. If we can become better tennis players or swimmers or dancers through lessons and practice, we should also, with help, be able to learn to write better.

2. If you write a good first sentence, then all the other sentences will follow in order.

False. This idea can lead to "writer's block." Agonizing over the perfect first sentence may prevent you from ever getting any further.

Brainstorming, freewriting, asking questions, and other techniques discussed on the following pages will help conquer what one writer has called "the tyranny of the blank page." Very few writers achieve perfection with the first sentence they write.

3. All you do is follow a step-by-by procedure which includes making an outline, choosing a topic sentence, and writing down details.

    False. Actually this is a *half-false* statement. Those steps may help some people because they are attempts at planning writing, but they oversimplify the process. Writing does not proceed in a straight line; it zigzags. Writers don't just plan, and then write, and then rewrite. They plan some, try to get some words on a page, think or plan some more, write more, cross out, rephrase, plan some more, and so on. In fact, good writers are even more "recursive"; that is, they zigzag even more than do inexperienced writers.

4. You should try to impress your reader with your large vocabulary.

    False. This idea has sometimes been encouraged by teachers in an attempt to stretch their students' vocabulary. It is true that you learn words by using them, but a paper that sounds like a thesaurus is hard to read. Sometimes the words do not even fit the ideas at all, so the writing becomes confusing. You want to strive to communicate with the reader, using the clearest, most understandable words you can.

Now, let us look at *your* writing attitudes and habits. Answer the following questions. Be honest—you will be surprised at how much answers will vary.

1. When you have to write something for school or work, how do you go about it?

    a. Where do you usually write?
    b. What equipment do you need? (e.g., three sharpened pencils, yellow pad of paper, a cup of coffee, etc.)
    c. When do you start to write an assignment?
    d. Do you use an outline, write rough drafts, look up words in a dictionary?

2. What strategies have you found useful to get started writing a paper?
3. What advice have you been given in school which you have *not* found very useful?

Compare your experiences with those of your classmates by discussing writing habits in small groups. Write down two or three ideas which help some group members to write, and report these to the class.

Let us look now at some basic principles of writing and some exercises which will help you to apply them.

CHAPTER 1

Basic Principles of Writing

Recently, studies of the writing process have identified some of the techniques used by good writers which *all* writers can learn. These hints may make the difference between being uncomfortable in a writing situation and being self-confident that you can do a good job. Below is a list of these principles, but remember: you may zigzag, rather than run right through the list!

A. Think about the writing assignment or situation.

B. Get started by playing with ideas.

C. Be specific.

D. Focus your ideas.

E. Select details that fit the focus.

F. Keep the focus clear.

G. Connect related parts.

H. Write an ending.

I. Rethink, reorganize, rewrite.

A. THINK ABOUT THE WRITING ASSIGNMENT OR SITUATION

Some assignments will be very general, and you will have to figure out what to do. Others will be defined quite clearly for you. In either case, ask yourself the following questions:

What does the assignment ask you to do?
Who will read it?

Though these questions may seem obvious, many writers do not ask them and instead plunge right ahead, only to discover later that they took the wrong path.

EXERCISE 1. What is the difference between these two assignments?

  a. Identify the four reasons President McKinley gave for going to war with Spain.
  b. Which reason for going to war with Spain was the most important?

EXERCISE 2. What do each of these italicized words or phrases mean as they relate to writing situations?

  a. *Trace* the events that led to the development of the airplane.
  b. *Select one* of the following essay questions.
  c. *Evaluate* the effectiveness of John F. Kennedy as president.
  d. *Identify* each part of the circulatory system and *explain* its function.
  e. *Compare* the *major* features of English government with those of American government.
  f. *Describe* the personality and appearance of Daisy Buchanan in *The Great Gatsby*.
  g. *Summarize* the first chapter of your economics text.
  h. *Define* what psychologists mean by intelligence.

EXERCISE 3. What does each of these questions ask you to find?

  a. What was the importance of Henry Ford's introduction of the assembly line to American industry?
  b. Discuss the consequences of the Civil War.
  c. Select one objective of American labor and discuss the problems involved in achieving it. In your opinion, has the labor movement made significant progress in achieving it?

EXERCISE 4. Let's suppose that a writing situation asks you to evaluate blue jeans.

1. What difference would it make to you if you were evaluating blue jeans for a friend, your mother, a foreign student from Russia, a buyer for a discount chain like K Mart, or a buyer for a major department store like Bloomingdales or Saks Fifth Avenue?
2. What different information would you give?
3. How would your reader (or audience) change the way you write?
4. Would you use the same form of writing (letter, list, formal report, etc.) for each person on the list? Why or why not?

EXERCISE 5. Following are two invitations issued by a company to two different groups to attend the same press conference announcing a new technological development.

1. What differences are there between the two invitations?
2. How can the audience (or intended readers) account for the differences between the two invitations?

August 26, 19–

Dear News Editor:

On Thursday, September 24, we are going to announce an important discovery that may revolutionize the manufacture and use of present batteries.

The discovery is said to be the most revolutionary breakthrough in battery technology since lead acid batteries came into use a century ago. With this new technology, batteries will be much lighter, much smaller in size, and much more powerful than conventional units now in use.

XYZ Company, which is sponsoring the press conference, sees a vast array of potential uses for the new batteries. These include long-range power for electric cars, rechargeable lightweight hand tools, miniature electronics, etc. Other applications might be in the medical field, military, outer space, etc.

We'd like you to attend this conference in Suite B of the Hotel Smith on Thursday, September 24, beginning at 10:30 A.M. You will have the opportunity to hear all about the new technology, ask questions, and see a demonstration of the new batteries.

Cocktails and luncheon will follow the demonstration.

Please let us know via the enclosed self-addressed postcard whether you will join us at this important press activity.

Date: September 24, 19–
Time: 10:30 to 11:30 A.M.
Cocktails at 11:30, Lunch at noon
Place: Hotel Smith
Suite B
Park Avenue

Cordially,

Dear Life-style Editor:

Imagine the ordinary flashlight at a fraction of its size and many times more powerful. Or an electrically powered automobile that will take you to the country and back without a recharge. Or an electric lawn mower with the power stored under the seat.

This isn't science fiction. We're announcing a major breakthrough in battery technology—a discovery that will captivate your imagination and affect every area of life.

Please join us for cocktails and lunch on Thursday, September 24, when XYZ Company, a division of ABC Corporation, will preview this revolutionary battery development. You'll be given an idea of this technology's vast potential—lighter in weight, stronger in power, and nearly maintenance-free.

We look forward to seeing you. Please call to let us know whether you or another member of your staff will be able to join us.

Thursday, September 24
10:30 to 11:30 A.M.
Cocktails at 11:30
Lunch at 12:00
Hotel Smith
Suite B
Park Avenue

Sincerely,
Jane Doe
Life-style Department

RSVP: 333-1234, Ext. 100

Summary: The purpose of the assignment and the intended reader will determine, in large part, what you will say and how you will say it.

Once you have thought about the assignment, you are ready to get started.

B. GET STARTED BY PLAYING WITH IDEAS

Studies show that the most experienced writers spend a lot of time thinking about the writing assignment and playing with ideas, whereas beginning writers often plunge right in.

Let us see how techniques for getting started can help you to write more easily. None of these works for everybody all the time, but try a few of the exercises and see what happens. Some of these techniques may apply to particular writing situations. For example, the first one, freewriting, may be most helpful when you know quite a bit about a subject from personal experience. It helps to break the "logjam" of ideas in your mind. Other techniques that follow may be more helpful at directing you to find out more—that is, to ask questions that might require reading or other information gathering in order to answer them.

EXERCISE 1. *Freewriting.* The idea of this technique is to let your mind range over a subject or over any topic that comes to mind and to write down those thoughts quickly without any attempt to be complete or correct. You might call it "uncensored writing," and what it does is either help you discover what you already know about a subject or discover some new areas of interest that you may be able to develop into a paper. Usually a time limit is helpful, say 5, 10, or 15 minutes. If you really write for 10 minutes without stopping, you will be surprised at the number of words that you have written.

Try it. Write for 5 minutes on your favorite (or least favorite) place. Your instructor may collect and read several students' efforts to show how productive and individual freewriting can be.

EXERCISE 2. Another way to get started is to ask questions about your topic and jot down the answers. This technique may help you find out what you know and don't know about unfamiliar subjects.

Let us say that your psychology professor asks you to write about the influence of heredity and environment in the development of a person's personality. What questions could you ask? List some.

Let us say that you choose your own topic but can't get started. You might ask yourself questions that your *reader* would logically ask and jot down the answers.

For example, suppose that you decide to write a letter about what your college is like to a friend considering this school. Here are some questions your reader might want answered.

1. Where is it located? How close is it to a big city? What is the immediate environment?
2. How large is the campus? What facilities does it have for recreation?
3. Where do students live, on or off campus?
4. What academic programs does it offer? How good are those programs?
5. What is the student body like? Where are they from? How many students are there?

Can you think of any other questions?

EXERCISE 3. There are several other question-asking techniques which can help you to get started. One is the popular reporter's questions: Who? What? Where? When? Why? How?

Suppose that your English professor asked you to write a paper on the most unforgettable person you have ever met. What kind of information would the answers to the questions provide?

How could you turn those answers into material for a paper?

EXERCISE 4. Still another question-asking strategy asks you to examine a subject from many different angles in order to discover a perspective you may not have thought of before.

Assume that your subject is your hometown. You ask, what can I say about that? Try asking these questions:

1. Where did it come from? How did it develop?
2. What does it look like?
3. How does it compare with others like it?
4. What have other people said about it?
5. What is my feeling about it?
6. What importance does it have?
7. What would I do to change it?

Can you find a subject to write about that somehow involves your hometown? List two or three.

Would these questions work for another subject? Try them on one of these: baseball, capital punishment, your college or university, the Equal Rights Amendment, our national parks.

EXERCISE 5. Another way to get started on a subject is to take notes or make lists. If the subject can be observed, then watching and jotting down notes might be a good idea.

Assume that you have been asked to report on a place where people go to eat. Observe the number of people, the time of day, the types of people who eat there, other types of behavior, and so on.

EXERCISE 6. You may find that just talking about an assignment and your ideas on the topic will help. Talk to a friend, go to a writing center on your campus, or if your instructor agrees, discuss an idea in small groups in your class.

Sample topic: What should be the content of a brochure designed to recruit more students to your campus?

These are just a few techniques to help you think about a topic more confidently. The important idea here is to do some preliminary thinking *before* starting to write the paper. You will write more confidently and more easily and will get better results.

C. BE SPECIFIC

As you work with ideas and generate material on a subject, strive for the most specific information you can get. That way the reader will more nearly understand the subject the way *you* understand the subject. If you try to communicate your *specific* experience with *general* words, the reader will get only a fuzzy idea of what you mean.

For example, let's say that you saw a car leaving the scene of an accident. Would you tell the police you saw "a car"? Or would you say that you saw a faded-blue late-model Chevrolet with a dented left fender?

Very specific information is necessary to identify the car. That information often comes from modifiers—words added before or after the word you wish to identify. Look at some other examples of words helping to identify "car":

Shiny car
Freshly washed car
Car with one headlight

Note also that the noun "car" can be made more specific:

A blue '57 Chevy
An elegant black Cadillac
A silver Pontiac Trans Am

EXERCISE 1. Make each phrase below more specific by adding modifiers or by making the root word itself more specific. Think of a specific example of each of these that you have encountered and describe it.

  a. A man
  b. A man wearing a suit
  c. A fat lady
  d. A bus
  e. A restaurant
  f. A gas station
  g. A small child
  h. A doctor's waiting room

     i. A house
     j. A school
     k. Participation in a sport
     l. Walking down the block
    m. Drinking a soda

Being more specific is harder work than being general. You may have to observe something, interview someone, do research in the library, or try to remember the specific details of an incident that happened to you. But the results will be worth the effort. Instead of a blob or fuzzy outline, the reader will get the whole picture.

EXERCISE 2. Write down all the specific details you can about a place you know well. Make no effort at this point to write a finished paragraph; just try to capture what this place looks like, smells like, sounds like, and so on.

EXERCISE 3. Now ask yourself, what more would someone want to know about this place? Where can I be more exact so they can picture what it is like? Add additional ideas.

EXERCISE 4. Exchange your list with a classmate to see if he or she has any questions left unanswered about what this place is like.

D. FOCUS YOUR IDEAS

Though it may seem strange, after being so specific in writing details, you now need to be general! That is, you need to give your ideas a focus or controlling idea so that the reader will know what's coming, and so that he or she can make sense of all the specific details.

Sometimes the focus is provided for you by the instructor or by the nature of the assignment. For example, if you are asked on a history midterm to compare the effectiveness of George Washington and Thomas Jefferson as presidents of the United States, your focus is clearly going to be on how well each man did as president. Nevertheless, a focus statement at the beginning of your answer explaining your main point will convince your reader that you know what you are saying. Such a statement will also act as your guide to the selection of details. (A focus statement in this case might read: "Although both Washington and Jefferson accomplished certain goals as president, Jefferson is acknowledged to have been more effective.")

If you do not have a suggested focus but are working on an assignment "from scratch," you may have generated details, free-floating ideas, or bits of paragraphs which will need something to unify them. You should try to find something common to all the details which can be stated as a sentence. A reader will then be able to follow the main idea in the focus statement and the supporting details which follow.

Below are several exercises that will give you some practice (1) in moving from details to the focus statements, (2) in finding a focus statement in a model paragraph, and (3) in formulating your own focus sentences.

EXERCISE 1. What do the following groups of details have in common? Can you write a sentence which expresses that commonness? Write a focus statement which could serve to begin a paragraph about a subject described by these details.

Two hot ovens
A long, white counter
A black griddle
A refrigerator with cold drinks in it
Tubs of tomato paste, cheeses, onions, tomatoes, and green peppers
Sweaty men in white aprons stained with tomato sauce

Two tennis courts with fences around them
A large baseball diamond
A sandbox with climbing apparatus in the center and small animal statues to ride on
A tire swing on a long rope
A tire bridge strung together with twisted steel cables and stretched across a small, shallow creek
A large, open, grassy field bordered by pine, maple, and fruit trees

EXERCISE 2. Take your details from Exercise 2 in item C (the description of a place) and look at them carefully. Is there a common principle that binds them together? That is, is the place that you chose basically run-down, neat and tidy, noisy, quiet and manicured? Write a trial focus statement.

Note: Your focus does not always have to come in a statement at the beginning of the paragraph or essay, but it is convenient for the reader to see it there. Also it helps *you* keep in mind what it is you are talking about. But as long as the focus is clear throughout the piece of writing, it doesn't matter where the focus statement is or even if you have one.

EXERCISE 3. Read the following passage. What is the focus statement? Could the writer have done without it? What other purpose does it serve?

An arsenic-contaminated environment affects not only man but animals as well. A report of great interest came from Germany in 1936. In the area about Freiberg, Saxony, smelters for silver and lead poured arsenic fumes into the air, to drift out over the surrounding countryside and settle down upon the vegetation. According to Dr. Hueper horses, cows, goats, and pigs, which of course fed on this vegetation, showed loss of hair and thickening of the skin. Deer inhabiting nearby forests sometimes had abnormal pigment spots and precancerous warts. One had a definitely cancerous lesion. Both domestic and wild animals were affected by "arsenical enteritis, gastric ulcers, and cirrhosis of the liver." Sheep kept near the smelters developed cancers of the nasal sinus; at their death arsenic was found in the brain, liver, and tumors. In the area there was also "an extraordinary mortality among insects, especially bees. After rainfalls which washed the arsenical dust from the leaves and carried it along into the water of brooks and pools, a great many fish died."

Rachel L. Carson
Silent Spring

One more clue: Good focus statements often contain an attitude word which gives the reader a sense of the direction the piece will take. Note in the exercise above that Rachel Carson uses the word "contaminated," which lets the reader know that the effect arsenic has is not a positive one.

EXERCISE 4. Write a focus statement for each writing situation below, remembering to make each a complete sentence which contains the main point you are trying to "prove." An attitude word or phrase (such as "worst," "most important," "least effective") often helps to establish the point you will make. Remember to consider your audience and your purpose for writing.

a. You are asked to compare two brands of blue jeans for a student consumer group.
b. You are asked to write an essay for your political science instructor explaining your opinion of capital punishment.
c. Your boss has asked you to justify your request for a raise.
d. You are to describe one personality trait of a person you know well.
e. A friend from another school writes to ask you what you like best (or least) about the school you are attending.

E. SELECT DETAILS THAT FIT THE FOCUS

Once you have decided what your focus is to be, you need to go back to your lists, questions, freewriting, and so on, to look for the material you will use to support your main idea. This is one of the "zigs" in writing we were talking about earlier.

It may help you to think of your job as similar to that of a television crew. They go out to cover a fire, a shooting, a craft fair, or whatever the editor decides is newsworthy, and they shoot quantities of film. If you ever have been filmed by a news crew, you know they take a lot of pictures. But how much is aired at news time? Perhaps 30 seconds to 1 minute at most! What happened to all the rest? It ended up on the cutting-room floor; only the pictures needed to convey the message remained.

EXERCISE 1. Now go back to the assignment on a place and put your focus sentence at the top of the column. Then list the details which support the focus. Leave out any that do not fit the focus.

You may find that you don't have enough details to explain your focus after listing them in this way. You then have two choices: either try to find more details *or* change your focus. Yes, this may be another "zig" in the zigzag of the writing process. You may even have to do *more* freewriting or use one of the other techniques to generate more details.

Practice Writing Assignment. At this point in studying the writing process, you should write a paragraph, following what we have learned so far. There are still three principles to go, but your understanding of these will benefit from your experience of having written something.

Therefore, write a short paper that characterizes a place you know well. That is, try to describe it or explain what it is like to someone who has never seen it.

Remember the principles:

A. Think about the writing situation: What is your purpose, and who will read your writing?
B. Get started by playing with ideas.
C. Be specific.
D. Focus your ideas.
E. Select details that fit the focus.

EXERCISE 2. Exchange papers in class and discuss the success of your first efforts. As you read your classmates' papers, ask yourself the following questions:

1. Is there a focus sentence in the paper? Where?
2. Are there specific details? List some. Are there enough, or are more needed? Suggest areas where more details would help make the writer's point.
3. Does the writer stay within the main focus of the paper? If not, where does the paper go astray?
4. What suggestions for improving content can you make?

F. KEEP THE FOCUS CLEAR

It is puzzling to a reader to begin reading about one thing only to end up reading about another. That is, a writer must fulfill his or her promise to the reader by staying on the subject.

It is easy to get sidetracked because our minds jump frequently from one idea to the other, *although we can follow our own train* of thought. Since we are so close to the thoughts in our own papers and can supply all the background and all the logical connections in our minds, we sometimes write many ideas jumbled together without a clear focus—what has been called "writer-based prose." But it is quite another matter to get someone else to make the same leaps without confusion. Without a focus, our readers may well find our ideas as difficult to follow as drivers would find driving a car in a strange city without maps or road signs to help them. What we must do is make our writing "reader-based." That is, we need to help the reader by introducing one subject at a time and discussing that topic with enough specific details for the reader to understand what we want to say before going on to something else.

EXERCISE 1. Read the following student paper as an example of the kinds of logical leaps students sometimes ask readers to make. What ideas do you think the writer was trying to get us to understand?

SNAP BELIEF

I used to have the belief that to be a part of the crowd one had to do everything everybody else did. These were drinking, pulling incomparable pranks, and causing general annoyance to my parents. As the years went by my ideas of this changed almost completely to reverse.

I think my beliefs most drastically changed when I was involved in an accident that caused the loss of one eye in another person. This caused me to withdraw from my friends. I started analyzing the actions of my friends and discovered that these actions were not the keys to growing up.

Drinking does not make a teenage boy a man. It disillusions his thoughts to where he thinks he is a man. The drinking of my friends did one thing for me; it showed me who my true friends were.

Pranks that involve possibly pain or hurt to other people I am totally against. When I look back and see how my friend could have lost his life instead of his eye, I began to wonder that maybe those harmless pranks we always pulled might have developed into something more serious.

The bother I may have caused my parents I saw in the way they worried about my brother. My brother has had ulcers through a third of his life, and in some cases they have threatened his life. He thought it was fun to drink and would get deathly sick from it. I knew how it bothered my parents so I swore that I would never cause my parents any hardship.

The most important thing that was brought about by my change in belief was that I became able to halfway analyze people. I would do this by looking for one important characteristic, maturity.

1. Try to write a clear focus sentence for this paper.
2. What details from the paper fit your focus sentence?
3. Make a rough outline of the points you would use.
4. What material would you leave out of the original paper?
5. What details would you add?

G. CONNECT RELATED PARTS

Sentence to sentence, idea to idea, paragraph to paragraph. This is another technique which helps your reader to follow *your* train of thought. You must connect.

Some of you may have learned the word "transition," which means moving from one thing to another. Transitions are like bridges between the gaps of ideas. If you can give your readers a bridge to cross, they will understand where they have just been, where they are going, and how they got from one to the other.

One way to connect ideas is to repeat the same words or use synonyms to reinforce the ideas.

EXERCISE 1. Read the following passage and underline words which are repeated or are synonyms for the same words.

CITIES NEED OLD BUILDINGS
JANE JACOBS

Cities need old buildings so badly it is probably impossible for vigorous streets and districts to grow without them. By old buildings I mean not museum-piece old buildings, not old buildings in an excellent and expensive state of rehabilitation—although these make fine ingredients—but also a good lot of plain, ordinary, low-value old buildings, including some run-down old buildings.

Another way to link the ideas is to use words which specifically point to certain relationships.

Pronouns, for example, are words which "knit" together a paragraph. Their function, like that of synonyms, is to link ideas together without the monotony of simply repeating the same words. Look for the personal pronouns (I, me, she, him, etc.) and the impersonal pronouns (someone, anyone, each, many, etc.) in the passages above and below.

Each of the following words also serves to connect one idea to another or to refer the reader back to an earlier idea:

Adding	*Causing*	*Time*	*Contrasting*
also	because	first	however
and	therefore	afterward	yet
moreover	subsequently	meanwhile	but
next	as a result	then	on the contrary
in addition	for	until	although
	so		nor
	since		

Comparing	*Summarizing*	*Explaining*
similarly	in short	for example
or	on the whole	that is
	in other words	in fact
		to illustrate

There are many others in the language, but these will serve to alert you to their function—linking things together.

EXERCISE 2. Read the following passage and underline all the repetitions and circle the words which link ideas. Note how many the writer uses to make sure her reader understands her.

THE USES OF SIDEWALKS: SAFETY
JANE JACOBS

This is something everyone already knows: A well-used city street is apt to be a safe street. A deserted city street is apt to be unsafe. But how does this work, really? And what makes a city street well used or shunned? . . .

A city street equipped to handle strangers, and to make a safety asset, in itself, out of the presence of strangers, as the streets of successful city neighborhoods always do, must have three main qualities:

First, there must be a clear demarcation between what is public space and what is private space. Public and private spaces cannot ooze into each other as they do typically in suburban settings or in projects.

Second, there must be eyes upon the street, eyes belonging to those we might call the natural proprietors of the street. The buildings on a street equipped to handle strangers and to insure the safety of both residents and strangers, must be oriented to the street. They cannot turn their backs or blank sides on it and leave it blind.

And third, the sidewalk must have users on it fairly continuously, both to add to the number of effective eyes on the street and to induce the people in buildings along the street to watch the sidewalks in sufficient numbers. Nobody enjoys sitting on a stoop or looking out a window at an empty street. Almost nobody does such a thing. Large numbers of people entertain themselves, off and on, by watching street activity.

In settlements that are smaller and simpler than big cities, controls on acceptable public behavior, if not on crime, seem to operate with greater or lesser success through a web of reputation, gossip, approval, disapproval and sanctions, all of which are powerful if people know each other and word travels. But a city's streets, which must control not only the behavior of the people of the city but also of visitors from suburbs and towns who want to have a big time away from the gossip and sanctions at home, have to operate by more direct, straightforward methods. It is a wonder cities have solved such an inherently difficult problem at all. And yet in many streets they do it magnificently.

EXERCISE 3. Underline repetitions and circle transitions in your paper about a place.

H. WRITE AN ENDING

Your readers appreciate knowing that your paragraph or essay had ended, and if your essay is long, like a term paper or report, they may also appreciate a summary of main points. Remember that the last thing the reader sees is your ending, so that it is your last chance to get your ideas across.

There are several kinds of endings, depending on what your essay is about. You may wish to restate your main idea or focus, summarize the main points or pieces of evidence, explain the significance or importance or implications of your ideas, or tell a story or anecdote that illustrates what you have been discussing.

EXERCISE 1. Look at your paper about a place. How could you end it?

I. RETHINK, REORGANIZE, REWRITE

This principle is important all the way through the writing process, not just at the end. As you have already discovered, you have probably gone back to take a look at notes or observations, reobserved, written some more, revised that writing, and so on. As was mentioned before, studies show that more experienced writers are even *more* recursive (that is, they zigzag more) than are beginning writers. That idea runs against our common feeling that experts get it "right" the first time. They don't. They work and polish and write things many times before they are satisfied. And the changes they make are often substantial ones—changing a focus entirely to make a point clear to a specific audience or restructuring paragraphs for greater emphasis on a point. We often associate revising with just proofreading, that is, looking for spelling and punctuation mistakes. That is a part of the process, but only a part.

EXERCISE 1. To illustrate the need for rethinking, read this passage from a student's final history examination on the Hundred Years' War. Even if you don't know the subject, what changes could you make to improve the passage?

The internal problems of peasant revolts and taxation with economic unrest, and famines, led to the ending of this war because both sides were weak and poor by now and it was a last ditch effort to a point, and the French had the upper hand. British lost all their possessions in France except Calais, which they lost later.

How do you go about rethinking? That is, what strategies are useful in getting a writer to evaluate his writing?

EXERCISE 2. One effective strategy is to write down what you are trying to do in a paper. What point are you trying to make? What idea do you wish the reader to understand? Write such a statement for your paper on a place.

EXERCISE 3. Now give this statement and your paper to a friend or classmate to read. Ask him or her if the purpose you were trying to achieve has been accomplished. Get suggestions from him or her on how you might more fully realize your goals.

Another aspect of revising is reorganizing—that is, putting ideas into effectively arranged sentences and paragraphs.

Reorganizing involves fulfilling your promise to the reader. Readers come to expect to see certain things in what they read. If a paper starts out by saying, "There are three reasons for expanding the parking lots on campus," the reader expects to read a discussion of the three reasons. If the paper says that determination in sports is just as important as ability, the reader will expect a discussion of determination and how it relates to ability in the success of certain athletes. And no reader wants to get halfway through a recipe to discover that a step has been left out or an ingredient missed.

A clear focus statement can help you keep your promise to the reader. While it is true that not all good writers have the focus statement at the beginning of every paragraph, it is also true that the clear statement of a main idea can help you stick to an issue and help your reader to follow your thinking.

EXERCISE 4. Read your paragraph about a place again. What does it say that you will be talking about? If it is fuzzy, try to make it clear.

Next, check the rest of the paragraph against the focus sentence. Does it develop the main point that you wish the reader to understand? Try not to let the mind's natural tendency to ramble influence your writing. Keep to the point.

Are there signposts to help the reader along the way? The use of "first," "second," "finally," "on the other hand," and other transitions helps readers to follow your logic.

Do you give the reader enough to go on? Is there enough evidence to convince him of the truth of your remarks? If you explain how stingy your Uncle Fred is, you need to make the reader "see" his stinginess by revealing

Uncle Fred's habit of putting used tea bags in the refrigerator for later use. Don't expect the reader to agree with you automatically; most people take a "show me" attitude. This fact is especially important on essay tests where the instructor wants to see the extent of your knowledge and how well you can use it.

Can you add more evidence or detail to your paper on a place?

If you rethink and reorganize, you will be rewriting to accommodate your new thoughts and new patterns of organization. Proofreading is the last step in this process, not, as many believe, the first. Proofreading is difficult for some students because they read the papers in their heads as they think they have written them rather than the actual words on the page as the reader will read them. Here are some strategies to help you proofread:

Strategy 1:   Read your writing out loud to yourself or someone else to *hear* the way the sentences sound.

Strategy 2:   Type your work. The way something appears in print often reveals sentences that are too short or too long, that are incorrectly punctuated, or that have some other problem. The people who advertise Smith-Corona are right! Typing does improve writing!

Strategy 3:   Read your paper backward; that is, read the last sentence first and so on. That will allow you to check each sentence without mentally filling in missing words.

Strategy 4:   Give yourself some time between writing a final draft and turning in a final copy. The delay will help you to see the paper from a fresh perspective and may help your rethinking and reorganizing efforts as well as your proofreading.

Figure 1.1 is a rough draft of a student paper about a place, with comments by the writer and by other students in the class suggesting areas for revision. Next you will see the paper after it has been substantially revised (Figure 1.2).

Figure 1.1
Rough Draft
Seaview Hotel

The Seaview Hotel was torn down during the

winter of 1980 after eighty years of service in

order to make room for twenty-four new motel

units. In her time the grand old hotel was a

Does this beginning provide the focus you want?

good details

high-class place, with strong white pillars
guarding the entrance, and crystal chandeliers
hanging in the dining room. Shiny maple
banisters ran four flights of stairs, which
were connected at each floor by hand-carved
posts. In the lobby, a high wooden desk
supported various signs: "Check-in 11:00 a.m.,"
"Quiet after 10:00 p.m.," "No smoking," and
there is a bell for service that was always
overworked. In the dining room large Persian
rugs were spread out on the floor, and
colored glass beads stretched the length of
the windows from ceiling to floor. During the
last two years of service the Seaview showed
signs of old age because of neglect from the
owners. Instead of a family resort hotel, the

need Transition

need more accurate word

Seaview was transformed into a cheap party

need more accurate word

house for kids who further <u>decimated</u> the once
<u>nostalgic</u> place. The front porch slanted down
to the right side of the hotel, where it was
being supported by a few stacked cinder blocks,
and a group of bushes on that side had become

good physical description

a target for empty beer cans. The ceiling of
the lobby contained water stains and fallen
plaster resulted from a stopped-up toilet
in the first floor bathroom that worked only

when the handle was held down for a long period
of time. The Coke machine in the corner of
the lobby would only take quarters and a good
swift kick to the side before producing a
dusty old bottle of soft drink. The ice
machine required service on a regular basis
because it spewed out huge chunks of ice
instead of making small cubes. At least half
of the fifty rooms had holes in their screens
big enough for birds and insects to get through.
Today, all signs of the hotel have been erased
except for an occasional reservation sent in by
some old couple who managed to save a rate
schedule from the 1930s.

Student's comments:

I wanted readers to see the hotel the way I saw it when
it was still nice, and after it had fallen apart. I think some
of that came through pretty well. But I need to make it clearer
from the beginning what I am trying to do and not focus on the
fact that the hotel is no longer there.

Figure 1.2
Second Draft
Seaview Hotel

I remember the Seaview Hotel as a high-class place, with
strong white pillars guarding the entrance and shiny maple

banisters which ran four flights of stairs connected on each floor by hand-carved posts. The dining room featured crystal chandeliers and Persian rugs, and colored glass beads stretched the length of the windows from ceiling to floor. In the lobby, an eighty-year-old wooden desk held signs that said "No smoking" and "Quiet after 10:00 p.m." Two years ago, the grand old hotel showed signs of the neglect of its new owners. Instead of the family resort it had been, it became a cheap party house for groups of kids on Senior Week orgies. Everywhere I looked, the hotel seemed to be falling apart. The front porch slanted down to the right side of the hotel, where it was being supported by a few stacked cinder blocks, and a group of bushes on that side had become a target for empty beer cans. The ceiling of the lobby was water stained, and fallen plaster resulted from a stopped-up toilet in the bathroom on the first floor. The Coke machine in the corner of the lobby would take only quarters and a good kick to the side before producing a dusty old bottle of soda. And the ice machine regularly spewed out huge chunks of ice instead of small cubes. The rooms were neglected too. At least half of the fifty rooms had holes in their screens big enough for insects and even birds to get through. The Seaview had become so decayed that when I heard it was to be torn down to make room for a modern motel, I was both sad and relieved. Restoring it to its former beauty would have been better, but tearing it down was better than watching its continuing decay.

Figure 1.3 is a longer student paper on a place. Note that the longer paper begins with an introduction, which sets the scene for the paper and prepares the audience for the announcement of the topic. Make comments in the margin about what you find effective and what you would tell a fellow classmate to change. Look for changes in emphasis or even contradictions. Does the ending fit the rest of the paper?

Figure 1.3
Muir Woods

From the ferry boat, in San Francisco Bay, you can see tall buildings and pavement in the city; but across the bay, there is a place, called Muir Woods, which still remains untouched by man. Last summer I visited many different areas in and around San Francisco, but for me Muir Woods was the most impressive.

Redwood trees are native to northern California. The timber of the redwood is valued for its lightness, strength, and resistance to decay. Because of its value, the redwood has come close to extinction. Therefore, in 1968, Congress declared Muir Woods a national park.

The forest is located across the bay from San Francisco, in a small town called Salsaulito. Muir Woods is at the very top of a very tall mountain. To get there, you must travel up a long and dusty road which winds and circles around the mountain. The road itself is very dangerous because it is very narrow, with barely enough room for two cars. In fact, if you glance down several hundred feet, you will see a group of wrecked cars to prove it.

What I found so interesting and unique about Muir Woods is not only the forest itself, but the drive up there. Along the mountain can be found three different growth areas. At the base of the mountain, you can see shades of yellow, green, and brown grass, blowing in the wind. Here, the air is hot, the sun is brilliant, and the grass grows tall and dry. The second area that you drive through is a tiny section of eucalyptus trees growing along the road. The third section, of course, is the forest of redwood trees, in which you find Muir Woods.

Muir Woods resembles a jungle rain forest. The air is damp and misty, and the leaves of redwood trees are always coated with water droplets. This is because of the dense fog which continually descends from the surrounding mountains and into the bay.

restatement

The first time I went to Muir Woods, I couldn't believe my eyes. The sun was gleaming down through the redwoods which stood over two-hundred feet tall and twenty feet in diameter. I felt like an ant in comparison to those tall, red trees towering above me. Below, the soil is soft and moist. It is also red.

There are various paths which you can choose. Some go up along hills; some slope down. Alongside the main path, there is a stream which flows and breaks off into the tiny tributaries which accompany the other paths.

Although there are many tourists and joggers all about,

the only sound you can hear is the rolling and brushing of the stream. It's almost as if the air is taking in all of the sound for itself. The atmosphere is so peaceful and serene that you can walk for hours and be unaware of the passing of time. The only thing that you see are the beautiful reds and greens of the trees; the only thing you feel is overwhelming calmness.

Muir Woods allowed me to see what nature really is. Because Muir Woods has no trash, no concrete, and no pollution, I feel it is one of the few paradises left on the Earth.

Figure 1.4 shows another student paper written in "street" slang. What is effective about the language and details? What changes would you suggest?

Figure 1.4
Aunt Janie's

Finally, I was going to enjoy some real fun. According to my late Grandpop Nat, the supposedly exciting big city and its honky-tonk bars, lit with the knock-out smell of Thunderbird, strong enough to make Ray Charles see three lone men dance the funky-chicken to the "Star Spangled Banner"; and the sound of local yokels holding up the corner singing "do-wop" music to the sound of the taps on their Vaseline-shined roach killers wasn't nothing compared to Saturday night downtown at Aunt Janie's. Aunt Janie's, located in Grandpop's hometown of Maysville, South Carolina, was a restaurant, grocery store, and post office during the week, but on Saturday night it was the party place for everyone in town. And there I was,

big-time city teeny-bopper, anxiously waiting to be captured
by the "Good Time Fairy" of the country.

It did not take long for me to realize why everyone chose
to be entertained at Aunt Janie's--it was the only source of
entertainment in the old hick town. Anyone who was anyone came
downtown to enjoy the foot-tapping, head-shaking sounds of the
jukebox, which operated automatically by the kick of Mr. Ned's
size 14EE "baby coffins." Even Miss Alice, the town old maid,
took the night off from chasing stray, dirty, and hungry mutts
to enjoy the fresh air of two-for-a-nickel cigars smoked by the
gray, stray, dirty, and love-hungry old men chasing her.
Not even J. J. Johnson racing about in his chalk-white orthopedic
shoes or Ol' Lady Taylor searching for her "eyes," which she
left on her bureau, cared that the grease which sizzled Aunt
Janie's famous trout sandwiches was as old as Christmas.

It was ironic for this place to leave me with a sense of
comfort and enjoyment, because in all truthfulness it was the
filthiest place I ever saw, except a seafood joint in
Baltimore thrice condemned for violations of every sanitary
code in the books. The license and inspection people would
go crazy in that place. There was no running water inside
the place, although there was a pump just outside with a
rusty handle and faucet. The lack of inside lavatory facilities
accounted for the distinctive aroma in the rear left corner,
nearest to the back door which led to the outhouse several
feet away. In the back right-hand corner--the post office by

day--was the only part of the room which had linoleum laid down on the otherwise sawdust-covered floor. The three renovated barn stalls converted to eating booths were always filled to capacity as the Saturday night jammy continued.

As I called it a night and walked out of Aunt Janie's, I slowly began to realize that Grandpop was right--I had been missing the real fun of life. The box played on, and Mr. Ned continued to kick it off. But the good old sounds and familiar spots of the city were good enough for me.

CHAPTER 2

Strategies for Writing

THE FOUR BASIC PURPOSES IN WRITING

People write for many reasons and to achieve many goals. Some may write only for themselves (in diaries); some may write for thousands (magazine and newspaper writers, speech writers, novelists). But most writing that is done in academic or business life can be understood as fulfilling one of four purposes. Each is described briefly below and will be discussed more fully with examples later in the text.

Purpose I. Writing to Inform: *Explaining.* To explain an idea to someone, to define a word or term, to report evidence (facts), to inform.

Purpose II. Writing to Support a Point: *Substantiating.* To show that a conclusion you have drawn about a subject is valid; to "prove" that your opinion is "correct."

Purpose III. Writing to Judge: *Evaluating.* To judge something as good or bad according to clearly stated standards or criteria.

Purpose IV. Writing to Persuade: *Recommending.* To persuade someone to do something or think about a subject in a different way. To give your advice about an opinion or course of action.

DEVELOPMENT STRATEGIES TO ACHIEVE YOUR PURPOSE

Writers have many ways to develop ideas to achieve their purposes in writing. A single strategy may be used to develop one paragraph or a whole essay, but most frequently strategies are combined to achieve the writer's purpose. What follows is a list of common strategies for developing ideas and some suggestions for organizing your thoughts when using these strategies.

1. Narration

Writers use narration to tell a story, either to illustrate some point they wish to make or perhaps to gain the reader's interest before moving into a more complicated explanation. For example, you could tell the story of being frightened by a menacing German shepherd to explain your fear of all dogs. Or as the writer of "Killer of the Unprepared" (p. 41) does, you can use a story as an introduction to a longer essay.

Narration is usually organized chronologically, beginning when the incident started and ending when it ended, but breaks or flashbacks (going back to a previous time) may occur. Though most student writers are quite comfortable with narration because it may be familiar to them from past writing experiences, there are some guidelines to observe. If you have ever sat next to a gossipy person on a bus who told you his or her life story, you are aware that knowing when to start and stop your tale is necessary to keep the reader's attention. You can't include every small detail of the incident (what everyone was wearing, who the relatives of all the participants are, what everyone had for lunch) unless those details are relevant to the point you are making. On the other hand, your wish to involve the reader in your story requires specific details that will enable the reader to picture the incident as you are telling it.

A narrative strategy may begin with the point you wish to make, followed by the story, or it may simply begin with the incident and then conclude with the overall focus. Examples of both of these patterns may be found in the student writing presented later in this chapter.

2. Process Analysis

When a writer needs to explain how to do something (such as change a tire) or how something works (such as how the heart pumps blood to the body), she needs to use this strategy.

Like narration, process analysis is organized chronologically so that the reader can follow the steps of the procedure.

Knowing who will read the process analysis is very important in preparing to write the paper because the writer must suit the material to the audience's experience and needs. For example, explaining how the heart works to sixth graders would be quite different from explaining its workings to a group of medical students.

A writer of process analysis must also be complete. Have you ever tried to follow directions to someone's house only to find out that a fork in the road has been left out, and you do not know which way to turn?

If you expect a reader to follow the steps of a procedure, you must be sure to give *all* the steps. Furthermore, make sure that the steps are in order. It does no good to tell someone after he has poured the batter in a pan that the pan should have been greased and floured first. Careful attention to transitions ("first," "next," "another step," "finally") will help the reader understand the procedure.

Finally, anticipate the problems that might prevent your reader from understanding the process. Define any unfamiliar terms either to begin with or as you go along. If this is a how-to-do-it process, tell the reader what materials she needs to get started and anything she should be sure *not* to do (such as removing the oil filter from her car without first putting a bucket under it!).

Organizing by process is usually quite straightforward, but there are some options you may wish to consider. If this is a how-to-do-it paper, you may want to explain why learning this process is beneficial to the reader and what makes you qualified to teach it. If this is a how-something-works paper, you may want to give your readers some reasons for their needing to understand the procedure.

3. Examples

This strategy is commonly used in answers to essay examination questions. The writer makes a statement and then backs it up with specific references to the text or notes given in lecture. For example, if a student were asked to respond to the statement that the slave Jim is the most consistently moral character in *Huckleberry Finn,* she could cite several examples of Jim's putting others before himself, including standing Huck's watch for him and helping the doctor take care of Tom after he was shot, though it meant Jim's recapture. In an essay exam the student tries to provide many examples to show the instructor the depth of her knowledge.

In other writing situations, examples are used to illustrate a point so that the reader will understand it. Therefore, it is important to choose examples which clarify, not obscure an idea, and those which a reader can readily understand. A writer may use an extended example or several shorter ones; usually the most important one of the series goes last for emphasis.

This strategy is frequently combined with others because if you are comparing two things, examples of their similarity are important to show. Or if you are defining a word, examples of situations in which the word applies may become part of the definition. The use of examples may be found in just about any piece of writing.

4. Comparison and Contrast

This strategy is used to find similarities or differences between two subjects. We use it all the time in everyday life to decide which cereal, toothpaste, or soap to buy. Students are frequently asked to compare two American presidents, or psychological theories, or characters in a novel. It is important to compare or contrast things which are comparable—you could not compare automobiles with musical instruments very easily. It is also important to impose order on the details of the comparison, or the reader may become confused as to which subject you are discussing. Suppose that you wish to compare two colleges in order to decide which you want to attend. You decide that you will investigate the size, location, academic programs, and tuition for each one. Once you have compiled the data, you can organize the material in one of two ways:

Option 1. The Whole Method.   Write a general focus statement that introduces the subject of the two colleges. Then discuss everything about College *X* first, including size, location, academic programs, and tuition. Next provide a transition and discuss College *Y,* including (*in order*) size, location, academic programs, and tuition. Conclude by pointing out the most important similarities or differences that made you decide to choose College *X* or *Y.* (Usually the last one you discuss will be the one you favor.)

Option 2. The Alternating Method.   Write a general focus statement. Then discuss the size of College *X* followed by that of College *Y.* Next discuss the location of College *X* and then that of College *Y.* Third, discuss the academic programs at College *X* followed by those at College *Y.* Fourth, discuss the tuition for College *X* and then that for College *Y.* Conclude by summing up the best points of one of the colleges.

How do you know which option to choose? Each has advantages and disadvantages. The whole method is useful if you wish the reader to get an overall view of each subject (say two professors), but you aren't concerned with the reader's remembering each small detail. On the other hand, if you have a technical subject and are concerned with comparing subjects in a detailed way (say, machine tolerances to the 0.001 inch), then the alternating method is the option of choice. Otherwise, your reader will be hopelessly lost trying to remember technical details presented through the whole method. The disadvantage in alternating subjects is that the paragraph can become singsong (first this, then that; then this, then that). The remedy for this problem is to use clever transitions and vary the beginning of the sentences so they don't all sound alike. See the student essay "Football vs. Swimming" (p. 46) as an example of the alternating method and "The Park" (p. 44) as an example of the whole method.

Sometimes you don't need to give "equal time" to both halves of the comparison–contrast. If your reader is well acquainted with one subject (say, American football), then you could briefly mention the qualities of that subject in an introductory paragraph and spend the rest of the paper discussing the more unfamiliar subject (say, British rugby).

5. Analogy

If a writer decides to explain something unfamiliar to an audience in terms of something familiar, she is using an analogy. Analogy is a comparison made between two unlike objects which nevertheless may help make a reader understand an idea better. For example, the workings of the eye may be explained by comparing the eye to a camera. The writer shows how the camera takes a picture and then by comparison how the eye sees. The usefulness of this technique depends on the reader's already understanding the function of the camera. Otherwise, the writer will be explaining two complicated processes. But if a reader already has a knowledge of one, the other subject will be made clearer by the comparison. This strategy is best used to explain a difficult subject in terms people can more readily understand. Doctors use analogies to explain complicated disease processes to patients; for example, arteriosclerosis could be explained as "clogged pipes." Political analysts may explain political strategy in terms of games. What an analogy cannot do is prove anything; it is not evidence, only explanation.

The analogy is usually clearly announced to the reader: "Perhaps understanding how the eye works will be easier if we compare it to a camera taking a picture." The rest of the paragraph then follows, alternating the unfamiliar with the familiar.

6.   Analysis by Classification or Division

These strategies are ways of imposing order on chaos. Imagine a super-market where everything on the shelves was placed randomly without some logical order! If all the soup were not in one place and cereals in another, it would take us hours to do the shopping. Therefore, we impose order by classifying items in logical groups. If you are faced with writing a paper on a large unwieldy topic, such as television programs, you will probably want to narrow it, and one way to do that is to try to classify television programs according to type. There are, for example, morning programs, afternoon pro-grams, and prime-time programs. Another classification would be network and cable programs. Still another would group programs into content types: detective shows, sitcoms, soap operas, made-for-television movies, game shows, and so on. There are several classification schemes that can provide the basis for an analysis of a subject. What is important is not to mix schemes, such as morning programs and detective shows. Also, all the categories should make up the whole subject.

Once a writer has decided which way to classify the groups in a subject area, she then may describe them, compare them, and give examples of them. See the student esay "Bonanza!" (p. 42) for an example of classifi-cation.

A division strategy imposes order by dissecting a subject and looking at its component parts, much the way you dissected a frog or cat in biology class. The need for division occurs in technical subjects where an object or a part needs to be analyzed for defects or function or whatever. But other topics may also lend themselves to this strategy: What are the typical plot components of horror movies or what are the various offices and duties of a college administrator? Once a writer has divided a subject into its com-ponents, the rest of the essay might define each part's role in the whole, explain the process by which the parts work, or describe each part sepa-rately.

7.   Description

This strategy commonly becomes a part of every piece of writing. It in-volves giving the physical characteristics of a subject, such as color, shape, or size, as in describing what a room looks like or describing the physical appearance of a person. Description may also attempt to capture feelings, such as the peacefulness of walking along an empty beach or the distaste you may feel for your loud Uncle Fred.

Good description relies on the quality of specific details. As we discussed in Chapter 1, the good specific detail depends on observation and thought. Certainly the reader gets more out of a description of a corner drugstore which says, "The grayish sunlight streaming in the dust-covered, fingerprinted windows reveals chipped wooden shelves lining the walls of the tiny store" instead of "The light coming through the window shows lines of shelves on the walls."

A whole paragraph developed by description usually seeks to create a dominant impression in the reader's mind, that is, a basic idea of what the subject is like. Such paragraphs often begin with a focus sentence and then follow with details carefully chosen to create the impression desired. Details are usually organized according to distance (near to far, top to toe, right to left) or according to importance (least important to most important).

8. Definition

This strategy, too, can become part of a paragraph or be the cornerstone for developing a paragraph by itself. Writers frequently must explain the meaning of a term to a reader who is unfamiliar with the word. Sometimes the writer can provide just a synonym for the word, such as the substitution of "treasure hunting" for "coin shooting" in the student paper "Bonanza." Other times a dictionary definition may be needed which explains the word in relation to other similar words. Still other circumstances demand a more extensive discussion. These longer definitions may include one or more of these ideas:

a. The historical background of the word, showing where or when it originated and how it developed its present meaning
b. The word's use by certain groups in society and values or attitudes attached to it (What is a "wimp?")
c. What the word does *not* mean (A *true* friend does *not* lie)
d. A comparison or contrast of the word with other related terms
e. A narrative illustrating the word's meaning (for example, how you first learned what "hot" meant)
f. An explanation of a process that the word entails (What is photosynthesis?)
g. Use of analogy to define a word
h. Examples of the word's use in certain situations

In fact, there are many possible ways to define a word or term which use the strategies already discussed.

9. Cause and Effect

Human beings like to know why something happened, or given its oc-
currence, what consequence or effect resulted from the cause. To be effective, this strategy depends on good reasoning. The writer must be careful
to look at *all* possible causes and not jump to hasty conclusions. Supersti-
tions are often based on faulty assumptions of cause and effect. Does spill-
ing salt really *cause* bad luck, or is there some other more logical cause?
Sometimes, too, there may be both an immediate cause and a more fundamental but remote cause (a divorce, for example, may be caused by one
mate's infidelity, but a more fundamental cause may be the unfaithful
mate's midlife crisis and fear of aging). The writer should try to gather
evidence to support his assertions about causes, so that readers will not
simply have to take his word for it.

In a paragraph, a writer may begin with a cause (if known and easy to
substantiate, such as a traffic accident) and then detail the effects that were
the result of the accident (personal injury, possibly a trial, etc.) Or a writer
may begin with an effect (a mysterious death) and search for a cause or
causes, attempting to reach a conclusion. The writer must be aware that
sometimes cause and effect create a chain, with one thing leading to another
(tripping over a loose brick caused a person to fall, which in turn caused
a back injury, which in turn caused him to miss work, which in turn . . .).

Identifying Developmental Strategies in Student Essays

The following student paragraphs provide examples of these strategies.
Read each one and identify the strategy or strategies used.

1.

At first meeting, Bruce and Brian seem like exact copies of each other. On
the surface they are very much the same. However, as you get to know them,
they are really strikingly different.

Bruce and Brian are identical twins. When they were younger, their parents
dressed them exactly alike. No one could tell them apart. Both of them have
always loved the shore, and much of their lives has seemed to revolve around
it. They are both lifeguards for Long Beach Township. Also both are very good
surfers. At their winter home they are nicknamed the "barnacle boys." Aside
from surfing, they also love to snow ski and have become good enough to be
called experts.

However, once you get to know them, they seem so different that it is hard
to believe someone could even mistake one for the other. Brian likes sailboats,
distance running, and chemistry. Bruce, on the other hand, won't even leave

the dock on a boat unless it has power other than the wind. He hates running but loves swimming. And in school, he's as far from a chemistry major as you can get. He is an English major. . . .

2.

The ball stayed aloft endlessly, as if the many pairs of eyes fixed on it held it in this position. Then, as if through a time warp, gravity forced the slow descent of the ball. As time stood still, a stray hand stretched and strained in its vain attempt to swat the white sphere back into the air where, had it been properly hit, it would float for a few more eternal seconds awaiting a new flight. As it was, the hand, followed by the rest of the body, crashed to the floor and came to rest less than a foot from where the ball hit the floor with a hollow "thud." The gym took a breath and within a fraction of a second, a thundering roar filled the room. . . .

3.

The weeks before a concert are filled with excitement and endless questions: Who else is going? Whom should I go with? What should I wear? Which seats should I try to get? The night of the concert people are scattered about, fighting for parking spaces, having tailgate parties, scalping tickets, and dodging pushy salesmen who keep shoving programs and T-shirts under their noses. Inside there is loud music and general euphoria.

A concert event probably means something special to each person who attends, but I think people who attend concerts generally fit into four different categories: floaters, hangers-on, status seekers, and ardent admirers. . . .

4.

The art of making pottery is called ceramics. Most people think of ceramics as an elaborate, painstaking process that only professionals can do. Actually, there are techniques that enable anyone to participate in this craft. One technique is by using the coil method. Consider the process of making a simple vase as your first project.

First, you need to go to a pottery outlet or craft supply store to gather the materials you might not already have. . . .

Next, you should set up a place to work. . . .

5.

"A car is a machine; you should respect it, or it will get the best of you and possibly kill you," my father once said, long before I received my driver's license. I knew my father was right, for he was an ex-race car driver and learned the lesson from the many accidents he had. Yet for some reason, I never paid much attention to his little saying, and one night, I learned the lesson for myself.

It was a very dark night with a slight drizzle falling from the sky. I had just had a quarrel with my girlfriend and was driving a little frantically on the way home. Waiting at the intersection that is about 10 minutes from my house, I could see that the clock on the dash of my dad's beautiful light blue Grand Torino Sport read 10:50. When the light turned green, I took off like a flash with the tires spinning on the wet pavement. The next cross street was Keep Run Road, the road on which I live.

The speedometer read forty miles per hour as I entered the dreadful L-shaped turn. Knowing I was going too fast for conditions, I applied the brakes through the sharp right-hand turn, and the rear of the car skidded to the left. As I tried to correct and gain control of the car, I oversteered, and the rear of the car skidded to the right, just touching the grass on the right side of the road. The tires caught grip of the pavement, sending the car diagonally across the road toward a tree. I had just enough time to brace myself; my eyes were glued on the approaching tree. In what seemed a fraction of a second, the impact occurred, sending my knees through the lower section of the dashboard, and snapping my head into the windshield. I felt a trickle of blood running down my forehead and heard sizzling noises under the hood. I ran as far as I could from the car, thinking it was going to blow up, and looked at what I had done.

With only a cut on my head, I felt okay, but the car was in even worse condition than I suspected. The front portion of the car was badly mangled, with the dented hood sticking straight in the air and the indentation of the tree forced back to the engine. The windshield looked like a spider web where the impact of my head had occurred, and the fenders were bent back to the wheels.

My knees were shaking as I walked to the nearest house and knocked on the door. An older woman answered the door and asked if I was all right; I didn't answer and just asked if I could use her phone. "I was in an accident; I wrecked our car; it's totaled," I said to my mom through my tears over the phone. She asked if I was all right and where I was and told me she would be right there. The tow truck arrived shortly after my parents and carted the mangled piece of machinery away. After speaking to the police, my parents drove me home and tried to comfort me by saying they understood what I was going through and that I would be all right.

As I lay down to sleep that night, tears formed in my eyes as the accident flashed through my mind in slow motion. I thought about my father's little saying, and then realized he was right, for I had just learned my lesson. I drove too hard, too fast, and did not respect the car, and it got the best of me. To this day, I have not come close to having another car accident.

6.

Animation is the art of bringing movement to a series of inanimate objects. Animation could be something as simple as the self-made cartoons of stick figures on the corners of notebook pages to Walt Disney classics such as *Fantasia*. To bring a cartoon to life is a very long and tedious job. After the characters and script are established, the sound track is formed. This consists of the characters' voices, the sound effects, and the music score. Now the tough part begins. The animators start drawing the pictures, which are called cels. . . .

7.

Bernoulli's principle is a fundamental principle in fluid mechanics. The law states that the higher the speed of a flowing fluid or gas, the lower the pressure. As the speed decreases, the pressure increases. Named for Daniel Bernoulli (1700–1782), Bernoulli's principle has many applications in everyday life that may not seem evident.

The lift of an airplane wing is a prime example of Bernoulli's principle. The airplane wing is designed so that the speed of the air on top is greater than the speed of the air below. Since according to Bernoulli the pressure of the air must be greater below the wing, there is a net force upward called lift.

ORGANIZATIONAL STRATEGIES TO ACHIEVE YOUR PURPOSE

Frequently, a writing situation requires that a paper must be longer than a paragraph because there are more varied and complex ideas to discuss than 150 to 200 words will allow. Writers are then faced with the question of how to organize several paragraphs into a readable, coherent whole.

Although some students may have learned strict rules for paragraphing, the practice of where to begin a new paragraph varies widely among academic and professional writers. We all know that journalistic paragraphs, for example, are extremely short to accommodate column size and reader impatience. The standard explanation is that each paragraph should discuss a new aspect or subheading of the overall topic. Thus, if one were writing on the reasons for choosing a college and had three main reasons, a paragraph could be devoted to discussing each reason in detail. But such a scheme does not always work. Perhaps one reason is more important than the others, and the less important ones may be briefly listed in one paragraph while the main reason (subdivided as appropriate) may be discussed over two or three paragraphs. You must remain flexible in determining how many paragraphs to use and what to include in each one. Now that you have been appropriately cautioned, Figure 2.1 shows a *sample* organizational diagram which you might find useful as a general plan.

Figure 2.1
Sample Essay Plan

Introduction

Provides background for the reader, gives the context in which the rest of the paper will be read, and may include an incident to interest the reader. The focus sentence often comes at the end of this paragraph.

Introduction
Focus Sentence

Body

Discusses the focus sentence in detail according to the audience for the paper and the writer's purpose for writing. Some internal organization is helpful: chronological order (what came first, second), the order of importance (with the most important going last), spatial order (how things are arranged from left to right, from near to far, etc.)

Transition	First,
Point 1	To begin with,

Transition	Next, Second,
Point 2	On the other hand, In addition,

Conclusion

Restates the focus sentence or main point and summarizes the evidence. It may also make clear the importance of the subject or idea, suggest implications the paper may raise, direct the readers to study further, or urge them to belief or action.

Transition	Third, Most important,
Point 3	Next,

Transition	Finally, Therefore,
Conclusion	To sum up,

Sample organizational plans for each of the four purposes are found in Chapters 3–6, but this general plan will help you analyze the remaining student essays and write your own short essay at the end of this chapter.

On the next few pages are four student essays which demonstrate how development strategies may be combined to accomplish a purpose. Read each essay, trying to identify the development strategies used in various paragraphs. Note how each essay is organized and whether it conforms to the sample plan we've just looked at or departs from it. Following each essay are questions for you to answer which point to the principles we learned in Chapter 1 as well as to the strategies we've discussed in Chapter 2.

Identifying Organizational Strategies in Student Essays

KILLER OF THE UNPREPARED

I hear voices ahead. I look up but cannot see past Scott's backpack. My three hiking companions and I shuffle to the side of the muddy trail, yielding the right of way to the voices. Two female hikers approach us from the opposite direction. As they pass we exchange greetings, such as "Hello" and "Lousy weather for a hike." Then the girls continue on their way, we on ours. The rain begins to fall harder. It seems so cold. I try to open and close my numbed hands quickly. To my dismay the act takes seconds to do just once. This disturbs me because the cold rain and impaired coordination could indicate hypothermia.

Hypothermia is the bodily condition of severely low temperature, usually caused by exposure to adverse weather. Hypothermia is the major cause of death among outdoor enthusiasts, yet most people have never heard of hypothermia, much less how to prevent it. These facts have earned hypothermia the nickname "killer of the unprepared." Even dictionaries appear unfamiliar with the word. *Webster's New World Dictionary* defines hypothermia as a "subnormal temperature of the body, often induced artificially to facilitate cardiac arrest." This definition ignores the fact that hypothermia kills people.

We usually associate hypothermia with cold weather, but the weather does not have to be bitterly cold. If a person lacks adequate clothing, even the typical temperatures of a summer evening in the mountains combined with a soaking rain can bring on hypothermia.

But what is hypothermia? To explain the process we must first understand that the body is a sensitive machine. The torso or "core" of the body must remain at a constant temperature of 98.6 degrees. When the core overheats, the excess heat is distributed to the limbs, away from the core. In addition, the body's pores open to allow perspiration. The perspiration evaporates and thus cools the body.

When the core becomes too cold, the reverse process takes place. Everyone has experienced cold hands; this occurs because the core has borrowed sufficient heat from the limbs to keep itself warm. If the core is still too cold and the limbs cannot supply any more heat, the core temperature actually begins to drop. When the core temperature drops from 98.6 to 97 degrees, the victim begins to shiver. This is the first stage of hypothermia.

At about 95 degrees the shivering increases and muscular coordination deteriorates. At this point the victim's thought processes diminish. As the core temperature approaches 92 degrees, the victim shakes violently, loses the ability to move the muscles, and no longer thinks rationally. Unconsciousness occurs at about 87 degrees. At this stage the victim is probably beyond recovery. Finally, death occurs before the core temperature falls below 75 degrees.

All afternoon my three friends and I have hiked through a torrent of icy rain.

Although we wear ponchos, our legs and arms have remained exposed to the rain since this morning. The cold greatly concerns us. We have all noticed the "slow motion" effect which inhibits our coordination.

Soon, Gary, who hikes in the lead, says, "I see a cabin up ahead. I think we have hiked far enough." Our resulting silence indicates a unanimous decision to spend the night at the cabin.

Immediately upon entering the cabin, we throw off our ponchos and place them outside on the porch. Preventing hypothermia is our prime concern. With this objective in mind we change into warm, dry clothes and then build a fire in the fireplace. The fire is especially important in preventing hypothermia. Not only does a fire physically warm the body, but the act of building a fire, keeping it roaring, and then sitting in front, staring hypnotized at the flames, has many positive effects on a person's mental attitude. After building the fire, we boil a pot of water and make tea, thus warming our bodies from the inside. Later that night we cook dinner. All these steps help remove the threat of hypothermia.

The next morning the sun shines. We decide to take the day off from hiking and dry out our wet gear instead. As we hang the clothing on a line, a forest ranger trudges up from the trail.

He inquires, "Did you fellows meet two girls hiking on the trail yesterday?"

Feeling a little nervous, as anytime an authority figure asks a question, we tell him that we had.

He continues, "Apparently, last night when the girls got to a campsite they were so cold that they ignored dinner and just crawled into their sleeping bags—wet clothes and all."

After pausing a moment he says, "They died."

Questions

1. Which strategies were used in this essay and in which paragraphs?
2. Can you find a focus statement that tells you what the essay is about? If so, write it down.
3. What specific details help you to understand the subject or make it more interesting to you, the reader? List some.
4. How did the order of the details help you to understand the subject? Make a brief outline of the main points.
5. What connections did you notice which helped to connect the paragraphs or ideas within the paragraphs? Underline the repeated words or synonyms. Circle the transitions or words that link paragraphs or ideas to each other.
6. What is the purpose of the ending?

BONANZA!

One day last September, while I was driving to work, my gaze fell upon a small, old park which I had never noticed before. Aha! I exclaimed to myself, that little park looks like a great place to look for lost valuables with my metal detector. The only thing I was able to do at work that evening was to daydream about treasure hunting in that park. Early the next morning, I was at the park methodically scanning the ground with my detector. By midafternoon, I deduced that no one had ever searched the park before because my goodie-bag was nearly full of coins, jewelry, relics, and junk.

When I returned home, I immediately ran over to my best friend's house to show him my finds. For a long time my friend had wanted to try detecting, but he was skeptical as to whether he would find anything worthwhile. I figured that the results of that day's hunt would surely convince him that coinshooting was both worthwhile and lucrative. I spilled the contents of the bag before him and I began to sort them out.

The first thing I did was to separate the large number of coins from the rest of the piles. I usually do not bother to check the dates on the coins while I am in the process of detecting, because checking dates wastes too much time. When I did get around to checking, I was surprised to discover some very old coins. I had located three Indian Head pennies, dated 1874, 1894, and 1907; two Liberty Head nickels, dated 1889 and 1905; an 1871 two-cent piece; and a 1900 Barber dime. The rest of the coins were all dated later than 1920. The silver coins which I found included four Washington quarters, a Standing Liberty half-dollar, six Mercury dimes, and about a dozen Roosevelt dimes. Since the price of silver has risen to nearly forty dollars an ounce, these silver coins are worth approximately fifteen times their face value, or $49.50. I was also fortunate in finding several Buffalo nickels and several early wheat cents. The remaining coins were mostly later wheat pennies and memorial pennies. Added to this were a number of new quarters, dimes, and nickels which I could spend immediately. I had managed to collect a grand total of eighty-eight coins on this particular excursion.

After examining the coins for a while, I isolated the few pieces of jewelry that I had accumulated. The most valuable piece of jewelry that I found that day was a 14-carat-gold wedding band. I later sold this ring for its gold value of forty-six dollars. The other jewelry items had less monetary value, but were equally interesting. The most intriguing piece was a watch-fob medal which commemorated the fiftieth anniversary of the light bulb. The next best finds were two antique silver religious medals and a silver chain. Along with these more precious articles, there were a few pieces of costume jewelry, two gum machine rings (one with a diamond), and a cheap earring.

When I go detecting, I always enjoy finding a few interesting relics, and I was definitely not disappointed that day. To me, a relic is any object (other than coins, jewelry, or junk) that represents past history. Over the years, at least two horses succeeded in losing one of their shoes in the park. Although the two horseshoes were practically worthless, they made a nice addition to my relic collection. Horses were not the only ones to lose interesting relics in that park. I dug up an ancient U.S. Mail lock that apparently had fallen from some unfortunate postman's mailbag long ago. The brass lock emerged from the ground in excellent condition.

The rest of the relics were probably lost by children. I unearthed three very old penknives (two with ivory handles and one with a rotted, wooden handle), a lead toy horse, and, possibly the most fascinating find of the day, a miniature bisque "Frozen Charlotte" doll. I found the doll quite by accident in the same hole with a bottle cap.

Once I had separated the cream of the crop, the only thing left was a huge pile of junk. Junk is a problem all treasure hunters must put up with to be successful. Digging a big hole only to find a worthless hunk of metal has to be the most frustrating aspect of coinshooting. The junk that I dug up on that fall day consisted mostly of pull tabs, tinfoil, and bottle caps. I had also dug up a number of unidentifiable pieces of scrap metal. I did with this junk as I do with all garbage—I threw it away.

That day last September was by far the most successful of my coinshooting career. I hope that someday I will be able to find an equally prime area to detect. Virgin areas such as that park are getting harder and harder to find today because of the increasing number of metal-detecting enthusiasts. The beginner should not be discouraged by this fact, for anywhere people congregate now or have congregated in the past will yield lost valuables. Also, even though other coinshooters may have been there first, it is virtually impossible to hunt out an area which has been used for many years. I know that that small park still holds treasures, and come summer, I will harvest more of its treasures.

Questions

1. Which strategies were used in this essay and in which paragraphs?
2. Can you find a focus statement that tells you what the essay is about? If so, write it down.
3. What specific details help you to understand the subject or make it more interesting to you, the reader? List some.
4. How did the order of the details help you to understand the subject? Make a brief outline of the main points.
5. What connections did you notice which helped to connect the paragraphs or ideas within the paragraphs? Underline the repeated words or synonyms. Circle the transitions or words that link paragraphs or ideas to each other.
6. What is the purpose of the ending?

THE PARK

It was always hot at the amusement park. That's what I remember most about the summer afternoons when my big brother and I would go there to escape the boredom of the beach. The entire park was covered with asphalt, and even on cooler days, the ground would be burning like the surface of a giant black skillet. The only place we could go to escape the heat was to the refreshment stand where we could buy snow cones or Coke for a dime, if we were lucky enough to find an open space at the counter. If we didn't spend all our money on candy and snow cones, we would buy a ride ticket at the main booth and be set for the rest of the day. With this ticket we had our choice of hundreds of rides, such as the red and green "Whirling Saucer," the dangerous "Scooper Loop," or the menacing "Flying Spyder," just to name a few.

Best of all, however, was the old wooden roller coaster that twisted around the park like a monstrous serpent. When our car climbed to the crest of the main hill, the track would shake as if it were going to break into a thousand pieces. Then suddenly, the blue sky would fall away, and for a split second, we could see all the way across the park to the beach and ocean before careening down the other side. We always saved the roller coaster until the end of the day when the crowds had thinned out some, and we could get a car to ourselves for one last ride before going home.

A few years later, when I was taking my older brother, who had enlisted in the Navy, down to Newport to meet his first ship, we decided to stop by the park just to see how it was doing after such a long time. As we drove up toward the beach, I could see the outline of the roller coaster, assuring me that the park was still there, just like always. After parking the car, we jogged across the dunes toward the entrance booth where you could buy tickets to the rides in the park. As we got close, I could see that the booth was gone, and a tall chain-link fence ran over where it used to stand, enclosing the entire park.

Beyond the fence, a cool breeze was whipping small tornadoes of sand across the deserted park. The sand had long since taken over the asphalt, and even the refreshment stand had been covered up to the roof by the drifting white crystals. The only thing that the sand hadn't covered were the rides, and even they were not unchanged. Their paint had long since been chewed away by the wind and sand, leaving the bare metal to rust in the salty sea air. The rides looked ridiculously out of place now, all by themselves, like some strange spaceship that had crashed and been deserted.

The old roller coaster still stood up among the ruins, but the main hill had been broken up and lay in a huge pile of shattered planks and twisted rails. I could not see any sign of the blue cars which used to ride along the track at one time. The only sounds to be heard were the two or three sea gulls that occasionally broke the silence with their sarcastic, shrill screams.

It was getting late and I still had to take my brother back to the base to catch his ship. I took one last glimpse at the place where a giant amusement park had once stood, and sadly nodded my head. We finally got in the car and drove off. As my brother climbed out of the car, he said, "Take it easy. I'll see you in a couple of years."

"Yeah, see you in a couple of years," I whispered. As I got back in the car,

I wondered what my brother might be like in a couple of years, and if he was going to change as much as the park that I once knew.

Questions

1. What strategies were used in this essay, and in which paragraphs?
2. Can you find a focus statement that tells you what the essay is about? If so, write it down.
3. What specific details help you to understand the subject or make it more interesting to you, the reader? List some.
4. How did the order of the details help you to understand the subject? Make a brief outline of the main points.
5. What connections did you notice which helped to connect the paragraphs or ideas within the paragraphs? Underline the repeated words or synonyms. Circle the transitions or words that link paragraphs or ideas to each other.
6. What is the purpose of the ending?

FOOTBALL VS. SWIMMING

There are many disagreements as to which is the harder sport: football or swimming. This particular question was brought up on numerous occasions throughout my senior year in high school. The so-called football jocks would insist that the swimmers were nothing but a bunch of wimps because all they ever did was swim back and forth in the pool, making waves.

Since I was a participant on both the football and swimming teams for four years, I would many times find myself acting as judge in determining which was the harder sport. The parties in dispute would trap me in the hall and say, "Tell them, Dave. Isn't swimming harder than football?" Each time this happened, I would simply go into a lengthy discussion expressing my views about the length of the season and the training involved for each sport.

The football season ran from the last two weeks in August straight through to the second week in November—approximately a 12-week season. The competitive swim season, on the other hand, ran from the first week in November straight through the second week in March—approximately an 18-week season. Therefore, I explained, the swim team practices almost a month and a half longer than the football team does. The football players would then reply, "Aw, Dave, that don't mean nothin'; we bust our asses during the season while the swimmers just jump in the pool and take a bath every night after school." Having had to do the swimmers justice, I'd say, "OK, let's break down each team's season and see what we come up with."

"All of you would agree that both of your varsity teams go through a pre-season workout which is probably the hardest stage of practice throughout the entire year. The football team practices three weeks before playing the first game. During this period, a typical practice, which lasts one and a half hours, consists of running, blocking, and tackling techniques, repeated drills of offensive and defensive plays, and calisthenics. The swim team, however, practices two hours per day, six nights a week throughout both the preseason and dual-meet season. A typical preseason practice includes a variety of kicking, pulling, swimming different strokes, sprinting, and long-distance training, totaling anywhere from five to six thousand yards per day.

"During the competitive season, training done by each team varies slightly from the preseason training. The football team almost always has a Friday night game. Thus, practice on the Monday following a game would, in reality, be a loosen-up practice to recover from any bumps or bruises received during the game. Tuesday and Wednesday practices are geared toward both offense and defense in preparation for the coming game. On Thursday, the team has a light practice under the lights. At this practice only sweatpants and a helmet are worn. In all, the team has only two hard practices (if that's what you want to call them) per week. But the swim team has not one, but two competitive meets per week, usually on Tuesdays and Thursdays. This leaves four hard workouts per week for each practice geared toward each individual swimmer's stroke. During the dual-meet season, the practices are cut slightly to approximately fifty-five hundred yards a day."

After my explanation, the football players retorted, "All right, their season and practices are longer than ours, but we work a lot harder during our practices than they do in theirs!" I quickly said, "I'm glad you raised that point again, because you are absolutely wrong. The main difference between football and swim practice is the rest factor. The football players may run or perform a strenuous exercise, but 90 percent of the time, the exercise doesn't last longer than a minute, which is not long enough to produce oxygen debt. On the other hand, swimmers practice continuously. For example, all swimming is done in sets such as ten two-hundred-yard swims with a fifteen-second rest interval in between each two hundred. Once a set is completed, the standard time of one minute is allowed before starting a new set. This one-minute rest period is as long as the typical exercise period for the football players. As you can see, the swimmers practice almost a full two hours in a state of oxygen indebtedness while the footballers hardly ever attain this state."

Now the football players were totally turned off and insisted that I was full of bull and didn't know what I was talking about. The clincher to the whole argument always came when the football players had to take the required swim class for nine weeks. The first day of class proved many players wrong, because everyone had to be timed for fifty yards—a measly two laps. They would swim incredibly slow times and would be huffing and puffing at the finish of their marathon swim. The honest, diligent player would say, gasping for air, "How the hell do you swimmers swim two hundred and fifty laps every night?"

Questions

1. Which strategies were used in this essay, and in which paragraphs?
2. Can you find a focus statement that tells you what the essay is about? If so, write it down.
3. What specific details help you to understand the subject or make it more interesting to you, the reader? List some.
4. How did the order of the details help you to understand the subject? Make a brief outline of the main points.
5. What connections did you notice which helped to connect the paragraphs or ideas within the paragraphs? Underline the repeated words or synonyms. Circle the transitions or words that link paragraphs or ideas to each other.
6. What is the purpose of the ending?

WRITING ACTIVITY

Choose a topic below to develop into a short paper using one or more of the writing strategies discussed in this section. Your audience for this activity is your instructor and/or your fellow classmates.

1. Write about an incident that affected you in some way.
2. Write about the most unusual person you have ever known.
3. Explain to someone how to do something which you learned as a hobby or on the job.
4. Analyze the kinds of people you see at a shopping mall, a rock concert, a country fair, or a sporting event.
5. Write about how you see yourself in relation to some other member of your family. How are you similar or different in appearance, taste, attitudes, and so on?
6. Write about television advertisements. Are they humorous? Tasteless? Sexist? Be sure to use specific details to support what you say.
7. Write about a time when you were afraid of something.
8. Explain why you chose to come to this school.

Beginning the Assignment

After you have chosen a subject, use freewriting, observation, asking questions, or one of the other techniques you studied in Chapter 1 to get yourself started. Jot down lists, freewrite, or otherwise get started. Don't forget to take your purpose in writing and your audience into account as you think about what you will write.

Certain of the topics listed above lend themselves to certain of the techniques discussed earlier. Topic 4, for example, lends itself to observation, as does topic 6. Topics that ask you to write about a personal experience (1, 2, 7, and 8) may respond well to freewriting. You may wish to discuss the ways to get started in small groups in your class or with your instructor.

Selecting a Strategy

What organizational strategy suggests itself from the material you have gathered or from your freewriting? Select a strategy or a combination of strategies and jot down in a preliminary order the details you have developed so far.

Writing a Draft

Put your ideas and plans now into written form as a first draft. Many writers find that their ideas take shape only when they write them down, not simply when they are ideas in their heads. Also, you will be revising this first draft to produce a really complete and coherent final copy. Think of a possible introduction and conclusion for your paper as well.

Revising Your Writing

Answer these questions about your first draft:

1. Does the paper have (or need) an introduction? If you have written one, does it help the reader understand the topic you are discussing? Does it lead to the focus sentence?
2. Is there a focus sentence?
   a. Does it clearly indicate what the paper is about?
   b. Does it have an attitude word in it or is an attitude strongly implied?
3. Do subsequent paragraphs support the focus or main idea?
   a. Are they all clearly related to the main point?
   b. Is there enough evidence to be convincing?

      c. Is the evidence or detail specific enough to be interesting and persuasive?

4. Are there clear connections between paragraphs to let the readers know where they have been and where they are going?

5. Is there a conclusion, which reminds the reader of the essay's main points or which explains some implications of the main idea?

6. Is the writing free from errors in spelling, punctuation, and sentence structure?

PART II
Writing Purposes and Assignments

As discussed at the beginning of Chapter 2, the four basic purposes in writing are explaining, substantiating, evaluating, and recommending. Each builds on the other. That is, to prove something, you will probably have to define or explain it first. To evaluate, you will have to supply evidence to substantiate your claims that something is better than something else. To recommend, you will have to explain, substantiate claims, and evaluate. These interrelationships are shown more clearly in the following diagram:

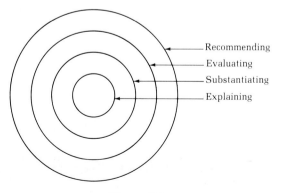

Figure II.1
Interrelationship of Writing Purposes

In the pages that follow, each purpose is explained using professional and student examples. Writing assignments for each purpose are designed to give you practice in several writing situations, moving from the simpler assignments to the more complex ones.

CHAPTER 3

Writing to Inform: Explaining

Explaining includes defining a word or a term, exploring what an idea means to someone, reporting information, or describing a process.

This purpose underlies many essay examination questions in college because instructors want to know if you can explain the major ideas learned in a course and can remember material from the texts or lectures to illustrate your explanation.

Sample questions taken from examinations include:

1. Define what social scientists mean by "rites of passage." Illustrate rites of passage for a particular culture. (from anthropology)
2. Explain the idea of "balance of power." (from history)
3. Define "imperialism." Explain how it has become a controversial and often a derogatory term. (from history)

In the world outside college, explaining becomes important anytime someone wants to know how to do something, such as file for income tax, install a garage door opener, or teach a new employee how to handle new accounts. We seek information about the newest advances in the treatment of diabetes, the status of the dollar abroad, and who the new players are on our favorite sports team. We don't always stop with gathering information; that is, we may go on to express our opinion about the evidence, evaluate the evidence, or try to recommend that someone do something about a situation we have discovered. In other words, the purposes in writing may overlap and become quite complex. Nevertheless, we can think of situations where our *main purpose* is to inform or explain.

Listed below are some ways that explanations can be organized. Note that these are *sample plans,* not absolute rules to be followed inflexibly. In fact, you may be able to think of still further options.

Sample Organizational Plans for Explanatory Essay

A. Introduction to the idea being explained

Option 1: To interest the audience recount an incident which illustrates the concept.

Option 2: Stress the importance of the idea to your readers so that they will read the rest of your explanation.

Option 3: Use a formal definition of the word or concept as might be found in the dictionary to create a common understanding of at least one meaning before you write an explanation which expands on or changes the commonly held definition.

Option 4: Explain what the concept or word does *not* mean so as to dispel any misconceptions about its use ("Juvenile diabetes does not necessarily strike only children but is the name given to the most severe type of the disease.")

Option 5: Begin directly with the explanation and dispense with an introduction as such.

B. The focus sentence is usually placed at the end of the introduction.

C. Main points

Option 1: Develop your subject by explaining how it works or came to exist. (process analysis)

Option 2: Analyze the subject by breaking it down into parts (division) or by examining categories (classification).

Option 3: Compare the idea, object, or word to other, more familiar ideas and show its similarities, differences, or both (comparison, contrast, or analogy).

Option 4: Explain by providing examples of the idea as seen in people's behavior, in incidents involving the concept, or in an object's physical qualities.

Option 5: Use a longer story (narration) to show what something means.

D. Conclusion

Option 1: Restate the main points raised in the essay.

Option 2: Explain the importance of the idea to give your readers a reason to remember what you have said.

Option 3: End with a case study, incident, or other application of the idea to experience.

Option 4: Suggest further study if warranted.

The professional examples which follow are concerned *primarily* with explaining something to an audience. As you read, try to determine the audience each writer is trying to reach. How does the idea of such an audience affect the details which the writers choose? What strategies do the writers use to accomplish their purpose (explaining)? Following each essay are some discussion questions which ask you to consider these and other points.

The Black Death

Barbara Tuchman

In October 1347, two months after the fall of Calais, Genoese trading ships put into the harbor of Messina in Sicily with dead and dying men at the oars. The ships had come from the Black Sea port of Caffa (now Feodosiȳa) in the Crimea, where the Genoese maintained a trading post. The diseased sailors showed strange black swellings about the size of an egg or an apple in the armpits and groin. The swellings oozed blood and pus and were followed by spreading boils and black blotches on the skin from internal bleeding. The sick suffered severe pain and died quickly within five days of the first symptoms. As the disease spread, other symptoms of continuous fever and spitting of blood appeared instead of the swellings or buboes. These victims coughed and sweated heavily and died even more quickly, within three days or less, sometimes in 24 hours. In both types everything that issued from the body—breath, sweat, blood from the buboes and lungs, bloody urine, and blood-blackened excrement—smelled foul. Depression and despair accompanied the physical symptoms, and before the end "death is seen seated on the face."

The disease was bubonic plague, present in two forms: one that infected the bloodstream, causing the buboes and internal bleeding, and was spread by contact; and a second, more virulent pneumonic type that infected the lungs and was spread by respiratory infection. The presence of both at once cause the high mortality and speed of contagion. So lethal was the disease that cases were known of persons going to bed well and dying before they woke, of doctors catching the illness at a bedside and dying before the patient. So rapidly did it spread from one to another that to a French physician, Simon de Covino, it seemed as if one sick person "could infect the whole world." The malignity of the pestilence appeared more terrible because its victims knew no prevention and no remedy.

The physical suffering of the disease and its aspect of evil mystery were expressed in a strange Welsh lament which saw "death coming into our midst like black smoke, a plague which cuts off the young, a rootless phantom which has no mercy for fair countenance. Woe is me of the shilling in the armpit? It is seething, terrible . . . a head that gives pain and causes a loud cry . . . a painful angry knob. . . . Great is its seething like a burning

---

Barbara Tuchman is a two-time Pulitzer Prize winner and a history writer. She was a foreign correspondent for *Nation* magazine and has written extensively about World Wars I and II. This excerpt was taken from her 1978 book *A Distant Mirror: The Calamitous Fourteenth Century.*

cinder . . . a grievous thing of ashy color." Its eruption is ugly like the "seeds of black peas, broken fragments of brittle sea-coal . . . the early ornaments of black death, cinders of the peelings of the cockle weed, a mixed multitude, a black plague like halfpence, like berries. . . ."

Rumors of a terrible plague supposedly arising in China and spreading through Tartary (Central Asia) to India and Persia, Mesopotamia, Syria, Egypt, and all of Asia Minor had reached Europe in 1346. They told of a death toll so devastating that all of India was said to be depopulated, whole territories covered by dead bodies, other areas with no one left alive. As added up by Pope Clement VI at Avignon, the total of reported dead reached 23,840,000. In the absence of a concept of contagion, no serious alarm was felt in Europe until the trading ships brought their black burden of pestilence into Messina while other infected ships from the Levant carried it to Genoa and Venice.

By January 1348 it penetrated France via Marseille, and North Africa via Tunis. Shipborne along coasts and navigable rivers, it spread westward from Marseille through the ports of Languedoc to Spain and northward up the Rhône to Avignon, where it arrived in March. It reached Narbonne, Montpellier, Carcassonne, and Toulouse between February and May, and at the same time in Italy spread to Rome and Florence and their hinterlands. Between June and August it reached Bordeaux, Lyon, and Paris, spread to Burgundy and Normandy, and crossed the Channel from Normandy into southern England. From Italy during the same summer it crossed the Alps into Switzerland and reached eastward to Hungary.

In a given area the plague accomplished its kill within four to six months and then faded, except in the larger cities, where, rooting into the close-quartered population, it abated during the winter, only to reappear in spring and rage for another six months.

In 1349 it resumed in Paris, spread to Picardy, Flanders, and the Low Countries, and from England to Scotland and Ireland as well as to Norway, where a ghost ship with a cargo of wool and a dead crew drifted offshore until it ran aground near Bergen. From there the plague passed into Sweden, Denmark, Prussia, Iceland, and as far as Greenland. Leaving a strange pocket of immunity in Bohemia, and Russia unattacked until 1351, it had passed from most of Europe by mid-1350. Although the mortality rate was erratic, ranging from one fifth in some places to nine tenths or almost total elimination in others, the overall estimate of modern demographers has settled—for the area extending from India to Iceland—around the same figure expressed in Froissart's casual words: "a third of the world died." His estimate, the common one at the time, was not an inspired guess but a borrowing of St. John's figure for mortality from plague in Revelation, the favorite guide to human affairs of the Middle Ages.

A third of Europe would have meant about 20 million deaths. No one knows in truth how many died. Contemporary reports were an awed impression, not an accurate count. In crowded Avignon, it was said, 400 died daily; 7,000 houses emptied by death were shut up; a single graveyard received 11,000 corpses in six weeks; half the city's inhabitants reportedly died, including 9 cardinals or one third of the total, and 70 lesser prelates. Watching the endlessly passing death carts, chroniclers let normal exaggeration take wings and put the Avignon death toll at 62,000 and even at 120,000, although the city's total population was probably less than 50,000.

When graveyards filled up, bodies at Avignon were thrown into the Rhône until mass burial pits were dug for dumping the corpses. In London in such pits corpses piled up in layers until they overflowed. Everywhere reports speak of the sick dying too fast for the living to bury. Corpses were dragged out of homes and left in front of doorways. Morning light revealed new piles of bodies. In Florence the dead were gathered up by the Compagnia della Misericordia—founded in 1244 to care for the sick—whose members wore red robes and hoods masking the face except for the eyes. When their efforts failed, the dead lay putrid in the streets for days at a time. When no coffins were to be had, the bodies were laid on boards, two or three at once, to be carried to graveyards or common pits. Families dumped their own relatives into the pits, or buried them so hastily and thinly "that dogs dragged them forth and devoured their bodies."

Amid accumulating death and fear of contagion, people died without last rites and were buried without prayers, a prospect that terrified the last hours of the stricken. A bishop in England gave permission to laymen to make confession to each other as was done by the Apostles, "or if no man is present then even to a woman," and if no priest could be found to administer extreme unction, "then faith must suffice." Clement VI found it necessary to grant remissions of sin to all who died of the plague because so many were unattended by priests. "And no bells tolled," wrote a chronicler of Siena, "and nobody wept no matter what his loss because almost everyone expected death. . . . And people said and believed, 'This is the end of the world.' "

Discussion Questions: "The Black Death"

1. How does the writer begin the essay? Does the beginning help the reader understand the writer's main point?
2. Can you find a sentence of definition that explains in much the same way a dictionary would the meaning of "bubonic plague"?
3. Who do you think Tuchman's readers are? Why do you think so?
4. What strategies are used to develop the definition of the black death and its consequences?
5. What is the purpose of the statistics in the eighth paragraph? What other details do you find particularly convincing?
6. Circle the transition words or phrases in the essay. These words serve to link ideas together or signal a change of focus or idea so the *reader* will be able to follow the *writer's* train of thought.
7. How does the writer end this portion of the essay? How does the ending help the reader understand the writer's main idea?

Into the Wild Blue Yonder

By Lloyd Byers

If you were a lad in the early 1920's, lived on a farm or in a small town almost anywhere in the country, you knew what you were going to be when you grew up—a barnstormer.

Like the cowboys and G-men of yesterday and the space pilots of today, those barnstormers were a breed apart, half god, half man. They started coming soon after World War I. Most of them had old Curtis "Jennies," or JND4's. They traveled singly or in pairs and were more than instrumental in bringing the air age to the common man.

Say you are 14 in the summer of 1921. You live in Smallville, and it is a warm day in late August. You and a bunch of fellows are playing half-heartedly in the shade of the blacksmith shop. The rest of the town seems to be sleeping. Suddenly you hear a hum in the distance. You pause and look westward as the humming becomes a distant roar. Then you see it—a *plane!* As it becomes larger in your sight, you see that it is losing altitude, coming down toward Smallville. The plane circles the town and all of a sudden Main Street is full of people. You are jumping up and down in indecision. Will he land on the pasture east of town or the stubble field west of town? Remembering the new fence at the end of the pasture, you take off at a gallop toward the stubble field.

Now the plane is so low you can see the two heads in the cockpits. Sure enough, they are landing in the stubble field. You are the first one there and as soon as the Jenny lands, you are running behind it. The prop blast is blowing straw and dust at you and ballooning the legs of your overalls way out. They taxi about 100 yards and then swing around facing you. The prop is ticking over slowly now and you smell the heady aroma of gasoline and castor oil. The fabric on the plane is vibrating and shiny. There are patches all over the poor old Jenny and through a hole in the wing-covering you can see a control wire leading to the aileron. Then they get out. The goggles are pushed up on the helmet. Their faces are white where the goggles were, brick red below. Their eyes are always sky blue and there are many crinkly lines leading from the corners of them. Their teeth are always so very white, as are the scarves knotted so casually at their throats. They pull themselves from the cockpits and you see the whipcord breeches and the mirror-like leather puttees. They turn the motor off and the pilot beckons you over.

Heaven.

The pilot asks you if there is a hardware store in town where he can get some stove gas for the plane. You nod "yes" and he asks you to go with him. Proudly you do, and as you leave the field, the other sky-

Lloyd Byers lives in Fargo, North Dakota, and is a retired postal worker. He served as a paratrooper during World War II.

man is talking to the growing crowd. You hear him tell about the joys of flight and how pretty Smallville is from the air. You hear him offer some lucky man there the chance to be the first man in town to fly, and for only three bucks.

You help get the gas and talk your Uncle Joe into hauling it out to the field in his Model "T." You help gas up the Jenny and watch in jealous awe as three, then four lucky ones produce the three dollars and go up. The shadows are lengthening now and the pilot says only one more ride. Adam Gant, the undertaker, holds up three bills and the pilot buckles him in. Then the pilot looks down at you and sees the fierce longing and maybe the beginning of a tear. Adam is skinny and so are you, so he buckles the two of you in the cockpit together.

Oh, the joy . . . the ecstasy! The nothingness feeling as you leave the ground. The strange, crushing numbness you feel as the earth gets smaller. You let out your breath and look around. The checkerboard fields, the snake-like river, the ribbons of roads and the toy town enchant you. But it's all over too soon. The stubble field comes up to meet you and Adam's elbow makes you bite your tongue. But what good is a tongue? You couldn't talk anyway. The barnstormers say goodbye and you nod numbly.

The Jenny is just a speck in the sky that gradually disappears, but still you watch. The field is empty now and so are you. You trace the track of the rudder bar across the field. You see the stubble trampled where the crowd stood. You try to relive the past hour but you just cannot. An hour goes by and still you stand there. Your mind is still soaring up there with *them*. Your stomach has forgotten supper. Your hands have forgotten milking time. Your heart remembers flight, and you'll never be the same again.

Discussion Questions: "Into the Wild Blue Yonder"

1. To what does Byers compare barnstormers? Does his comparison help you understand his feelings about the barnstormers?

2. What is the main idea of the essay? Write down the focus sentence(s) that contain(s) the main idea.

3. Why does Byers address the reader as "you"? Is this choice an effective one?

4. What is the predominant strategy used in the essay? How well is the strategy suited for the writer's purpose?

5. What specific details are used to support the main idea? What is the effect of the description of the pilots: "Their eyes were always sky blue . . ."?

6. Circle the transition words or phrases in the essay. How do the transitions reflect the organizational strategy chosen to develop the essay?

7. How does the writer end the essay? How does the ending help the reader understand the writer's main idea?

If Birds Can Fly, Why Can't I?

Alan Lightman

Human physical capacity is greatly restricted by natural laws, nowhere better illustrated than by our inability, despite vigorous and patient flapping of the arms, to fly. But the problem here is not simply the lack of wings. Scale up a pheasant to the size of a man and it would plummet to Earth like a rock. Or consider Icarus. In the very plausible picture of him in my childhood mythology book, each attached wing equals his height and is about one-quarter as wide—not unlike the graceful proportions of a swallow. Unfortunately, to fly with those wings the boy would have to beat his arms at one and a half horsepower, four times the maximum sustained output of an athletic human being. Icarus and Daedalus may have been willing to utterly exhaust themselves in their aerial escape from Crete, but most of us would like to go with better equipment.

Weight, shape, and available power all play a part in the science of flying. Let us begin with the most obvious requirement for flying: A lifting force must counterbalance the weight of the animal in question. That lift is provided by air. Air has weight and, at sea level on Earth, pushes equally in all directions with a pressure just under 15 pounds per square inch of surface. To achieve lift, an animal must manage to reduce the air pressure on its top surface, thereby creating a net pressure pushing upward from below. Birds and airplanes do this with properly formed wings and forward motion. The curvature and trailing edge of a wing force air to flow more rapidly over its top side than its bottom, causing net upward pressure in proportion to the air density and to the square of the forward speed. Thus with every doubling of the speed comes a quadrupling of the lift pressure. No motion, no net lift pressure. Birds couldn't fly on the moon, where the air density is essentially zero. (Under the moon's reduced gravity, however, creatures could jump six times as high as on Earth, which might be a happy substitute.)

Once you've got your lift pressure of so many pounds per square inch, you want to have as many square inches of wing as practical. For example, a lift pressure of 1/100 pound per square inch (obtained by flying at about 35 miles per hour) pushing on a wing area of 400 square inches will yield a total lift force of four pounds, enough to buoy the weight of the average bird. There is a convenient trade-off here: The necessary lift force can be

---

Alan Lightman, a physicist at the Smithsonian Astrophysical Laboratory and professor at Harvard University, investigates a common question to discover the scientific answer. His column appears in *Science* magazine.

had with less wing area if the animal increases its forward speed, and vice versa. Birds capitalize on this option according to their individual needs. The great blue heron, for example, has long, slender legs for wading and must fly slowly in order not to break them on landing. Consequently, herons have a relatively large wingspan. Pheasants, on the other hand, maneuver in underbrush and would find large wings cumbersome. To remain airborne with their relatively short and stubby wings, pheasants fly fast. Illustrated with some actual numbers, which I got from a helpful man at the Audubon Naturalist Society who happened to have the birds in his office, an average great blue heron weighs in at six and a half pounds with a wing area of about 800 square inches, while a typical pheasant has three times the weight to wing area. However, the pheasant flies at an average 50 miles per hour, more than twice the speed of the cruising heron.

How a bird propels itself forward, without propellers, is not obvious. This mystery was clarified in the early 19th century by George Cayley, father of the modern airplane. (Leonardo da Vinci spent years studying the art of flying and may well have understood the propulsion of birds. But his notes went undiscovered until a hundred years ago and, as was typical, were left unfinished—although he did, as legend has it, launch one of his pupils from Mount Cecere in a flying contraption, which promptly crashed.) Birds, in fact, do have propellers, in the form of specially designed feathers on the outer halves of their wings. These feathers, called "primaries," change their shape and position during a wing beat. On the downstroke they move downward and forward; on the upstroke, upward and backward. The primary feathers, operating on the same physical principles as the rest of the wing, produce their lift in the forward rather than in the upward direction.

Flying, like other physical activities, costs energy. A frictionless bird, having attained level flight and satisfied with its course, could glide forever without moving a muscle. All the flapping, and expense of energy, is made necessary by air drag. Depending on a craft's aerodynamic design, the drag force is about 1/20 of the lift force. To counteract drag, a heron must pay out energy at the grudging rate of 1/50 of a horsepower, leaving behind its calories in the form of stirred up pockets of air. Heavier birds of the same proportions have to use even more power for each pound of weight. Quadruple a bird's dimensions in every direction, keeping the shape identical, and its weight and volume increase by 64 times, while the power required to fly is 128 times larger. The only way around this law is to change shape. For example, if you hold the bird's volume and weight fixed but increase the wing area four times, you can fly with half the power. For the long migration flights, birds save power by flying together in formation, each member in the rear partially boosted by the rising air current trailing the bird ahead and taking turns in the lead positions. But for solo flight, weight and shape inescapably determine the power needed to fly. These are the facts of life for aviation.

We now turn to biology, where we find that, pound for pound, living creatures are highly inefficient at producing useful power compared to internal combustion engines. A human being can maintain a maximum mechanical power output of only about 1/200 that of an engine of the same weight. For biology to reach 12 horsepower, the output of the little engine on the Wright brothers 1903 airplane, requires the services of an elephant.

The predicament of limited biological power lessens, however, as we proceed to smaller and smaller size. Lighter animals have more power for each pound of weight than heavier ones. Begin with a 950-pound horse, which has at its disposal one horsepower. Now reduce the weight of the animal. For every 50 percent reduction of weight, it is found that the power available for work diminishes by only 40 percent. By the time you're down to less than an ounce, you realize that the 4,000 mice that weigh the same as a man have nine times the total power. Embarrassing perhaps, but not unexpected. Unlike most engines and machines, the muscles in animals generate more heat than useful work. Since heat production cannot be sustained at a greater rate than the animal can cool, and cooling is generally accomplished via the skin surface, animals will produce heat, and mechanical power, approximately in proportion to their surface area. Power to weight is thus the ratio of surface area to volume. It is then simple mathematics that smaller objects have greater surface area to volume than larger ones. Being very small does have its own drawbacks, like the obligation to eat for most of the day, but that's another story.

Now, as the power needed to fly increases more rapidly with increasing weight than the power generally available—unless some spectacular change in body shape is effected—lightweight creatures clearly have the edge for flying. Nature seems quite appreciative of this struggle between physics and biology. Although birds have been experimenting with flight for a hundred million years, the heaviest true flying bird, the great bustard, rarely exceeds 31 pounds. The larger, gliding birds such as vultures are carried partially by rising hot air columns. The 345-pound ostrich never leaves the ground, apparently having chosen sheer bulk and fast ground speed over flight for defense.

Never having seen a 200-pound bird aloft, the British industrialist Henry Kremer must have felt his money safe for a long time when in 1959 he offered a prize of 5,000 pounds for human-powered flight. In 1973, after many serious but unsuccessful attempts in Britain, Japan, Austria, and Germany, the "Kremer prize" was increased to 50,000 pounds. According to the rules set up the Royal Aeronautical Society of England, a winning flight would have to traverse a figure eight around two pylons half a mile apart, never touching Earth, and cross the start and finish point at least 10 feet above the ground. And, of course, the human pilot would have to furnish the power.

On August 23, 1977, at Shafter Airport near Bakersfield, California, an athletic young man climbed into a fragile, ungainly craft named the Gossamer Condor, strapped his feet to a pair of bicyclelike pedals connected to a propeller, and captured the prize. The entire flight lasted almost seven and a half minutes.

What Paul MacCready, the designer of the craft, had done was to create an extraordinarily lightweight structure of enormous wing span. To keep the wing as light as possible, it was fashioned from Mylar stretched over aluminum struts, with piano wire for bracing and cardboard for the wing's leading edge. The entire craft, including fuselage and wing, weighs 70 pounds. To this you have to add the weight of Bryan Allen, 135 pounds. Allen is approximately six feet tall: his wing was 96 feet long and 10 feet wide. Never has Mother Nature conceived a flying creature remotely approaching such disproportions. For numerical comparison, the pheasant has a wing area per mean body area of just over one, the heron has five, and the great bustard has 12. The Gossamer Condor (with pilot) has a wing area per mean body area of 90.

In many ways, human beings circumvented the difficulties of aviation long ago, at Kitty Hawk. And internal combustion engines date back even earlier. But in our dreams, when we soar into the air to escape danger or to simply bask in our strength, we fly as birds, self-propelled. It may be awkward to imagine ourselves installed with a hundred feet of wing, but that's what Nature asks, to fly like a bird.

Discussion Questions: "If Birds Can Fly, Why Can't I?"

1. What do Lightman's examples of the pheasant and Icarus help you to understand?
2. The first sentence of the second paragraph sets up the organization of the essay. What are the three main points Lightman makes about flying? Which paragraphs take up the first point? The second? The third?
3. Though scientific, is this essay intended for the technical specialist or for any interested reader? How can you tell?
4. What specific details are used to support the three main points? Construct a brief list or outline of the facts that support each.
5. Circle the transition words or phrases in the essay.
6. How does the writer end the essay?
7. This essay may tell you more than you wanted to know about how birds fly. Could you summarize the essential content of the essay in one paragraph or less? What are the advantages and disadvantages of such a summary?

If I'm Late, Start The Crisis Without Me

Gail Sheehy

The crisis model of young people caught in a turbulent passage between their late teens and early twenties has come to be equated with the normal process of growing up. We all recognize hallmarks of this sensitive condition: kids who are at once rebellious, listless, and jumpy. Kids who are seized by sudden and riotous swings of mood. When cramped by anxiety, they cannot sleep or work. They may suffer from mysterious maladies and hold to inflexibly high ideals. Often they seem to be gripped by a negative view of themselves and by hostility to the family. They are likely to drop out of school, the job, the romance, or to stay in and be actively resentful.

In short, it's like having flu of the personality. And since we all think of flu as something to be inoculated against, obvious questions are raised.

Is all this psychic havoc typical of development during the Pulling Up Roots period? No.

In that case, is tumult essential at some later time if one is to achieve identity? Probably yes.

Can't a person get through life without suffering one of these mental blitzes? Yes, if you are willing to let others define you and take care of you—and provided there is always someone whose interest lies in doing so.

Let me explain my answers. First, because the behavior of those late adolescents who are in turmoil is so upsetting to them and alarming to their parents, it can't help but draw the greatest share of our attention. Yet among the general population in this age group, the classic crisis of identity is rather rare. That was the conclusion of a survey of recent studies of adolescent development made by a Harvard research director, Stanley H. King. In his own study of Harvard students, King found the most common pattern to be a gradual and progressive identity formation.

The typical student was a young man who, when faced with present problems, coped in ways he had found to be successful in past experiences. He made friends easily and was able to share his feelings with them, which helped him to work out gradually the kinks in his relationship to the family. Mood swings he would have, but he was not at their mercy. By throwing himself into sports, theater, writing, fun, or enjoying a good laugh at

---

Gail Sheehy graduated from the University of Vermont in 1958 and was a fellow at Columbia University in journalism in 1970. She has written articles for many of America's most popular magazines, including *Esquire, Ms,* and *Rolling Stone.* Her novel *Lovesounds* was published in 1970. Among her interests is the study of contemporary problems, such as the stages of adult development, which she explores in *Passages* (1976), from which this excerpt comes.

himself, he worked off his depressed feelings. Nearing college graduation, many of his previous self-doubts, as well as the inflexible armor that may have covered them, had begun to fall away.

He knew by now that he could have an effect on people and events and therefore felt a surge of confidence, competence, and personal power. His interests had deepened, interests that did not violate his values. From taking the old, arrogant "I'm absolutely positive" stands, he had relaxed enough to be able to enjoy the prospect of personal freedom to change his moral decisions.

But let us not forget that King was looking only at young men, and at some of the most highly privileged young men in the nation. When these Harvard seniors come to *know* they can have an effect on people and events and thereby feel an increase in self-esteem and a sense of power, they are absolutely correct in their assumption. For most college students outside the privileged corridors of Ivy League schools, and certainly for young women, there is no such guarantee of graduating into the "old boy" network that to a large degree runs the country. And for those who don't have a college diploma, a good deal of scrambling is required simply to get a toehold in the system, never mind assembling an identity.

If a full-blown identity crisis is uncommon during this passage, and evidence of a gradual, progressive identity formation comes only from Harvard men, then where do most of us stand? J. E. Marcia, associate professor of psychology at the University of British Columbia, made an important addition to Erikson's work by distinguishing four "normal" positions in which people are likely to find themselves during the identity formation process.

Some will be in the *moratorium* group. They have not yet made commitments or invested much of themselves in other people, and about their own values they are still vague. But even while delaying their commitments, they are actively struggling toward finding the right ones. They are in a crisis that has yet to be resolved and are taking a stop-out.

The *identity-foreclosed* group appear very sure of what they want to be. They have made commitments without a crisis, but not as a result of a strenuous search. They have passively accepted the identity their parents cut out for them. The son of a Republican investment banker, for example, becomes a runner on Wall Street and joins the young Republicans. Or the daughter of a suburban California housewife and a landscape architect marries a young man in the local nursery business. Predictably, people with foreclosed identities are more authoritarian than any other group. I call these *locked in.* Until recently in our culture, this was the slot into which most young women were trundled early.

The *identity-diffused* group have shrunk from the task of defining what they want or how they feel. Parents, teachers, or friends expect from them something other than what they can give or want to be. They are not able to rebel against their parents (or other authority figures) or to struggle with them toward resolving the conflict. They perform well enough in school and social roles. But they always feel like misfits. Often, in the early attempt to define themselves, they become immobilized by feelings of inferiority or alienation. But unlike those in moratorium, they do not seem driven to do much about it and are not in a state of crisis. Young women with the opportunity to attend college are frequently, by graduation, in a state of identity diffusion.

The *identity-achieved* group has been in crisis and come through it. They have developed a sustained personal stance with regard to their sense of purpose and view of the world. They are also likely to be a good deal older.

As young people try to fit themselves into, or prove themselves outside of, such categories, they usually pipe up with at least two more questions.

Suppose I do have all the Sturm und Drang *up front. Will it unhinge my later development?* On the contrary. It will probably facilitate it. Students who come down with a classic personality upheaval at this age generally recover quickly, before the senior year of college is out. And they are likely to become well-integrated adults. Harvard psychiatrist George Vaillant, who has been deciphering the results of a fascinating study of 268 men across the span of thirty-five years, find that a stormy adolescence, per se, was no problem to the normal progression of the adult life cycle. In fact, it often boded well.

If I don't have the crisis at identity-crisis time, must it erupt during a later passage? If you're lucky. A crisis appears to be necessary before identity can be fully achieved.

Discussion Questions: "If I'm Late, Start the Crisis . . ."

1. a. How does the writer begin the essay? Does the beginning help the reader understand the writer's main point?
   b. What purpose does the analogy serve in the second paragraph: "it's like having flu of the personality"?
2. What is the main idea of the essay? Does Sheehy have a focus sentence? Can you state the main idea in a sentence or two?
3. Was the essay written expressly for people in their late teens and early twenties? What word choices suggest that this is the writer's intention? On the other hand, who is being referred to as "we" and "they" in the first paragraph? Note other pronoun uses in the essay. Is it entirely clear who her audience is?
4. a. What organizational strategy develops the "most common pattern" of identity formation (the seventh and eighth paragraphs)?
   b. What organizational strategy does Sheehy use to discuss people during the "identity formation process" (the eleventh to fourteenth paragraphs)?
5. a. What references to authorities does Sheehy make in the essay?

    b. Why are such references important to her credibility?

6. Note the sentence in the ninth paragraph: "But let us not forget that King was looking only at young men, and at some of the most highly privileged young men in the nation." What is the effect of that sentence? Why is it important to what comes after it?

7. Note that the answers to the three questions at the beginning of the essay and the two questions at the end are sentence fragments (incomplete sentences). Are they justified? Why or why not? What difference is there between a sentence fragment written on purpose as a stylistic device and one that occurs for no apparent reason?

8. What do you think of Sheehy's technique of beginning and ending with questions?

9. Can you apply Sheehy's explanation of the identity-forming process to your own experience or to that of your friends?

Inside the Supreme Court

Potter Stewart

It is certainly accurate to say, with such a change in its membership, that the institutional personality of the United States Supreme Court has greatly altered [since 1958]. But it is also accurate to say the institutional character has changed remarkably little—in 21 years or in 50 years.

I came to the Court at the beginning of the 1958 term. In that term the aggregate of the cases on the calendar numbered about 1,800. In the term that ended last July we had to deal with over 4,500 cases—an increase of 150 percent. How does the Court manage such a huge volume of cases? The answer is that since 1925 we have had the authority to screen the cases and select for argument and decision only those which, in our judgment, raise the most important and far-reaching questions. By that device we select annually only about 200 cases in all.

Each Justice receives copies of every certiorari petition [a request to the Court to hear a case] and response. Each Justice, without consultation with his colleagues, reaches his own tentative conclusion whether the petition should be granted or denied. The first con-

sultation comes at the Court conference at which the case is listed for discussion on the agenda. We sit in conference almost every Friday during the term. Those conferences begin at 9:30 and continue through the day, except for a half-hour recess for lunch. Only the Justices are present. There are no law clerks, no stenographers, no secretaries, no pages—just the nine of us. The conferences are held in an oak-paneled room with one wall lined with books from floor to ceiling. Over the mantel of the marble fireplace at one end hangs the only picture—a portrait of Chief Justice John Marshall. In the middle of the room stands a rectangular table, large enough for the nine of us. Upon entering, each of us shakes hands with his colleagues. This handshake tradition originated many years ago. It is a symbol that harmony of aims, if not of views, is the Court's guiding principle. Each of us has his own copy of the agenda of the cases to be considered, and each has done his homework and noted on his copy his tentative view in every case as to whether review on the merits should be granted or denied.

The Chief Justice begins the discussion of each case. Then discussion proceeds until each Justice has spoken. Voting goes the other way, if there is any need for a formal vote following the discussion. When any case receives four votes for review, certiorari is granted, and that case

Potter Stewart was an Associate Justice of the Supreme Court. This article explaining how the Court decides on its cases was delivered as an address to the Cincinnati Bar Association and draws on an article by Justice Brennan which appeared in the *New York Times Magazine* in 1963.

is then transferred to the Argument List. This "Rule of 4" is not written down anywhere, but it is an absolutely inflexible rule.

Oral argument ordinarily takes place about four months after the petition for certiorari is granted. Each party used to be allowed one hour for argument, but in recent years we have limited oral argument to half an hour a side in almost all cases. Counsel submit their briefs and record in sufficient time for the distribution of one set to each Justice two or three weeks before the argument. We follow a schedule of two weeks of argument, followed by two weeks of recess for opinion writing and the study of petitions for review. The Friday conference discussion of the dozen or so cases that have been argued that week follows the same procedure described for the discussion of certiorari petitions, but, of course, the discussion of an argued case is generally much more extended. Not until the discussion is completed and a vote is taken is the opinion assigned. The senior member of the majority designates one of his colleagues or sometimes himself to write the opinion of the Court. This means that the Chief Justice assigns the opinions in those cases in which he has voted with the majority, and the senior associate Justice in the majority assigns the opinions in all other cases. The dissenters agree among themselves who will write the dissenting opinion. But each Justice is free to write his own individual opinion, concurring or dissenting.

The writing of an opinion is not easy work. It always takes weeks, sometimes months. When the author of an opinion for the Court has completed his work, he sends a printed copy to each member, those in dissent as well as in the majority. Often some of those who voted with him at the conference will say that they want to reserve final judgment pending circulation of the dissent. It is a common experience that drafts of dissenting opinions change votes, even enough votes to become the majority. Before everyone has finally made up his mind, a constant interchange goes on while we work out the final form of the Court opinion. There was one case this past term in which I circulated 10 printed drafts before one was finally approved as the opinion of the Court. The point is that each Justice, unless he disqualifies himself in a particular case, passes on every piece of business. The Court does not function by means of committees or panels. The process can be a lonely, troubling experience for fallible human beings conscious that their best may not be adequate to the challenge. A Justice does not forget how much may depend on his decision. He knows that it may affect the course of important social, economic and political currents.

Unlike Congressional or White House decisions, Americans demand of their Supreme Court that the written and oral arguments of the issues be completely open to the public, and that its decisional process produce a written opinion, the collective expression of a majority of the Justices, setting forth the reasons that led them to the decision they reached. These opinions are the exposition, not just to lawyers, to legal scholars and to other judges, but to our society, of the basis upon which the result in any case rests.

Discussion Questions: "Inside the Supreme Court"

1. What distinction is being made between institutional personality and institutional character in the first paragraph?
2. What is the main idea of the essay? Write down the focus sentence(s) that contain(s) the main idea.
3. For whom was the essay written (the audience)? How can you tell? What accommodations for audience do you find in the essay?
4. What predominant organizational strategy does Justice Stewart use to explain the main idea? Why did Justice Stewart choose the details he did to explain how the Court works?
5. Circle the transition words or phrases in the essay. These words serve to link ideas together or signal a change of focus or idea so that the *reader* will be able to follow the *writer's* train of thought.
6. How does the writer end the essay? What purpose is served by Justice Stewart's reminder to us that the Court's opinions are based on a "decisional process" and presented publicly in written form?
7. Can you think of other explanations that you have read of the way institutions conduct their business? Could you explain to someone how your student government operates or how to register for a class?

ASSIGNMENT 1: THE EXPLANATORY ESSAY

1. Choose a word or idea learned in one of your classes to explain to someone who has not taken the course. The reader could be a friend, a brother or sister, a parent, or someone else you know well. You will need to illustrate your explanation using details that your reader will be able to understand.
2. Explain a term associated with a hobby, sport, or other interest you have which people new to the subject should know if they want to participate. You may assume that the reader is someone you know well.

One may begin an essay of explanation with the word or term to be defined and then go immediately into an explanation of the meaning, with perhaps an example or illustration to make it understandable to the reader. Essay examination answers often follow this organizational pattern because the writers are under time pressure and must "stick to the facts" as clearly and concisely as they can. In other instances, however, a writer may use an introduction to "set the scene" or to interest the reader in the explanation to follow. Two of the student writers in the following examples chose that course. You might consider what effect an introduction might have on a reader of *your* paper.

If you choose to have an introduction, the word or term to be discussed usually follows and is then explained through one or more strategies. In the following student papers, definition, process analysis, examples, comparison, and analogy are represented. When you think of your topic, decide on which strategy or combination of strategies will interest and instruct your reader.

After each paper you will find a series of questions to guide your discussion of each student paper and to help you focus on the ways these student writers coped with this assignment.

STUDENT ESSAYS

CONSERVATION OF MATTER

The Law of Conservation of Matter proves that matter can't be thrown away. Matter may change forms, but will never disappear. All the cycles in nature demonstrate this law to be true.

The water cycle shows that all the water that is now present on Earth is the same water that was present since Earth's beginning. The water molecules that are in a glass of water you're drinking could be the same molecules that were in a glass of water that Christ drank. Water that is present on Earth evaporates and forms clouds and rain. Rain pours down from the sky, and the whole cycle starts again. All water ultimately ends up in the ocean. Sun shines on the water, so the water evaporates. The reason the rain from the evaporated water isn't dirty is that when water evaporates, all the dirt and other junk are left behind. Another kind of water that is evaporated is human perspiration. Plants have a process called transpiration that is like human perspiration in which water is also evaporated. The water cycle shows how we never lose water molecules.

The carbon dioxide–oxygen cycle also demonstrates how matter is always conserved. All animal life requires oxygen. Human beings could never exist without oxygen. Plants evolved before animals, because they don't need oxygen, which wasn't present on Earth's surface at the beginning of time. Plants took in the carbon dioxide that was present and mixed this with water. As a result of this process, oxygen was given off. This is shown in the following chemical equation:

$$6CO_2 + 6H_2O \rightarrow C_6H_{12}O_6 + 6O_2$$

The last element in this equation ($6O_2$) is the oxygen that was given off. Because of this oxygen, animal life evolved. Animals also help the plant life, because when they breathe in oxygen they give off carbon dioxide. This carbon dioxide goes to the plants. All of this demonstrates how carbon dioxide and oxygen are used over and over again and are never destroyed. We also get carbon dioxide from plant and animal remains. When plants and animals die, they get buried in the earth. These remains turn into fossil fuels like coal and oil. These fuels are burned so that the carbon dioxide existing in these fuels is floating around the atmosphere. The carbon dioxide present in animals and plants millions of years ago was never destroyed. It was conserved.

The last cycle that demonstrates how matter is conserved is the nitrogen cycle. Nitrogen is in the air, but we can't use it directly to make proteins. Plants have nitrogen in a form that animals can use. Animals eat plants. Plant protein is converted into animal protein. We eat animals which are high in protein. The wastes of animals are high in nitrogen. These wastes, which are used as fertilizers, go into the soil to help plants grow. Nitrogen is therefore never destroyed. This cycle, along with all the other cycles, show how matter can never be gotten rid of. It is continuously recycled for further use.

Discussion Questions: "Conservation of Matter"

1. How does the writer begin the essay? Does the beginning help the reader understand the writer's main point?
2. What is the main idea of the essay? Write down the focus sentence(s) that contain(s) the main idea.

3. For whom was the essay written (the audience)? How can you tell? What accommodations for audience do you find in the essay?

4. What organizational strategies did the writer use to explain the main idea? List them by paragraphs.

5. What specific details are used to support the main idea? Are there enough details to convince a reader that the idea is valid?

6. Find the transition words or phrases in the essay.

7. How does the writer end the essay? Does the ending help the reader understand the writer's main idea?

8. If this essay was written to explain a concept to someone who had not taken a course in chemistry, is the chemical equation in the third paragraph useful? Why or why not?

9. At the end of the second paragraph, are the ideas of perspiration and plant transpiration explained clearly enough? Should there be some connection between these ideas and the concluding sentence of that paragraph?

10. Some people would say that the last paragraph is choppy; that is, that the sentences are clipped and not logically connected to each other. A choppy style forces the *reader* to make connections and transitions, which is not really the reader's responsibility. Can you smooth out the sentences by adding transition words or phrases?

THE BENDS

In a sport-minded world, no sport compares with that of scuba diving. It is a totally unique and fascinating experience. It is a chance to explore areas of the Earth never before seen by man and to accept the challenges of the untamed ocean. Although diving is one of the most exciting fantasies within man's grasp, it can turn into a hellish nightmare if a person doesn't know what he is doing. Decompression sickness or caisson disease, better known as the "bends," is just one of the many problems one can encounter.

What exactly causes the bends? It is a result of increased pressure on the body. As one descends to depths beyond thirty-three feet, the body begins to absorb nitrogen faster and faster. The longer the diver stays down and the deeper he dives, the more nitrogen he absorbs. Clearly, this nitrogen must be released again. The way by which it is released is the same as the way it is absorbed. If, however, he ascends too rapidly, the nitrogen is not given a chance to escape, and it goes out of solution, forming nitrogen gas bubbles in the body's tissues and bloodstream. It is generally the same effect as the bubbling of uncapped soda. The result of these bubbles forming is dizziness, severe pain leading to paralysis, and possibly death.

Clearly, anyone who dives should know the necessary precautions to take in order to prevent the bends. First of all, every dive should be carefully planned.

If one is going deeper than thirty-three feet or making more than one dive in twenty-four hours, there are decompression charts to consult. They will determine if one must stop during ascent to allow the excess nitrogen to be driven out of the body. Therefore, it is very important to plan a dive, and dive the plan. Also, the deepest dive should be first. A second important item is to ascend slowly, at a rate no faster than sixty feet per minute. A wise method of judging the rate of ascent is to ascend more slowly than the smallest bubble ascends. Another, rather obvious, precaution is to allow for the air needed to ascend and to make any necessary decompression stops. If one doesn't watch the pressure gauge showing how much air is left in the tank, and he runs out of air while still on the bottom, an emergency ascent will have to be made. As a result, the risk of getting "bent" is greatly increased. Thus it is very important to know how to prevent the bends before ever entering the scuba world.

If, by chance, someone does get "bent," it is equally important that one know how to deal with this situation. An important fact to remember is that 50 percent of the victims of the bends get bent within thirty minutes; 85 percent within the first hour after diving; and after six hours, there is no chance of becoming bent. The first aid administered to a bent victim is pure oxygen until such time as the victim gets to a recompression chamber. In such a chamber, the person is, in a sense, "taken back down" and "brought back up" slowly as to allow the escape of nitrogen. In other words, the person is put through an increase in pressure, as in the ocean, until the nitrogen bubble goes back into solution, is driven off, and the bends is cured.

Obviously, the condition known as the "bends" is a very serious matter to understand before ever considering scuba diving. If, however, one does understand why people get bent and what to do to prevent decompression sickness, diving can be a most memorable experience. It is, after all, a means of entering into a different world, an environment totally alien to the one in which we live. By entering this strange environment, we encounter many risks and dangers; the bends is just one of these.

Discussion Questions: "The Bends"

1. How does the writer begin the essay? What psychological motive could there be for beginning with the positive values of scuba diving before giving the warning about the bends?
2. What is the main idea of the essay? Write down the focus sentence(s) that contain(s) the main idea.
3. For whom was the essay written (the audience)? How can you tell? What accommodations for audience do you find in the essay?
4. Is the process of absorbing nitrogen clearly explained in the second paragraph? What more explanation, if any, would you want?
5. What is the function of the last sentence in the third paragraph? Is it effective?

6. Is the second sentence in the fourth paragraph (about the time table for victims of the bends) necessary? Why or why not? Would it be better placed elsewhere in the paragraph or left out altogether?
7. What organizational strategies did the writer use to explain the main idea? List them by paragraphs.
8. What specific details are used to support the main idea? Are there enough details to convince a reader that the idea is valid?
9. Find the transition words or phrases in the essay.
10. How does the writer end the essay? Does the last sentence raise a new topic, "other dangers," that would be better left for another essay? Can you think of an effective way to end the essay?

CULTURE SHOCK

A social anthropologist, while doing research for his doctorate from the University of California, goes deep into the deserts of Saudi Arabia to study a Bedouin nomadic tribe called the Al Murrah. Their pastoral existence is characterized by aspects of life that the anthropologist is not accustomed to, and he finds that he isn't quite sure if he can adapt to these "harsh" living conditions. The tribe eats with their hands, they don't sleep in beds, and they are constantly traveling by camel. Can he, too, live like this? This reaction is not uncommon; he had experienced culture shock.

"Culture shock" is defined as the reaction of a person or animal to a new way of life, to a new culture. This reaction can be to all different aspects of life; for example, the way people dress, their religious beliefs, the food they eat, dialect and language, and their marriage customs. This "shock" is caused by the fact that most people are only keenly aware of the values and traditions of their own culture and cannot readily accept those of another culture.

The effects of culture shock have cultural advantages and disadvantages. The most important advantage is that it allows a person to center on his own culture. It is important to first know and understand the culture of one's own society, along with its values and morals. The primary disadvantage of the effects of culture shock is the development of ethnocentrism, which means the attitude of refusing to make a correct evaluation of another culture.

As you can see, culture shock is a very natural and common response to a different society's attitudes, beliefs, and behavior. It is experienced by the average person traveling abroad, as well as the highly trained professional anthropologist doing research in a foreign country. It is experienced by both the observer and the person under observation. An illustration of culture shock by both the observer and the observed could be a young woman from the United States, dressed in designer blue jeans and a revealing little cotton shirt, and a young woman of the same age from a small village in Iran, dressed in a long robe covering her whole body with a veil covering her face, coming in visual contact with one another and gasping with horror. Both young women experienced culture shock. In all instances, culture shock is a common and spontaneous social experience.

Discussion Questions: "Culture Shock"

1. How does the writer begin the essay? Does the beginning help the reader understand the writer's main point?
2. What is the main idea of the essay? Write down the focus sentence(s) that contain(s) the main idea.
3. For whom was the essay written (the audience)? How can you tell? What accommodations for audience do you find in the essay?
4. Is the reference in the second paragraph to "the reaction of . . . [an] animal to a new way of life" helpful to the reader's understanding of culture shock or confusing? How do animals experience culture shock? Is the focus of the writer on all creatures or just on human beings?
5. Is the third paragraph detailed enough to let you, the reader, understand the advantages and disadvantages of culture shock? Do you as reader have questions left unanswered by this brief paragraph? Are there other places you would like more details?
6. Do you find the examples of the anthropologist (in the first paragraph) and the two young women (in the fourth paragraph) effective? Do you want to know more about these instances, or would you like more such examples? Discuss your reasons for your opinions.
7. What organizational strategies did the writer use to explain the main idea? List them by paragraphs.
8. Find the transition words or phrases in the essay.
9. How does the writer end the essay? Does the ending help the reader understand the writer's main idea?

RUNNER'S KNEE

One of the most common afflictions of long-distance runners is runner's knee. It is more properly known as chondromalacia patellae, which comes from the Greek words for "cartilage" and "softness," and the Latin word for "a small plate" (the kneecap). It is associated with excessive wear between the kneecap and the end of the upper leg bone, the femur. When the bones mesh properly, the kneecap moves smoothly within an indentation at the lower end of the femur. But occasionally the alignment is incorrect, and instead of staying in the hollow, the kneecap grinds against the slope of the indentation. The kneecap's cartilage becomes worn if the grinding is prolonged, resulting in pain, stiffness, and swelling.

Many doctors recommend that a person stop running in order to cure chondromalacia. This is not always necessary. Runner's knee can be relieved by cutting down on mileage, doing strengthening exercises for the quadriceps muscles (the large muscle in front of the thigh), and running on a surface that slopes downward toward the injured side. Running on a road with a high crown helps. Run with traffic for chondromalacia of the right knee; run against traffic for chondromalacia of the left knee.

Some doctors believe that, despite its name, runner's knee is a foot problem, caused by faulty weight-bearing characteristics. Chondromalacia often disappears when a runner wears orthotics, or inserts. Orthotics change the foot's support patterns, thus shifting the relationship between kneecap and femur.

According to other doctors, chondromalacia is caused by a condition known as Morton's toe. Named after Dr. Dudley Morton, author of a 1935 study called "The Human Foot: Its Evolution, Physiology and Functional Disorders," this is a condition in which the first toe is shorter than the second. Problems can develop in the heel, leg, knee, and back when the first toe fails to support, because it normally absorbs twice the stress of the other four toes combined. This is not a sure cause of runner's knee, since many people with Morton's toe never develop problems.

In any case, runner's knee can usually be cured without having to go to the doctor. With stubborn cases, however, it is advisable to visit a doctor, preferably a podiatrist who specializes in treating athletes.

Discussion Questions: "Runner's Knee"

1. Why does the writer include the Latin and Greek terms for runner's knee? To what type of reader is the Latin and Greek term "more proper"? Why would it be wise for a runner to know both terms?
2. The second paragraph is about ways to cure runner's knee, while the third and fourth paragraphs are about different causes. Should the paragraphs be rearranged in order to proceed more logically? Note that the third paragraph also contains a possible cure—that of wearing orthotics. Does that fact affect the way you organize the paragraphs?
3. What organizational strategies did the writer use to explain the main idea? List them by paragraphs.
4. What specific details are used to support the main idea? Are there enough details to convince a reader that the idea is valid?
5. Several sentences in this essay do *not* use transitions to link them with previous sentences. Are there some places where inserting such transitions would make the writing easier to read?
6. What reason can you find for the ending of the essay? Is it consistent with the assumed audience for the essay?

WRITING ACTIVITY

Beginning the Assignment

Now that you have had a chance to see other students' essays, think about what you will write. Use freewriting or asking questions or any of the other "getting started" ideas discussed earlier. Consider what your reader would want to know about your topic, and jot down details which will satisfy her need to know.

Writing a Draft

Decide on a strategy or strategies to use which will explain the term you have chosen.

How will you get the reader involved in your topic? Think about an introduction.

Try to be as specific as possible in discussing the term. You want your reader to understand the word or phrase as well as you do.

How will you end your discussion? Do you need to summarize the main points or to give an explanation of the term's importance or the implications of understanding the term?

Revising Your Writing

After writing a rough draft, ask yourself the following questions about how well your paper has fulfilled the assignment *or* get a fellow classmate to read your paper and answer these questions. Your instructor may ask you to turn in the answers.

1. Has the paper clearly indicated what it will explain?
2. Is the paper written so that the audience can understand it? That is, are there enough details to explain what the word means?
3. Do the details support the focus? That is, does everything stick to the point of the paper?
4. What strategy or strategies were chosen to develop the paper? Were they appropriate for the subject?
5. What connections were made between paragraphs to serve as signals to let the reader know what he had just read and what he was going to read?

6. How does the paper begin? How does it end? Do the beginning and ending serve to introduce and then reinforce the definition so that the reader will not forget it?

7. Are the sentences error-free and easy to read? Do spelling and punctuation follow accepted usage?

ASSIGNMENT 2: THE SUMMARY

Frequently, students in physical science or social science classes are asked to write a summary of an article read for an outside reading assignment. Students in liberal arts classes may be called upon to summarize material as part of a paper or as an essay examination answer. And some study-skills instructors recommend writing summaries of reading material as a way of helping students remember what they read.

For this assignment, you are to choose a chapter or article from one of your textbooks to summarize in a short paper for the instructor of the course. If you have no course textbook suitable for this assignment, find a magazine or journal article acceptable to your composition instructor and use it to write a summary.

Whatever the purpose, a summary requires you to do several things. First, you must read the material and find the main points. How do you pick out main points?

1. Pay attention to headings, subheadings, and anything in dark type or italics.

2. Look at the first sentence of each paragraph. Sometimes these alone can serve as an outline for the article.

3. Note any definitions given by the author.

4. Read the beginning and ending of the article carefully to get a sense of the author's purpose (stated in the beginning most likely) and his or her main ideas (often repeated in the conclusion).

5. Make check marks in the margin or underline as you read so that piecing together the information will be easier later.

How do you know what to leave out?

1. Omit several examples of one point or shorten a long example. The reader should be given *some* detail so that the content of the article is clear but not so much that he or she is really reading the article, not a summary.

2. As a general rule, include all definitions of important terms in the summary.

After you have read the material and have an idea of what it says, you will write the summary. You may wish to reorganize the content to group main points or subpoints together. Don't feel that you must follow the text's organization. You may have your own way of presenting the main ideas. Also, try to summarize in your *own words.* Use the author's words *only* when necessary and then *only* by using *quotation marks* around everything directly quoted.

One further caution: Don't evaluate the text or give your opinion. Just present the information in a clear but condensed form.

Read the student examples which follow and the questions following each example; then begin your summary with the "Writing Activity" page after the sample summaries.

STUDENT ESSAYS

CHARACTERISTICS OF RECREATIONAL SERVICE LEADERS

It is incorrect to assume that all recreational leaders come from one mold; however, certain traits must be present in order for a potential leader to emerge. A potential leader can be identified through observation. It is easy to recognize an individual who interacts easily with his peer group, for he does not attempt to dominate his peer group. He is the one who can meet the emotional needs of the group, thus earning their confidence and having influence with them.

Although there are many characteristics associated with leaders, there are two necessary characteristics. First, an individual must have the desire to become a leader. Second, an individual must have intelligence. A leader must be more intelligent than his followers, but not too intelligent as to be above the average of the group.

Intelligence allows a potential leader to have understanding and to have the ability to perform. In this way, intelligence is the key to leadership. There are three aspects of intelligence that involve personal contact with the group: social intelligence, moral intelligence, and communicative intelligence.

Social intelligence involves showing understanding and showing knowledge in human relations. Included aspects of social intelligence are sympathy and empathy. Sympathy is the sharing of another person's sorrow or trouble. Empathy is characterized by a person's ability to place himself in another's place.

Moral intelligence is the ability to determine between right and wrong. This is the one aspect of intelligence that can be taught and learned. Morals are developed early in life which allow a person to develop a strong moral intelligence. An individual cannot pretend to have a set of standards; he must practice these standards each and every day.

Communicative intelligence is like a two-way street. The leader must be able to contact his followers, and his followers must be able to contact the leader. Only through communication can a leader influence his followers and make them aware of his goals. It is important that the leader not try to dominate his followers, thus closing off communication in the slightest way.

As was mentioned before, there are no set characteristics for a leader; however, there are a few qualities that are more prevalent than any other qualities. All of the following qualities function in combination with intelligence: loyalty—being faithful to an individual, a group, or a cause; integrity—being sincere, which leads to truth; discretion—being free to judge or choose with caution; reliability—depended upon and being worthy of trust; responsibility—being morally obliged; tolerance—being able to endure; talent—being natural due to an innate ability; sociability—being able to get along well with others; perseverance—being able to persist in spite of difficulties; and initiative—being able to take the first step in any undertaking.

There are four personal attributes, like the above qualities, that do not characterize a leader, but these attributes help a leader advance in his career. They are a well-groomed appearance, a skill in public speaking, a strong educational background, and a sound mental and physical health. In conclusion, an individual must use intelligence together with the aspects and qualities mentioned in order to be a leader.

Discussion Questions: "Characteristics of Recreational Service Leaders"

1. What point does the paper establish in the first paragraph? Why is that important?
2. List the two main characteristics of a leader. Is the first characteristic explained as completely as the second? Does it need to be? Why or why not?
3. The seventh paragraph is a list of other leadership characteristics, most of which is one long sentence. Is the sentence effective? Why or why not? Is each characteristic defined well enough for you to understand?
4. Several sentences in the essay sound too formal or "stilted." Locate sentences that do not sound right to you and suggest ways to edit them.
5. Are there places in the essay where *more* transitions or linking words would help a reader to understand this summary?
6. Do you as a reader understand the three different kinds of intelligence? If not, what would you like to know? Would more examples and details help your understanding?
7. How does the writer end the essay? Does it add necessary information or take away from the qualities already discussed?

SUMMARY: MUSIC—AN APPRECIATION, CHAPTER 9, "ROCK"

During the mid-1950s, a new type of popular music developed, termed "rock 'n' roll." Its main influences were the rhythm and blues music of American blacks, and the country and western, or folk, music of rural, white Americans. Rock music is characterized as being vocal music accompanied by a hard, driving beat, typically in the strong 4/4 time signature, featuring an electric guitar. The form of rock music is typically in the 32-bar "AABA" style of alternation of parts that is based on short melodic patterns having simple harmonic progressions of usually three to four chords.

Although rock still exists ubiquitously today, it has gone through essentially three stylistic stages of development, namely the rhythm and blues era, the experimental era, and the refinement and revival era.

The first era, that of rhythm and blues, was the beginning of rock. It was ushered in by the film about rebellious youths, called *Blackboard Jungle* (1955), which featured Bill Haley and His Comets. The style of music during this period was essentially an expurgated, white version of the black's rhythm and blues. Bill Haley and His Comets were the first group to write a rock hit single. Other big names in early rock were Chuck Berry, Elvis Presley, and the Platters.

The next stage in rock music began with the American tour of the Beatles in 1964, and the "British Invasion" that ensued, involving the Rolling Stones as well as many more of their countrymen. The British at this time dominated the American popular music scene; and because of this influence, rock groups explored a wider range of inspirations and instrumentations. Stylistically, this involved incorporating electronic effects, classical instruments, Eastern instruments, and unconventional chord patterns into their music. This British-influenced music contained a larger folk element, and also contained lyrics that served as social commentaries. This diversification of style generated many subcategories of rock, such as acid rock, hard rock, jazz rock, and classical rock, to name a few. The important musicians of this era were Jimi Hendrix, the Beatles, the Rolling Stones, Bob Dylan, and the Who (who wrote the first rock opera, *Tommy*). This era ended with Woodstock, the breakup of the Beatles, and the deaths of Jimi Hendrix, Janis Joplin, and Jim Morrison, who were prominent performers of this time.

The third era began about 1971 and was marked by a revival of rock's roots in rhythm and blues, and by a refinement of the previous British techniques. Some of the major artists of this time were Billy Joel, Linda Ronstadt, and David Bowie. This music was characterized as being heavily amplified, highly theatric, and heavily reliant on the recording studio and electronics as creative instruments.

Though rock music has stylistically changed throughout the years, its theme as music for and about the young people of society has remained constant. This differed from pre-1950s popular music, which had practically universal appeal, but lacked the social impact and the diversity of rock. Hence rock's importance lies in its concentration on the young, its rebelliousness, its experimental quality, and its reflection of life's issues.

Discussion Questions: "Summary: *Music—An Appreciation*"

1. The first paragraph defines "rock." What are the essential characteristics of rock music? Do any terms of the definition need to be further explained?
2. Besides the basic definition, what other information does the summary provide?
3. What is the predominant organizational pattern of the summary?
4. You may be more familiar with the content of this summary, but the writer still helps you to understand the different eras in rock through the use of names of performers, titles of songs, and so on. Were there enough of these details to illustrate the three eras of rock? What, if anything, would you add?
5. Does the third paragraph seem too short? Is more detail (titles of songs, examples of the music's character) necessary?
6. Look at the beginning sentence of each paragraph. What function does each perform in the summary?
7. What purpose does the ending accomplish?

SUMMARY OF AN ARTICLE: CUSHING'S SYNDROME

DAVID E. SCHTEINGART, et al., "Depressed Mood and Other Psychiatric Manifestations of Cushing's Syndrome: Relationship to Hormone Levels," *Psychomatic Medicine*, Feb. 1981, 48, 3–18.

Introduction

This was a study involving thirty-five patients with Cushing's syndrome, prior to treatment. They were psychiatrically evaluated and their cortisol and ACTH hormonal levels were measured. Next, the relationships among the psychiatric disability ratings and the hormonal levels were analyzed. The statistical significance obtained will be discussed later.

Methods and Materials

Subjects.   There were thirty-five subjects: twenty-eight were white and seven were black. Seven were male and twenty-eight were female (the usual 1 : 3 ratio expected with this disease). Ages ranged from 19 to 59 years, with an average age of 35. All patients had excessive levels of cortisol. The etiology of their disease differed slightly, as did their levels of ACTH.

Procedures.   Through the use of a semistructured interview technique, a standardized set of questions, and a mental status examination, the patients were psychiatrically evaluated prior to treatment. An overall score of psychiatric disability was obtained based on two factors: the total of the raw scores for the forty-five items in the symptom review and mental status examination and the "clinical global judgment of the seriousness of the psychiatric symptoms and degrees of psychiatric impairment." This overall score ranged from 1 to 4 (mild, moderate, severe, very severe). "Severe" meant that they were showing more disabling affective signs than mild or moderate. "Very severe" meant that their behavior showed paranoid ideation and/or confusional states.

Results

The overall psychiatric disability scores were as follows: Thirty-four percent were rated as having mild psychiatric disability, 25 percent moderate, 20 percent severe, and 11 percent very severe psychiatric disability.

Through an analysis of variance, statistical significance was obtained between the overall disability scores and the "degree of cortisol elevation as measured by the cortisol secretion rate ($p = 0.00$), urinary free cortisol ($p = 0.00$), and plasma cortisol at 8 A.M. ($p = 0.02$)." Highest hormone levels were seen in the most severely disturbed group.

Summary

The subjects in this study, victims of Cushing's syndrome, also showed that a number of psychiatric disturbances were present. These included irritability, depressed mood, decreased libido, insomnia, poor concentration, and impaired memory. Severe ratings or psychotic and/or confusional states were not frequently present, but when they were present, they occurred with extra high levels of cortisol and ACTH.

Mild mood ratings were associated with high cortisol levels and low ACTH levels. Also, the ratio of cortisol to ACTH may relate to severe mood ratings.

Many of the features of Cushing's syndrome resemble those of primary depressive disease. The article suggests that changes in biogenic amines, electrolyte shifts, and/or neuroactive peptides may also be major contributors to both disorders.

Discussion Questions: "Cushing's Syndrome"

1. What is the purpose of the introduction?
2. This article uses a form common to technical and business reports. Note all the headings and subheadings (not generally found in papers for liberal arts courses). Do they help a reader? Why or why not? If the summary you are working on is scientific or technical, you may wish to use headings and subheadings in your paper.
3. The vocabulary in this essay is more technical than in the other summaries. It may be difficult for you to read some of the words. Should the writer have "translated" some of the terms, or considering that this was an assignment for a biology class, is the level of diction (choice of words) appropriate?
4. How effective is the ending?

WRITING ACTIVITY

Beginning the Assignment

As you read the article, pay attention to headings, dark type, and first sentences of paragraphs. Perhaps make check marks in the margins opposite important points. Jot down the main points in an outline or list and then see if you need to combine or regroup them.

Don't evaluate the text or give your opinion. Instead, present the information in a clear but condensed form.

Use your *own* words except where you feel that you *must* quote the text. Then use quotation marks.

Writing a Draft

You may find that your first attempts to summarize are long-winded. Ask yourself, what information is essential in this material? What shows that I have read and understood this material?

Revising Your Writing

Sometimes a way to look at a rough draft is to assess its strengths and weaknesses. We are often aware of what went well and what did not go well with a particular assignment. Look at your rough draft of the summary and assess its good points and weak points. Perhaps exchange the draft with a classmate and have that person evaluate your writing.

ASSIGNMENT 3: THE OBJECTIVE REPORT

You have been asked, as student reporter of the month, to explain the facts about any issue current in your community, to be published in a local newspaper. Your readers will be people from the community, but most probably are younger readers who will want to see what the student reporter of the month has come up with.

Though the facts a writer chooses will often reveal his or her opinion about an issue, try to remain relatively objective in your article. Your main purpose is to explain something to local citizens, not to argue a particular point of view.

Because the medium will be a newspaper, you may wish to use a more journalistic style. The first paragraph, for example, usually tries to capture the reader's attention through a short statement of what is "news" and often a case history or other "human interest" angle. Paragraphs are short, as are sentences. Background or people's opinions are generally found farther down the column (or page). And of course the journalist tries to answer the questions Who? What? Where? When? Why? How?

Two students' papers on the next pages respond to the assignment. Again, read them with an eye to what is effective and what changes could be made to improve them. How objective did the students remain?

STUDENT ESSAYS

MOYER'S LANDFILL

Moyer's landfill, a local dump in Lower Providence Township, was closed on Monday, April 6, 198–, the culmination of public concern for landfills and their complications.

The dump had long been a public eyesore for township residents, who for years had tried, unsuccessfully, to close it. Finally, on Monday, the Department of Environmental Resources did the job for them. The DER closed the dump because of numerous violations of environmental laws.

Moyer's, according to Wayne Lynn, Regional Solid Waste Manager, was closed because it was "generating leachate" and the operators were "discharging it, without a permit." The dump was also cited for dumping beyond its boundaries, as well as failing to finish the sloping and covering of filled portions, and for not seeding these areas to prevent erosion. Moyer's also neglected to provide litter and dust control. And finally, they failed to provide an approved system for controlling leachate—a poisonous liquid formed from decomposing trash and rainwater.

Township officials, as well as some DER officials, now state that the dump was closed because it was at capacity, a point not mentioned in Mr. Lynn's letter.

Whether the reason for closing the landfill, turned dump, was environmental or due to capacity, it still stands that this eyesore is closed for good. The DER is currently meeting with dump representatives to outline the final phase of closing the dump, which is expected to include the neglected grading, sloping, and seeding of this area, as well as leachate control.

The township itself seems determined to take advantage of the momentum gathered from the closing. At the last township meeting, the board of supervisors unanimously approved a proposal to convert a 113-acre tract of land, adjacent to the closed Moyer's landfill, to a residential area, thereby making it impossible to construct a landfill on that tract of land. This action comes just in time to halt Moyer's legal action to gain access to this land for dumping purposes.

Whatever happens, the fact remains that the original Moyer's landfill is closed for good and that action, in this small township, has begun to prevent similar occurrences.

Discussion Questions: "Moyer's Landfill"

1. How does the writer begin the article? Can you think of another way it might begin?
2. What reasons are cited for the DER's closing of the landfill?
3. Who would be interested in reading this article?
4. Several paragraphs in this article are short. Does the proposed place of publication (a local newspaper) have any bearing on the length of the paragraphs? Discuss. What determines paragraph length anyway? Is it completely arbitrary or are there certain "rules of thumb"?
5. If you were a local citizen, would this article (a) have interested you in reading it, and (b) have provided you with enough information about the issue?
6. What "loaded" words reveal the writer's opinion against Moyer's landfill? Could (or should) the writer have chosen more neutral words? What effect would an interview with the owner of the landfill have had on the article?

SOCIAL SECURITY SHUTOFF

Lisa G. was a senior at Edina High School in suburban Minneapolis until she made a startling discovery two weeks ago. She learned from her school guidance counselor that if she was not enrolled as a full-time college student by May 1, she would lose thousands of dollars in Social Security benefits. Today, Lisa is a freshman at the University of Minnesota.

Lisa is just one of hundreds of Minneapolis-area high school seniors—along with 100,000 other seniors across the country—who has been affected by the federal budget cuts. The cuts have brought about a change in a Social Security rule. Under the old rule, eligible students were able to collect educational benefits until they reached age twenty-two. A student became eligible if one or both parents were dead, disabled, or retired.

Under the new Social Security rule, however, all benefits will end when children reach age eighteen, unless they have matriculated as full-time college students by May 1, 1982. Students not enrolled in college by then will lose all future benefits, not just aid for the current year. While benefits vary widely, the average student receives $259 a month. Under the new rules, the payments will decrease each year, even if a student has enrolled in college by May 1. Even so, many recipients who beat the deadline will receive between $5,000 and $6,000 in aid, according to the *New York Times*.

In many cases, this could be the difference between going to college and not going to college. Because of this, many high school seniors will begin their college educations in the next few weeks. They will trade the relative leisure of their last high school days for benefits that allow them to go to college.

The rule change has met strong criticism, not only because it might mean that numerous future high school graduates may not be able to attend college, but because those affected were not notified. A spokesman for the American Association of State Colleges and Universities states: "We are shocked that the administration has done nothing to notify these families that the program is coming to an end. We are also inquiring whether it is a violation of federal law for the Social Security Administration not to notify families of a change in their benefits."

Social Security officials said that they had issued news releases about the change, but had not included notices to beneficiaries because that would have defeated the purpose of the cutback. "The intent of this change in the law is for such benefits to stop, not for us to find ways to help people get in under the system," said Jim Brown, a Social Security Administration spokesman.

The Social Security Administration said it decided not to notify any students individually about the impending cutoff until late February. At that time, officials concede, it would be too late for students to enroll in the winter-spring semester, which has already begun at most colleges.

Discussion Questions: "Social Security Shutoff"

1. How does the writer begin the essay? Does the beginning interest you more than the beginning of the previous article? Discuss.
2. Is the difference between the old rule on eligible students and the new rule clear to you? If not, what changes might have made it clearer?
3. Who would be most interested in reading this article?
4. If you were a local reader, would this article have interested you and have provided you with enough information about the issue?
5. Is this article more objective than the preceding one? If so, how was the objectivity achieved?

WRITING ACTIVITY

Beginning the Assignment

Whichever topic you choose to write on, remember to keep your reader in mind. Local residents will be interested in a lively discussion of a local issue as it *affects them*, especially their life-styles or their wallets. Remember: *Your primary goal is to present information, not to argue for or against something.*

Writing a Draft

After generating information through interviews, reading local news articles, and answering the journalists' "who, what, where?" questions, think about how you will organize your article. What would make an effective lead? Did you find out a startling fact or come across an absorbing human interest story? Is there an aspect to this issue which local residents will recognize as being important to their lives? Once you have your lead, think of how you will present the rest of the story, concentrating on an objective presentation of the facts. You may, through selection of material or your tone, reveal your attitude toward the subject, but the purpose of the article should remain chiefly explanatory.

Revising Your Writings

Get a classmate to read your rough draft and answer these questions:

1. Does the beginning effectively introduce the subject?
2. a. Does the discussion of the issue continue to hold my interest? Why or why not?
   b. Is there an angle or aspect that could interest me more?
3. Are there enough facts for me to understand the issue? If not, what questions do I have for the writer?
4. Did the writer stick to the point or wander away from it?
5. Does the ending wrap things up?
6. Are the sentences clear? Are there transitions from one idea to another? Are there places I needed to read twice to understand what was being said? Did I notice any mechanical errors?

MASTERY ASSIGNMENTS

Below is a list of topics related to the work on explaining which may provide you an opportunity to show what you have learned in Chapter 3. Try to keep in mind who the audience is for the assignment you choose and use the techniques you have learned to get started writing and to revise your writing.

1. Choose any current legislation or policy (the Social Security System reform, the revision of the minimum wage law to permit lower wages for students working during the summer, etc.) and show how it might affect any *one* group of people in a newsletter directed to that group. Do *not* argue for or against, just *explain* the legislation and its likely *impact* on the group.
2. Define a word or term that you use in everyday life to someone who lives elsewhere and doesn't understand what you mean by the word or phrase. The person could be your age or somewhat older and could even be from another country.
3. In a speech to a class of 10-year-olds at a local elementary school, try to explain how something works, such as a nuclear generating station, an x-ray machine or CAT scanner, an internal combustion engine, a computer, or any other relatively complicated device or process. You may wish to use diagrams to help your explanation, but be sure to explain the diagrams. Your paper will be the script for your speech.
4. Explain to someone what something meant to you by recreating the experience as if it were happening in the present (as in the essay "Into the Wild Blue Yonder"). Tell the story vividly so that it has the immediacy of living through it.

CHAPTER **4**

Writing to Support a Point: Substantiating

Writers frequently have to show through solid evidence or convincing reasoning that a conclusion they have drawn about a subject is valid. They attempt to "prove" that what they say is really true.

College instructors may ask students to write papers which take a stand and support that stand with evidence from class or research. In business, a person frequently must present evidence to back up an opinion about how well a product is doing or how badly new personnel are needed in a particular department. And, of course, substantiating is the lawyers' "stock in trade," for they must present evidence to a jury to substantiate their claims that a client is innocent or that another person is guilty. Such writing often entails explaining along with substantiating. It may be represented by two interrelated circles (Figure 4.1).

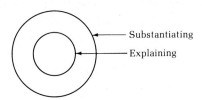

Figure 4.1
Relationship of Two Writing Purposes

That is, you often have to define terms, give background or explain the situation before you state an opinion and back it up.

Following are some sample questions drawn from examinations that require both explaining and substantiating:

1. What do you think were fundamental changes in America wrought by the New Deal from 1933 to 1940? (Here you need to explain what the changes were and why they were "fundamental.")
2. Some say that American literature from 1900 to 1940 shows an attempt on the part of the writer to come to grips with the change to a highly industrialized society. Do you agree? Use the works studied to support your conclusion. (To answer this question you must decide if the statement is valid and then explain how the works show or do not show this idea.)
3. Discuss the Progressive Era, defining its meaning, chronology, and achievements. What is the significance of the Progressive Era for us today? (This two-part question asks you to define and then to establish the importance of the period.)

Below is a sample organizational plan a writer might follow to accomplish this purpose. Remember that such plans are highly adaptable to the needs of writer and reader and should be seen only as suggestions.

A Sample Plan for a Substantiating Essay

A. The introduction explains the background of the issue or situation and defines any terms, if that seems necessary.
B. The writer's point of view or opinion is clearly stated in a sentence or two.
C. Evidence is presented to support the writer's point of view and is explained as needed. Strategies include details, examples, comparison–constrast, and cause and effect.
D. The conclusion usually restates the author's point, emphasizing the validity of the opinion in light of the evidence presented.

Do the following professional essays follow the typical plan? If not, what plan do they follow? Read each essay and decide. Following the essays are other questions for you to consider.

READINGS

Exploding a Myth

Tom Wicker

"As fear of crime has become epidemic in America," I wrote in a recent article, "the myth has spread that streams of criminals are going free because the exclusionary rule prevents the evidence against them from being used in court."

This evoked some angry letters from readers who insisted it was not a myth. And their letters reflect a substantial public protest against the idea that criminals are going free because the police made a mistake or committed "technical violations" of the Fourth Amendment in seizing the evidence of crime.

As one result, the Fifth Circuit Court of Appeals already has established an exception to the exclusionary rule, providing that unconstitutionally seized evidence is admissible in court if the police had a reasonable, good-faith belief that they were acting properly.

The Supreme Court now is considering the adoption of such a "good-faith exception," and five of the nine justices have indicated in past decisions some willingness to modify or abandon the exclusionary rule. Legislation is pending in

Tom Wicker writes a column for the *New York Times* and is one of its editors. A seasoned reporter, Wicker served on several newspapers in North Carolina and Tennessee before joining the *Times* in 1960. He frequently writes about contemporary political issues and is also a published novelist.

Congress to abolish it in the Federal courts.

But I repeat: It's a myth that many criminals are going free because the exclusionary rule bars the evidence against them from being used. And James J. Fyfe, for 16 years a New York City policeman and now an associate professor of justice at American University, told the House Subcommittee on Criminal Justice last month that "no empirical research" supports that myth.

Mr. Fyfe cited, instead, a National Institute of Justice study of 520,983 felony cases presented in the years 1976 to 1979 to prosecutors in California ("where the exclusionary rule is more stringent than in any other state"). Prosecutors rejected 86,033, or 16.51 percent, of these cases for various flaws—*but only 4,130, or 0.78 percent, of all felony cases because of search-and-seizure problems.*

Of these 4,130 cases rejected for search-and-seizure problems, nearly three-quarters (2,953) were drug-related. In contrast, of the 648,336 murders, rapes, assaults and robberies reported to California police during the period 1976–79, about 1 in every 2,500 (248 to be exact) resulted in prosecutorial decisions not to proceed because of search-and-seizure problems.

"Without ignoring the seriousness of these failed cases," Mr. Fyfe said, "it is fair to say that search-and-seizure problems have very little effect on California prosecutors' decisions to proceed with cases." And, he pointed out, the study shows that once a case gets to court in California, the effects of the exclusionary rule are no more impressive.

Of 15,403 felony dismissals in California superior courts from 1976 to 1979, only 575 were because of search-and-seizure problems. That's only four-tenths of 1 percent of the 157,147 felony cases processed through those courts in those years. In one month of 1982 (Aug. 20 to Sept. 20), only 10 of 519 preliminary hearings on felony cases in the Los Angeles District Attorney's Central Branch resulted in dismissals because of search-and-seizure problems.

There's no reason to suppose these findings aren't typical; Mr. Fyfe said they were supported by similar studies in San Diego, Jacksonville, Fla., and the Federal courts. And Peter F. Nardulli of the University of Illinois, James Eisenstein of Penn State and Roy B. Flemming of Wayne State University in Detroit have sent me confirming data from a three-state study they conducted over four years.

They examined felony court records in DuPage, Peoria and St. Clair counties in Illinois; Oakland, Kalamazoo and Saginaw counties in Michigan; and Montgomery, Dauphin and Erie Counties in Pennsylvania, obtaining data on 7,475 cases. They found that motions to suppress evidence had been raised "only infrequently" in preliminary hearings, and in about 5 percent of all cases at the trial level—most often in drug and weapons possession cases.

Of the 351 motions to suppress, 252 were denied and 51 were granted (the ruling in 48 instances could not be determined). Thus, of the 303 motions to suppress on which the rulings are known, just over 83 percent were denied. And of the 51 cases in which the motions were granted, convictions were nevertheless obtained in 11. So only 40 of 7,475 cases were lost, and Mr. Nardulli says that not all these acquittals were necessarily attributable to the suppressed evidence.

He concluded that if the exclusionary rule were abolished, "we would be able to realize an increase in conviction rates" of less than half of 1 percent. Such a marginal gain, he and Mr. Fyfe agreed, is not worth the risks inherent in easing the rule that now deters unconstitutional police searches and seizures.

It's true that this rule "protects some small number of criminals," Mr. Fyfe told the House subcommittee. "That is unfortunate, but it is a necessary and minor trade-off for the protection against judicial and police incompetence and arbitrariness that the rule provides for the rest of us."

Discussion Questions: "Exploding a Myth"

1. How does the writer begin the essay? Does the introduction involve you because you have believed the "myth" that criminals are going free on technicalities?

2. Does he define "exclusionary rule?" Where? What is Wicker's position?

3. How can you tell that Wicker feels he has a skeptical reader?

4. How does the writer substantiate his point of view? What development strategy or strategies does he use?

5. What specific details are used to support the main idea? Are there enough details to convince a reader that the idea is valid?

6. To be convincing, a writer must get the facts (details) from reliable sources (or ones that readers view as reliable). Where does Wicker get his information? Do you consider these sources reliable?

7. Find the transition words or phrases in the essay.

8. How does the writer end the essay? Does the ending help the reader understand the writer's main idea? Do you agree with Fyfe and Wicker about the need for the exclusionary rule?

Whatever Happened to Always?

Albert K. Schaaf

If you grew up in the 1930s and early 1940s, Franklin D. Roosevelt was always president of the United States. Joe Louis was always the heavyweight champion; Pius XII was always the pope; and J. Edgar Hoover was always director of the FBI. People didn't job-hop so much.

The Empire State Building was always the tallest building in the world. I don't know why Sears, Roebuck and whoever built the World Trade Center felt they had to build a few stories taller and confuse everybody.

Fiorello La Guardia was always mayor of New York.

Winston Churchill was always prime minister of England.

You could count on these things. They didn't change every two or three weeks the way things do today. They stayed the same for so long that even if you didn't pay any attention to them for years, they were still there.

The New York subway always cost 5¢.

Transit fares in Philadelphia (PRT or PTC, not Septa, for heaven's sake) were always two tokens for 15¢.

John L. Lewis was always president of the United Mine Workers.

James C. Petrillo was always president of the musicians' union.

Walt Disney pictures always opened at the Aldine Theatre.

There was always a stage show at the Earle Theatre.

The voice behind the movie newsreel was always Lowell Thomas.

There was always a newsreel. And a cartoon.

Neighborhood movies always changed every two days, except for the more important feature, which was presented Thursday, Friday and Saturday. They always cost 10¢ for kids, except when somebody dreamed up some strange tax that made the price 11¢. And movie theatres always had big screens with curtains.

Today, somebody hangs a window shade at the end of a long, plain hallway; the seats are arranged in an odd pattern because it's only half of what used to be a real movie theater; they charge you $4 to get in; they show the movie out of focus; and your feet stick to the floor.

Haile Selassie was always the emperor of Ethiopia.

The thing you played records on was always called a Victrola.

The mayor of Philadelphia was always a Republican, usually Bernard Samuel.

Albert K. Schaaf, a longtime resident of Philadelphia, contributed this article to *Philadelphia* magazine.

The *Bulletin* always had one-panel cartoons on the back page.

The *Saturday Evening Post* always had a "Little Lulu" cartoon on the next-to-the-last page.

Lionel Barrymore was always Scrooge on the radio at Christmastime. Jack Benny was always on the radio on Sunday night at 7 P.M. and Fibber McGee and Molly were always on Tuesday nights at 9:30.

Today, it seems to be mandatory to change the time of every television show every few weeks so you can't find them. If a show does last a few seasons, the star gets tired of it or something and they take it off so they can build all new sets for a whole new show based on another one-joke concept, featuring the same star.

Bette Davis was always in a new movie, and she was always mad at somebody.

The people who made Burk's hot dogs always gave you tickets for discount rides at Willow Grove Park. Except the little Scenic.

When you were sick, the doctor always came to the house, and he always gave you some kind of medicine he mixed in a glass of water your mother brought.

There was always a parade that went right by the corner on the Fourth of July, and everybody always put flags out.

The "wild man" in the circus was always from Borneo. The circus always played at 11th and Erie. Today, Borneo is part of a conglomerate called Malaysia, and I don't know what's at 11th and Erie.

Chiang Kai-shek was always the leader of China. I almost got used to Mao Tse-tung, but he died; then they changed the spelling of the names of all the people and places. Now you can't tell whether anybody is always anything or not.

Philadelphia was always the butt of jokes by well-known comedians. Now we've lost that distinction to Cleveland.

You can't count on anything anymore.

Discussion Questions: "Whatever Happened to Always?"

1. How does the writer begin the essay? What is the tone of the article (the author's attitude toward his subject)? What details or word choices set the tone?
2. What is the main idea of the essay? Where is the sentence expressing that idea?
3. For whom was the essay written (the audience)? How can you tell? What accommodations for audience do you find in the essay?
4. a. What organizational strategies did the writer use to explain the main idea?

    b. What is the effect of the comparison–contrast paragraphs used every so often? What difference would it have made if the writer had done without them?

5. What specific details are used to support the main idea? Are there enough details to convince a reader that the idea is valid?
6. Find the transition words or phrases in the essay.
7. Could you write a similar essay for *your* generation and *your* locality? What things would you include?

The Santa Ana

Joan Didion

There is something uneasy in the Los Angeles air this afternoon, some unnatural stillness, some tension. What it means is that tonight a Santa Ana will begin to blow, a hot wind from the northeast whining down through the Cajon and San Gorgonio Passes, blowing up sandstorms out along Route 66, drying the hills and the nerves to the flash point. For a few days now we will see smoke back in the canyons, and hear sirens in the night. I have neither heard nor read that a Santa Ana is due, but I know it, and almost everyone I have seen today knows it too. We know it because we feel it. The baby frets. The maid sulks. I rekindle a waning argument with the telephone company, then cut my losses and lie down, given over to whatever it is in the air. To live with the Santa Ana is to accept, consciously or unconsciously, a deeply mechanistic view of human behavior.

I recall being told, when I first moved to Los Angeles and was living on an isolated beach, that the Indians would throw themselves into the sea when the bad wind blew. I could see why. The Pacific turned ominously glossy during a Santa Ana period, and one woke in the night troubled not only by the peacocks screaming in the olive trees but by the eerie absence of surf. The heat was surreal. The sky had a yellow cast, the kind of light sometimes called "earthquake weather." My only neighbor would not come out of her house for days, and there were no lights at night, and her husband roamed the place with a machete. One day he would tell me that he had heard a trespasser, the next a rattlesnake.

"On nights like that," Raymond Chandler once wrote about the Santa Ana, "every booze party ends in a fight. Meek little wives feel the edge of the carving knife and study their husbands' necks. Anything can happen." That was the kind of wind it was. I did not know then that there was any basis for the effect it had on all of us, but it turns out to be another of those cases in which science bears out folk wisdom. The Santa Ana, which is named for one of the canyons it rushes through, is a *foehn* wind, like the *foehn* of Austria and Switzerland and the *hamsin* of Israel. There are a number of persistent malevolent winds, perhaps the best known of which are the mistral of France and the Mediterranean sirocco, but a *foehn* wind has distinct characteristics: it occurs on the leeward slope of a mountain range

Joan Didion graduated from the University of California at Berkeley and wrote for *Vogue, National Review,* and *Saturday Evening Post.* She has had three novels published and several books of nonfiction and collections of essays, the latest being *Salvador* (1983). This essay explains the character of Los Angeles and is from *Slouching Towards Bethlehem* (1968).

and, although the air begins as a cold mass, it is warmed as it comes down the mountain and appears finally as a hot dry wind. Whenever and wherever a *foehn* blows, doctors hear about headaches and nausea and allergies, about "nervousness," about "depression." In Los Angeles some teachers do not attempt to conduct formal classes during a Santa Ana, because the children become unmanageable. In Switzerland the suicide rate goes up during the *foehn*, and in the courts of some Swiss cantons the wind is considered a mitigating circumstance for crime. Surgeons are said to watch the wind, because blood does not clot normally during a *foehn*. A few years ago an Israeli physicist discovered that not only during such winds, but for the ten or twelve hours which precede them, the air carries an unusually high ratio of positive to negative ions. No one seems to know exactly why that should be; some talk about friction and others suggest solar disturbances. In any case the positive ions are there, and what an excess of positive ions does, in the simplest terms, is make people unhappy. One cannot get much more mechanistic than that.

Easterners commonly complain that there is no "weather" at all in Southern California, that the days and the seasons slip by relentlessly, numbingly bland. That is quite misleading. In fact the climate is characterized by infrequent but violent extremes: two periods of torrential subtropical rains which continue for weeks and wash out the hills and send subdivisions sliding toward the sea; about twenty scattered days a year of the Santa Ana, which, with its incendiary dryness, invariably means fire. At the first prediction of a Santa Ana, the Forest Service flies men and equipment from northern California into the southern forests, and the Los Angeles Fire Department cancels its ordinary non-firefighting routines. The Santa Ana caused Malibu to burn the way it did in 1956, and Bel Air in 1961, and Santa Barbara in 1964. In the winter of 1966–67 eleven men were killed fighting a Santa Ana fire that spread through the San Gabriel Mountains.

Just to watch the front-page news out of Los Angeles during a Santa Ana is to get very close to what it is about the place. The longest single Santa Ana period in recent years was in 1957, and it lasted not the usual three or four days but fourteen days, from November 21 until December 4. On the first day 25,000 acres of the San Gabriel Mountains were burning, with gusts reaching 100 miles an hour. In town, the wind reached Force 12, or hurricane force, on the Beaufort Scale; oil derricks were toppled and people ordered off the downtown streets to avoid injury from flying objects. On November 22 the fire in the San Gabriels was out of control. On November 24 six people were killed in automobile accidents, and by the end of the week the Los Angeles *Times* was keeping a box score of traffic deaths. On November 26 a prominent Pasadena attorney, depressed about money, shot and killed his wife, their two sons, and himself. On November 27 a South Gate divorcée, twenty-two, was murdered and thrown from a moving car. On November 30 the San Gabriel fire was still out of control, and the wind in town was blowing eighty miles an hour. On the first day of December four people died violently, and on the third the wind began to break.

It is hard for people who have not lived in Los Angeles to realize how radically the Santa Ana figures in the local imagination. The city burning is Los Angeles's deepest image of itself: Nathanael West perceived that, in *The Day of the Locust;* and at the time of the 1965 Watts riots what struck the imagination most indelibly were the fires. For days one could drive the Harbor Freeway and see the city on fire, just as we had always known it would be in the end. Los Angeles weather is the weather of catastrophe, of apocalypse, and, just as the reliably long and bitter winters of New England determine the way life is lived there, so the violence and the unpredictability of the Santa Ana affect the entire quality of life in Los Angeles, accentuate its impermanence, its unreliability. The wind shows us how close to the edge we are.

Discussion Questions: "The Santa Ana"

1. a. The beginning of the essay is an explanation of what the Santa Ana is. What details are provided?
   b. Why does she mention the "foehn" wind, the "hamsin," the "mistral" and the "sirocco?"
2. a. What point does Didion wish to substantiate after she explains the Santa Ana?
   b. Where does she make that point?
   c. Has she prepared the reader to accept this idea?
3. The second-to-last paragraph is about the effects of the Santa Ana in 1957. Why does Didion go into such detail in this paragraph? How does the first sentence of this last paragraph relate to the point Didion makes in the last paragraph?

Science Education and U.S. Technology

Sheldon Glashow

Americans win the lion's share of Nobel prizes in physics, chemistry, and medicine. This is frequently but wrongly quoted as evidence of the health of American science. In fact, it is interest earned by past investments. Prize-winning research was done ten to 25 years ago, when research was more generously supported than it is today. Prize-winning scientists received their crucial pre-college education in the first half of the 20th century. Since then, European investment in science education and research has been much larger, per capita, than ours. This will become apparent with the Nobel prizes of the next two decades.

This country was once the unquestioned technological hub of the world. Today, most of our industry is in deep trouble. Steel, ships, sewing machines, stereos, and shoes are lost industries. Japanese cars are generally thought to be cheaper and better made. Proud RCA has become a distributor of Japanese goods assembled in Korea. American Motors is controlled by the French government. We even buy Polish robots. Advanced electronics and computers are seen to be challenged by the Japanese. As we exhaust our heritage of capital and raw materials, Americans will no longer be able to afford the technological society to which they have become accustomed. We shall be left with our Big Macs, our TV dinners, and, perhaps, our federally subsidized weapons industries.

How is it that the forces of the marketplace have failed us? Is it too late for a technological renaissance? We have been leading our young people away from science and technology. The Vietnam experience, the failures of our nuclear power industry, and the threat of nuclear holocaust are partly responsible. The almost complete lack of pre-college teachers with competence in science and math has played a role. The forces of the marketplace have driven what few good ones there are into the desperate but better paying arms of industry. Who will our industries turn to next? Most of our high school students do not understand algebra or chemistry. We cannot count on them to reconstruct our technological society.

I was educated in the public school system of New York City. The State Regents exams demanded serious, substantive, and standardized curricula. Reading and math levels were tested often, and students were assigned in accordance with their skills. This sort of testing is unpopular today. Students are put into "open classrooms" and told to "do their thing." Self-

---

Sheldon Glashow, a Harvard physicist and Nobel Prize winner, expresses a concern over the state of American science.

expression is important; grammar and history, let alone science and math, are not. Our schools are fascinated by complicated and expensive scientific toys and "audio-visual aids." What they really need are scientifically literate teachers. Frogs, cow hearts, scalpels, siphons, a few leaves, pond water, the night sky, an inexpensive microscope, a good chemistry set, and some batteries, wires, and bulbs are enough to teach a lot of science. What my kids get is pre-packaged commercial pseudo-educational pap like "Magic Powders." But they cannot tell an oak tree by its leaf. Five hundred non-scientific Harvard undergraduates take my core course, From Alchemy to Quarks. Many of them cannot name one chemical element, or identify one planet or constellation. They will become famous sociologists or political scientists, but they are violently allergic to numbers. They suffer from "dysmetria," as do most Americans. Perhaps they are the people who will be entrusted with the U.S. budget a few years hence.

My father saw Halley's comet in 1910. Then he witnessed the explosive technological growth of this country, of which he was very proud. He explained to me when I was a child that Halley's comet would return in 1985, and that American scientists would voyage into space to meet it and solve its mysteries. He would not have been pleased to know that it will be the Russians, the French, and the Japanese who will launch the cometary probes. We could do it, of course, and do it best, but we have chosen not to. The torch of scientific endeavor has been passed to other peoples.

We were once the leaders in high-energy physics, my own specialty. We invented atom smashers, and, until recently, we had the biggest and the best. Since the opening of the Intersecting Storage Rings at CERN in 1971 and the CERN Collider in 1981, we have been completely outclassed by our Western European friends. The exciting field of electron-positron collisions was pioneered in France, Italy, and the Soviet Union in the 1960s, but we were triumphantly supreme in the 1970s. However, since 1978 we have been beaten by the Germans. Because Western Europe spends more than twice as much on high-energy physics as America, the future of this field in our country is not very rosy. Ironically, it is the force of the marketplace that impels the Europeans. Perhaps more clearly than we do, they see technology as the key to a healthy industrial society.

Discussion Questions: "Science Education and U.S. Technology"

1. What does Glashow say is deceiving about America's many Nobel prize winners?
2. What is the main idea of the essay? Write down the focus sentence(s) that contain(s) the main idea.
3. What does Glashow mean when he says in the second paragraph: "We shall be left with out Big Macs, our TV dinners, and, perhaps, our

federally subsidized weapons industries"? Does his choice of words indicate who his audience might be?

4. a. In the second paragraph, what is being contrasted?
   b. What is being contrasted in the fourth paragraph?
5. a. Are there enough details to convince a reader that the idea is valid?
   b. What is the effect of the writer's own teaching experience?
   c. Given his background, do you consider his own experience valid as evidence?
6. Do you find enough transitions between ideas? If not, where would you like to see some added?
7. What is the reason for his discussion of American and European high-energy physics in the last paragraph? How does this discussion help make his point?
8. There are implied recommendations in this essay (though we will be looking at recommendation in more detail later in the text). What are they? Are they specific recommendations?

Choosing Altruism: The Humanness of the Human Species

René Dubos

My confidence in the future of our species is not due to ignorance of its failings. My confidence is based on two different but related sets of facts. First, the human species has exhibited for at least 100,000 years certain traits which are uniquely and pleasantly human and which are more interesting than those that account for its bestiality. Second, the human species has the power to choose among the conflicting traits which constitute its complex nature, and it has made the right choices often enough to have kept civilization so far on a forward and upward course. The unique place of our species in the order of things is determined, not by its animality, but by its humanity.

In view of the fact that human beings evolved as hunters, it is not surprising that they have inherited a biological propensity to kill, as have all animal predators. But it is remarkable that a very large percentage of human beings find killing an extremely distasteful and painful experience. Despite the most subtle forms of propaganda, it is difficult to convince them that war is desirable. In contrast, altruism has long been practiced, often going so far as self-sacrifice. Altruism certainly has deep roots in man's biological past for the simple reason that it presents advantages for the survival of the group. However, the really human aspect of altruism is not its biological origin or its evolutionary advantages but rather the fact that humankind has now made it a virtue regardless of practical advantages or disadvantages. Since earliest recorded history altruism has become one of the absolute values by which humanity transcends animality.

The existence of altruism was recognized as far back as Neanderthal times, among the very first people who can be regarded as truly human. In the Shanidar cave of Iraq, for example, there was found a skeleton of a Neanderthalian adult male, dating from approximately 50,000 years ago. He had probably been blind, and one of his arms had been amputated above the elbow early in life. He had been killed by a collapse of the cave wall. As he was 40 years old at the time of his death and must have been incapable of fending for himself during much of his lifetime, it seems reasonable to assume that he had been cared for by the members of his clan. Several

René Dubos, a French citizen who earned his Ph.D. at Rutgers University in 1927 and became an American citizen in 1938, was a biologist. A prolific writer on biology, he came to write on topics concerning the human condition more generally. This essay is taken from his book *Beast or Angel? Choices That Make Us Human* (1974).

similar cases that could be interpreted as examples of "charity" have been recognized in other prehistoric sites. In fact, one of the first Neanderthalian skeletons to be discovered in Europe was that of a man approximately 50 years old who had suffered from extensive arthritis. His disease was so severe that he must have been unable to hunt or to engage in other strenuous activities. He, also, must therefore have depended for his survival upon the care of his clan.

Many prehistoric finds suggest attitudes of affection. A Stone Age tomb contains the body of a woman holding a young child in her arms. Caves in North America that were occupied some 9,000 years ago have yielded numerous sandals of different sizes; those of children's sizes are lined with rabbit fur, as if to express a special kind of loving care for the youngest members of the community.

Whether or not the words *altruism* and *love* had equivalents in the languages of the Stone Age, the social attitudes which they denote existed. The fact that the philosophy of nonviolence was clearly formulated at the time of Jesus and Buddha suggests that it had developed at a much earlier date. The Golden Rule, "Do unto others as you would have them do unto you," exists in all religious doctrines, even in those that have reached us through the very first written documents. It must therefore have an extremely ancient origin.

Discussion Questions: "Choosing Altruism"

1. Why does Dubos begin by defending his confidence in the future of humanity? What does he seem to expect his reader's attitude will be?
2. What is the main idea of the essay? Write down the focus sentence(s) that contain(s) the main idea.
3. Does Dubos define "altruism" in a clear, single sentence? When did you figure out what the word meant? Was the author assuming that the reader knew what the word meant? Should he have assumed that fact?
4. What predominant organizational strategy did the writer use to explain the main idea? What are the disadvantages of depending on this strategy? Why did Dubos choose to develop his argument this way?
5. What specific details are used to support the main idea? Are there enough details to convince a reader that the idea is valid?
6. Because Dubos is citing examples based on material from archeological finds, he must draw conclusions based on logical deductions rather than depend on incontrovertible proof. Are his conclusions logically drawn?
7. How does the writer end the essay? Does the ending help the reader understand the writer's main idea?

ASSIGNMENT 4: THE SUBSTANTIATING ESSAY

1. Defend any decision you have made, supporting your final choice with reasons and evidence.
2. Were you well prepared academically for college? Discuss specifically the strengths and/or the weaknesses of your previous education.
3. People we know and experiences we have shape our personalities and influence us in many ways. Write about a person or an experience which has had an important effect on you. Use specific details to show the reader what it was about the person or the experience that influenced you.

The audience for all of these topics is a general one—your classmates.

The following student essays are examples of the assignment. Prepare to discuss their relative effectiveness.

STUDENT ESSAYS

MY PREPARATION FOR COLLEGE

Upon graduation from high school, I was in the top 10 percent of my class. I was carrying about a 3.6 average. Although I wasn't voted the most likely to succeed, I felt confident that I would. When entering college, I felt that I had everything necessary to make it through. Little did I know.

My first class in college was Humanities I. When the syllabus was handed out, I nearly fainted. A list of eighteen books that I was required to read was listed. As I left the classroom, I debated dropping the course. I immediately set forth to my second class, where I received another syllabus. Here again was a list of books required to be read, just as for the first course. Only five this time, but as I added them to the previous eighteen, plus my textbooks, plus two courses still to go, I said, "Oh my god, what am I going to do?"

During my high school years, I was required to read a total of three books. My English classes centered around abstract subject matters such as death or reality. Very rarely was reading a book or writing a paper required. At that time, I had no idea whatsoever of the demands that would face me in college.

I struggled through my first semester of college. Not only did I have to keep up with the regular work, but I had to begin to teach myself how to read. With a book in one hand and a dictionary in the other hand, I pushed myself through lists of assigned material. Reading a book once was never quite enough. I usually found myself going through a book for the third time before the subject matter and details were clear to me. I had never thought that college would be easy, but this was ridiculous.

It was finally apparent to me that I was not the only one having these difficulties. Many of my friends were bogged down in their courses due to poor reading skills. Obviously, precollege schools are not doing their job, or they wouldn't be passing students who are only semiliterate. What is really sad is that as the pressure to read has been taken off high school students, they don't realize that their minds are being stifled in turn. I realize this now when I talk to old friends from high school who have such a limited range of knowledge. Their vocabularies, opinions, and subjects for conversations are limited because they don't read. Furthermore, they don't want to read. If I recommend a good book to them, they turn me down. It might take them three days to read the book! That's no fun. They don't know what it is to work at reading something that might stretch their minds.

I think that high schools should get on the ball and start teaching English. They should require students to read and understand a variety of material so that we have some background for our college courses. My preparation was deficient to say the least.

Discussion Questions: "My Preparation for College"

1. Why does the writer begin the essay with her high school place in class and grade-point average? Does this evidence affect her credibility with the reader? If she had been a poor student or had left out this information, would you have believed her criticism of her high school education?

2. What is the main idea of the essay? Write down the focus sentence(s) that contain(s) the main idea.

3. The intended audience for this essay was the class and teacher. Can you find examples of word choices or sentence style that indicates this informal audience?

4. What is the purpose of the fifth paragraph, particularly in regard to substantiating the essay's main point? Why does the writer bring in others' experiences?

5. What specific details are used to support the main idea? Are there enough details to convince a reader that the idea is valid?

6. Find the transition words or phrases in the essay.

7. How does the writer end the essay? Does the ending help the reader understand the writer's main idea? Does it go too far in recommending that something be done? Would it have been better merely to restate the point that the writer's preparation for college had been deficient?

YOU'RE AS OLD AS YOU FEEL

Prior to becoming a college student, I was faced with many questions about myself and my future. Often wondering about my future, I was depressed about aging and losing the happiness of youth and high school. These feelings were changed by working with a colorful and "young" man who happens to be eighty-two. Buck is currently the groundkeeper at a local swim club. He has been working there for twenty-four years and has worked for the owners for fifty-four years. I am one of Buck's boys or his "hard men," as he puts it.

One cold December Saturday morning, I arrived at the swim club. The sky was a gray blanket, and I sat in my car enjoying the heat that finally came on, wishing I were still in bed. I saw Buck approaching, an old man dressed in blue overalls and a heavy denim jacket slapping his arms against his body trying to get warm. Realizing I had to brave the cold, I left my car to say hello. Buck removed his leather work glove, that he bought for three dollars thirty years ago, revealing his strong, pudgy, workman's hands and the scar which drained some of his youth. The scar was the result of an electric saw accident which happened last year, severing vital nerves and causing partial paralysis in his fingers. He still complains that he is half the man he was. Shaking my hand, he flashed his boyish smile, revealing yellow teeth stained with brown chewing tobacco. His blue eyes lit up like a child's on Christmas. He seemed to really appreciate the new morning and his chance to work with his boys.

We waited in his truck for the other fellows to arrive. Talking to Buck is like talking to a living history book: he knows something about everything. We spoke about his days as a farmer and about leaving school in the fifth grade to support his family. We traded a couple of jokes and laughed about our boss's stupidity.

Today our job was to rake the leaves on the owner's twenty-acre estate. When the others arrived, we all loaded in the truck and headed on our way. Passing the newer of the two pools, I gazed at the bulging deck and the cracks in the concrete, which grow worse daily. The pool is only five years old and was a model for competitive swimming but now it decays because of stupidity. When it was being built, Buck kept telling our young bullheaded manager that the concerete was not set correctly, and it would belly. I reminded Buck of this, and he just laughed like Gabby Hayes and said, "The old farmer knows." This statement is true; he does know, but our manager, the boss's son, will not listen to Buck's wisdom. Half of our work is correcting our manager's mistakes.

We started by raking and blowing leaves behind the four-story brownstone house. The job is long, and the constant walking is wearing. After the leaves are piled, we have to dump them in the truck. Buck wanted to climb in the truck bed to straighten the pile of leaves. It is not easy to climb into the truck even for a kid, let alone someone his age. Carl and I gave him a boost in the truck. We lifted him awkwardly, and he lost his balance, rolled into the pile like a sack of potatoes and popped up out of the leaves grinning like a schoolboy.

With his trusty pitchfork in hand, he packed the leaves, and then it was time for lunch. On our way to the benches where we usually eat lunch, Buck started teasing Carl for throwing him in the leaves. Buck poked Carl in the shoulder, and they playfully grabbed and pushed each other like bear cubs. No one could guess from a distance that Carl is eighteen and Buck, eighty-two.

After lunch we had a job none of us were looking forward to. In the field beyond the thirty-foot holly trees lay a four-hundred-pound rock which had to be moved and loaded on the truck. It wasn't a fun job. I could not believe Buck would help lift it, but nothing seems to stop him. The five of us got an edge, took a deep breath, and turned red-faced as we lifted it in the truck. The whole time I worked there, we never did anything Buck didn't also do.

Even though most people his age would have retired twenty years ago, Buck works six days a week and feels young from his working. Buck proves that age is not a condition, but just a number, and people who are elderly do not have to act old and worn out. He certainly has inspired me to look forward to the rest of my life, instead of backward toward my high school years.

Discussion Questions: "You're As Old As You Feel"

1. What is the function of the introduction? How do you, as the reader, react to his observations? Does it strike a familiar chord in your thinking?
2. What is the main idea of the essay? Write down the focus sentence(s) that contain(s) the main idea.
3. What is the predominant strategy? How well does this work to show the writer's changing attitude toward age?
4. What specific details are used to support the main idea? Are there enough details to convince a reader that the idea is valid?
5. Find the transition words or phrases in the essay.
6. How does the writer end the essay? Does the ending help the reader understand the writer's main idea?

WRITING ACTIVITY

Beginning the Assignment

Which topic will you choose? Explore one of the suggested topics by freewriting or asking questions or making lists. Follow your interests as much as possible. What subject would you like to tell someone else about?

Writing a Draft

Take the freewriting material or the answers to the questions you asked and write a first draft of the assignment. Think about how you will develop and organize your topic.

Some Aids to Writing

1. What background does your reader need to understand the points you will raise? Perhaps you can provide this background in an introduction.
2. What are the main points of your discussion? List them in order.
3. What details will you use to support each point?
4. What point do you wish your reader to remember? Does your ending summarize or emphasize this point?

Revising Your Writing

Questions to ask of your first draft:

1. What is my main idea?
2. What evidence do I use to support my main idea? List details.
   a. Does all the evidence fit the main idea?
   b. Is there enough evidence and is it sufficiently specific to support the main idea? Add more evidence if needed.
3. Did I connect each of my subpoints or reasons to the main idea by using clear transitions? Check all transitional sentences.
4. Do I have a conclusion which leaves the reader with a summary of my main idea or an explanation of the implications or the importance of the subject I discussed? Check the conclusion.

ASSIGNMENT 5: THE ESSAY EXAM

Write down three questions from another course you are taking or have taken which might appear on a midterm or final exam. Your instructor will choose the one you will write on in class.

The questions should require you to draw conclusions or use evidence to support an idea.

How to Take an Essay Exam

General Instructions

1. Get a general picture of the examination before you start writing. How many parts are there? What is each question worth? How much time do you have?
2. Take up those questions first that you feel best qualified to answer.

Reading the Questions

3. Check the questions for important qualifying words such as *only, always, for the first time, major, most important.*
4. Pay attention to the exact wording of the questions.
5. Think about the questions before you answer them, but don't brood over them.
6. If you are asked to select "three reasons" or "four qualities," don't list more than are asked for.

Time

7. Budget your time carefully. For example, allow more time for a question worth 50 points than for one worth 10 points.
8. If you gain 5 points by treating one question at great length, and then lose 25 points by slighting the next two questions, you are 20 points behind.
9. Allow time for rereading and revision (about 10 minutes). But do *not* expect to recopy your answers. Instead, look for missing words which could make your answer confusing. Check spelling and punctuation. Cross out if you have to; it's better to be right than neat! Use a dictionary to help you proofread.

Organization

10. Use preliminary jottings or a scratch outline to organize answers that run to more than a paragraph in length. Jotting down information will also relieve your "short-term memory" so that you can concentrate on your writing. That is, if you have to remember facts while trying to compose an essay about them, it may be too difficult for

your brain to do so. Give it a break and concentrate on one thing at a time.

11. Be prepared to depart from the order of material in your textbook or in your lecture notes. (Many essay questions call for the synthesis of material from different parts of a course.)

Writing

12. Write a clear topic sentence which makes a statement that is an answer to the question. Then bolster general points with specific detail from lectures or readings. Your instructor is interested in what you have learned.
13. Do not pad weak answers with irrelevant material.
14. Once you have started writing on one of several alternative questions, try to make the best of it rather than shift to an "easier" question in midstream.

Now look at the student examples which follow. How well do you think the writers did? Note in the margins where they answer the question and where they provide details to support their answers.

QUESTION FROM A MANAGEMENT MIDTERM

Managers are classified into two categories: participative and authoritarian. Authoritarian is an old and traditional view of management, whereas participative management is relatively new. What is participative management? What are its advantages and disadvantages in a modern corporation or company?

Answer:

Managing has become a very intense and sophisticated field today. Over the years, there has been one accepted view of management: the traditional view of authoritarianism through legitimate power. Subordinates respected authoritarian managers because they believed and respected the formal rules of the organization and the power handed down to the managers through the generations. However, with the introduction of labor unions, subordinates now wanted to participate in organizational meetings and ideas. They wanted to take a part in the decisions of the company and they wanted more rules and regulations for their own protection. Thus the concept of participative management came into being.

Participative management is a relatively new concept of managing. However, many managers are finding it difficult to participate in this representative concept, and this is causing a tremendous amount of strain and conflict in many organizations. This is the major disadvantage of participative management in today's corporation. Authoritarian managers are afraid that if their corporations become too democratic, they will lose their authority over supervising and disciplining their subordinates. They feel that they will lose that respect and authority that has been traditional over the years through legitimate power. However, if executed correctly, participative management can be very advantageous to the manager and his subordinates. First of all, some managers are very content with having a representative company, for they were not that happy with using authoritarian methods. Many managers do not like being looked at as if they were villains. Furthermore, many feel a need to become socially involved with their employees and to become just "one of the guys." However, the biggest advantage of participative management is that it is a great work motivator. When subordinates are given a chance to partake in the decisions made at the top, they seem to work harder. The subordinates now feel that they are being respected not only as members of the company but also as human beings. They now feel special, and they are excited about the opportunity to make suggestions to the hierarchy. Thus they no longer hate their jobs and now they even look forward to coming to work.

Recently, surveys and questionnaires have been handed out to managers and subordinates all over the country. It has been found that about 80 percent of the applicants were content with this new concept of management. Furthermore, it also has been found that productivity has soared with the development of participative management.

QUESTION FROM A SOCIOLOGY MIDTERM

Explain how illness may be defined differently based on a person's situation, social structure, social class, and so on.

Answer:

When human beings begin to have symptoms that might be indicative of an illness, they will define the seriousness of the symptoms in different ways depending on external and internal factors. For some individuals, their particular social class and economic status will "allow" them to adapt to the sick role more easily. It is safe to say that a poor person is less likely to become sick, that is, adapt the sick role, than a person of higher economic standing. The reason is obvious and simple; a poor person cannot afford to become sick; therefore, he may ignore any symptoms he may have. He does not take the sick role and does not define himself as sick. A richer person experiencing the same symptoms can readily accept himself as sick because he is free of financial worry.

Another related factor that may influence how a person defines his sickness is social class. This is related to economic status. People with money are better educated because they can easily afford the cost of higher education and usually take advantage of it. Also, money enables people to have broader life experiences through travel, etc. On the other hand, a poor person is often not educated in such a way. The richer, more educated person would recognize and understand symptoms as signs that something is physically wrong. The less educated person may not recognize symptoms because he has a lack of knowledge about such things. Therefore, education plays a role in how people with the same symptoms define them differently.

Lastly, a person's culture and background may determine how and if he will take the sick role. For example, in Italian families, the role of the mother is an important one. Everyone in the family is dependent upon her, more so than in other countries. The mother is an extremely dominant figure in the family. She feels it is her job to hold the family together and that the family would fall apart if she weren't there. So, God forbid the mother of an Italian family becomes sick. She won't allow it. She does not accept the sick role. In some cultures, such as certain Indian cultures, medicine and illness are not highly valued. It is kind of amazing that in cultures such as these there is rarely any sickness. Sickness is simply not convenient to life-styles. Contrast this situation with that of a country such as the United States, where it is so easy to take the sick role with facilities and technology and drugs so readily available, and so consistently pushed on us. It seems in the United States that being sick is part of our culture, accepted and dealt with easily.

What everything said here comes down to is, that some individuals can become sick more easily than others based on outside factors such as economics, class, and social roles and education. And if people who don't take the sick role because of these factors survive anyway, doesn't that say something about the potential for human beings to handle illness on their own? This is a weakness in present health care. It lacks the ability to take into account the role that external factors play in illness. Also, modern medicine has only just begun to discover the workings of the human mind and its potential and what part it plays in illness. There is so much we do not understand but there has to be more than we're seeing simply based on the fact that two people with the same symptoms define their illnesses differently.

ASSIGNMENT 6: THE ANALYTICAL ESSAY

The following information might be used as evidence to support many different analyses or conclusions. Following the information is an article derived from it.

Read the information as carefully as you can. You may discuss in class what conclusions might be drawn from such information.

Following your discussion, you will choose an area on which to focus your attention. For example, you may wish to examine the data about students' political views, their attitudes toward social issues, their values, or many other things. Then you will write a generalization about freshman college students which you feel can be supported by the evidence. Finally, you will present your ideas in an essay which might make a suitable newspaper or magazine article.

Freshman Attitudes, 1981 (Percent)

	Two-Year Colleges		Four-Year Colleges				Universities		Predominantly Black Colleges	
				Private						
	Public	Private	Public	Nonsect.	Prot.	Cath.	Public	Private	Public	Private
Student's political views:										
Far left	1.9	2.2	1.8	1.6	1.5	1.3	1.2	1.3	5.5	3.3
Liberal	16.6	15.1	17.8	22.2	17.0	17.4	19.4	23.8	26.7	30.7
Middle of the road	64.2	60.4	60.1	53.3	53.2	61.0	57.1	48.4	45.6	46.6
Conservative	16.1	21.1	19.4	21.7	27.2	19.4	21.5	25.4	17.0	17.5
Far right	1.2	1.1	1.0	1.2	1.1	0.9	0.9	1.1	5.2	1.9
Student agrees strongly or somewhat that:										
Government isn't protecting consumer	72.6	75.0	71.5	69.8	68.4	69.2	66.7	62.3	78.5	79.2
Government isn't controlling pollution	77.5	78.9	78.2	79.6	77.2	78.7	76.1	76.6	77.8	79.7
Criminals have too many rights	70.5	67.9	68.7	67.3	70.2	67.3	68.3	66.7	56.4	55.8
Money is needed to solve urban problems	48.5	49.1	46.2	45.7	44.6	46.9	42.7	43.2	63.7	64.3
People should not obey laws that violate their beliefs	35.4	33.1	31.3	32.6	31.5	30.6	29.3	31.3	41.1	40.1
Inflation is the country's biggest domestic problem	81.8	80.5	75.5	76.4	76.5	77.5	76.3	71.1	81.5	81.1
The death penalty should be abolished	29.7	30.7	29.6	32.1	30.7	37.5	28.2	33.1	51.4	48.1
Government should provide a national health care plan	59.0	57.8	56.8	53.6	48.2	55.8	48.4	45.9	76.5	70.9
An energy shortage is causing a depression	81.0	80.8	82.0	82.1	81.0	80.3	80.8	79.4	81.8	83.3

Freshman Attitudes, 1981 (Percent) (Continued)

	Two-Year Colleges		Four-Year Colleges				Universities		Predominantly Black Colleges	
	Public	Private	Public	Private Nonsect.	Prot.	Cath.	Public	Private	Public	Private
Abortion should be legalized	53.8	47.0	55.2	59.0	41.9	31.9	58.9	58.2	56.5	60.5
Grading in high school is too easy	56.5	51.5	56.4	60.3	61.5	54.8	60.9	64.4	38.4	42.1
Women's activities should be confined to the home	30.0	31.1	27.0	23.4	30.5	23.4	22.7	19.8	44.4	31.4
Couples should live together before marriage	48.2	37.4	40.8	45.1	26.7	31.4	42.2	41.7	47.3	45.6
Large families should be discouraged	42.7	39.7	41.6	42.7	41.5	27.3	44.3	42.0	35.2	29.3
Divorce laws should be liberalized	48.8	43.8	45.1	43.4	29.8	32.0	42.6	39.2	60.2	56.2
It is all right for people who like each other to have sex	51.9	38.0	46.0	48.5	29.3	32.5	49.0	46.3	50.2	48.2
Women should have job equality	91.0	90.6	93.4	94.2	92.7	93.9	94.3	95.3	87.7	92.0
The wealthy should pay a larger share of taxes	74.0	70.8	73.1	67.8	69.8	69.5	67.9	60.2	74.7	79.1
Marijuana should be legalized	37.2	29.8	32.7	34.0	21.4	26.9	35.4	33.5	37.9	35.8
It is all right to bus to achieve balance	48.1	50.7	45.8	43.5	40.2	42.7	34.9	37.2	73.8	71.3
Homosexual relations should be prohibited	52.3	56.5	50.2	41.1	55.9	42.7	43.4	34.1	56.8	48.7

College has the right to regulate off-campus behavior	16.2	19.8	15.4	13.6	20.4	12.4	11.0	11.5	36.2	25.7
Students should help evaluate faculty	68.5	66.5	69.8	72.1	70.4	70.1	73.2	74.0	64.9	64.2
College grades should be abolished	17.6	16.3	14.8	14.2	13.7	14.0	12.9	12.6	31.5	19.4
Student publications should be regulated	45.3	51.5	42.9	37.1	48.4	40.9	33.7	28.0	63.8	54.5
Objectives student considers essential or very important:										
Achieving in a performing art	9.1	12.9	12.6	13.9	14.3	11.0	11.6	15.2	19.5	15.3
Becoming an authority in a field	69.8	70.2	74.6	73.9	71.4	72.1	77.0	75.9	75.4	84.0
Obtaining recognition from colleagues	52.0	52.4	55.7	56.4	49.5	56.4	58.4	59.6	62.0	68.1
Influencing the political structure	12.6	13.1	15.1	18.1	15.8	16.6	16.5	21.4	27.2	30.3
Influencing social values	28.8	34.8	32.5	33.4	39.3	35.9	30.4	33.3	41.4	48.8
Raising a family	64.2	66.4	66.5	66.4	71.5	73.1	66.8	68.8	57.0	64.5
Having administrative responsibility	40.1	38.9	41.2	35.9	34.8	39.2	41.1	36.2	51.1	51.1
Being very well-off financially	67.5	62.6	64.5	63.6	52.9	60.1	67.7	63.7	75.8	80.3
Helping others who are in difficulty	56.6	67.1	65.2	65.2	69.8	71.4	61.9	66.7	69.9	77.3
Making a theoretical contribution to science	13.2	10.2	13.3	16.8	12.0	13.7	17.0	21.0	21.3	27.3
Writing original works	9.5	12.5	12.4	14.6	13.0	12.3	12.5	16.3	17.4	18.1
Creating an artistic work	11.7	16.8	13.1	16.3	12.6	12.0	13.2	12.9	20.9	17.3

Freshman Attitudes, 1981 (Percent) *(Continued)*

| | Two-Year Colleges | | Four-Year Colleges | | | | | Universities | | Predominantly Black Colleges | |
	Public	Private	Public	Private Nonsect.	Prot.	Cath.		Public	Private	Public	Private
Being successful in one's own business	50.2	53.5	47.7	50.7	46.0	46.1		50.1	48.4	65.7	68.1
Helping to clean up environment	25.3	25.4	24.4	27.3	24.0	22.8		24.0	23.7	37.2	36.0
Developing a philo- sophy of life	42.4	49.6	49.9	55.2	57.0	56.2		51.6	58.7	57.9	65.5
Participating in community action	20.6	27.3	25.8	26.1	27.4	28.3		24.6	26.8	40.8	45.8
Promoting racial understanding	26.7	33.4	33.3	37.1	35.5	35.1		29.6	36.6	58.8	72.5
Keeping up with political affairs	31.3	31.9	39.2	47.0	41.8	44.3		46.1	57.0	45.4	54.1

STUDENT ESSAY

COLLEGE STUDENTS APATHETIC ABOUT THE ENVIRONMENT?

After analyzing the objectives that students consider essential or very important, I was astounded to learn that the issue "Helping to clean up the environment" was considered so unimportant. On a 100 percent scale the male freshman rated it at 27.0 percent and the female freshman rated it at an even lower 22.7 percent, with an overall average of 24.8 percent. How can this be? Is this attitude really valid, and if so, how can these students be so uncaring about their own environment?

Over the years the values, concerns, and attitudes of American youth change. Usually every 10 years there is said to be a change from the so-called "me" generation to the so-called "we" generation. During the "me" generation people's concerns are very self-centered and materialistic; they care more about their own personal wealth and well-being than about the well-being of society. During the "we" generation the opposite is found to be true. People are more concerned with the well-being of society as a whole than with their own personal well-being.

The 1980s are said to be "me" oriented, and I find this to be one of only two reasonable answers to the question of why these students are so uncaring about the environment. Their values and concerns must be very self-centered and materialistic.

The other reasonable answer might be that the students are actually unaware of the problems of our environment. Although the cliché "out of sight out of mind" might be hard to believe, in this case I find it to be very applicable because if people do not see the existing problems firsthand, they are prone to believe that there aren't any problems at all. It may be that all the publicity about toxic chemical dumping at Love Canal and problems with the water supply in many cities and towns just doesn't capture people's attention until they experience a problem themselves.

Whether "me" oriented or apathetic, the freshman students responding to the survey still surprise me. I find that my friends and classmates who are also college freshman place a higher degree of importance on the environment. In fact, I think if the students surveyed were given a chance to reevaluate this issue, their attitudes would change considerably.

Discussion Questions: "College Students Apathetic About the Environment?"

1. How does the writer begin the essay? Does the beginning help the reader understand the writer's main point?

2. What is the main idea of the essay? Is there one focus sentence? If not, should the writer have provided one?
3. Was the essay written for a specific audience? Should the writer have made it clearer to whom the essay was aimed?
4. Was there enough support for the writer's major points? Where would you have liked more support? Would it have been helpful to have found outside sources on the psychology of the "me" generation or on public awareness of environmental problems to buttress the arguments?
5. What do you think of the writer's ending? Is it reasonable given what he discussed in the essay?

WRITING ACTIVITY

Beginning the Assignment

Take notes on class discussion of the data. Then choose a hypothesis to support and write down relevant facts.

Writing a Draft

The chief problem with this assignment is deciding which data to use to support a hypothesis. You may feel overwhelmed by material and attempt to include as much as possible in the paper. Make a brief outline from your notes for your rough draft; and for each point you wish to make, be sure to have some statistical evidence from the data to support it. Don't include statistics which do not support any of your main points. In your conclusion try to put the data in perspective so that the reader will understand the implications of the information.

Revising Your Writing

As you read your draft, pay particular attention to making a clear statement of your hypothesis and then stick to that point as you marshal your evidence.

You may wish a classmate or your instructor to read this paper in draft form to make sure that you have stayed on the subject and substantiated your points.

Reread your ending too, judging whether it conveys to the reader the significance of the evidence that you have been discussing.

MASTERY ASSIGNMENTS

1. Based on your own experience, write an essay about what you feel are the chief concerns of today's college students. Use your own observations, interviews with fellow students, and material from class discussion of the last assignment to establish the validity of what you say.
2. Write an essay in which you support or refute the basic premise of one of these old sayings:

   > Money can't buy happiness.
   > Haste makes waste.
   > Look before you leap.
   > A friend in need is a friend indeed.
   > If at first you don't succeed, try, try again.

3. Write an essay commenting on Sheldon Glashow's opinion that modern students are not taught enough basic science and math. Support your agreement or disagreement by referring to your own educational experience and those of your friends.
4. Try to "explore a myth" as Tom Wicker did by examining a statement that many people take for granted (such as that all labor unions are crooked, that corporate executives make too much money, that people on welfare don't want to work, that children who read early will be superior students in school, and so on). Examine several sources to see if the statement is true or not. Present your findings in an essay or (if your instructor agrees) a research paper.

CHAPTER 5

Writing to Judge: Evaluating

Evaluating involves establishing criteria or standards and then measuring the subject in question against these criteria or standards. To fulfill this purpose, you will probably have to include elements of the other two purposes. The diagram might look as shown in Figure 5.1. That is, you will frequently need to explain or define and provide evidence before you can judge something. This purpose and the next one (recommending) are commonly used in reviews of books, movies, and restaurants; in business reports dealing with new products or methods of production, or solutions to problems which may have arisen; and in academic writing.

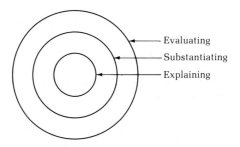

Figure 5.1
Relationship of Three Writing Purposes

Following are two sample questions taken from examinations:

1. Write a review of a film emphasizing its usefulness within the framework of an anthropology class studying explanations of the universality of beliefs in human societies. [This question demands that you be able to define universality of beliefs and then decide whether a film is useful or not in explaining these beliefs.]
2. Select one of the theories in the psychology text, state the central points of the theory, and evaluate the theory in terms of empirical evidence discussed in the text or in class. [This question clearly requires clarifying before evaluating. That is, students must select a theory and explain what its main points are before they can go on. Evidence of the theory's validity (substantiating) is necessary before they can finally judge the worth or value of the theory.]

Below are a sample organizational plan for an evaluating essay and further discussion on writing an essay to accomplish this purpose.

Sample Plan for an Evaluating Essay

A. Introduction

1. Explain the object or idea to be evaluated, giving whatever background the reader may need to understand the evaluation.

2. If desired, explain your background or experience to make your evaluation believable.

3. If desired, state the criteria for evaluating directly. (As mentioned below, criteria are often implied in the judgment itself.)

B. Focus Sentence. This follows the introduction and tells the reader the writer's judgment of the issue. However, some writers may wish to examine the aspects of an issue or object before announcing their evaluation at the end of an essay.

C. Main Points

The idea or object to be evaluated is compared with the criteria, and the results are presented in detail with enough specific information to convince a reader of the validity of the idea.

D. Conclusion. Usually the conclusion restates the focus sentence or, as mentioned above, is the focus sentence itself.

When we evaluate anything, we set up criteria or certain standards to measure how well a specific item or subject measures up to an ideal. For example, if you are buying a pair of shoes you will most likely be looking at style, fit, quality of materials, good workmanship and price, and if you find shoes that match the standards you have in mind, you will probably buy them.

Criteria are not always directly stated, however. If you go shoe shopping, as in the above example, you may not actually compare each pair of shoes to your list of criteria but rather examine each shoe as a whole, accepting or rejecting it. If a companion were to ask you though, "Why didn't you buy those?", you would probably answer that the shoes didn't measure up to one of your standards: "They didn't fit; I didn't like the material; the style doesn't look good on my foot."

Criteria are there, then, whether directly stated or implied, every time someone says, "I liked that movie," or "This cheese tastes awful."

Another aspect of evaluation is its dependency on personal values or taste. What might fit someone's standards might very well violate someone else's. So your friend may buy shoes you find unattractive, and you may laugh at a comedy film that he or she finds totally unfunny.

What then is a reviewer to do if personal taste or personal standards determine one's evaluation? The answer lies in the previous purpose: substantiate. If the evaluators give enough evidence to show *why* they like a movie or why they feel that a restaurant deserves four stars, their readers will have enough information to compare their views of the subject with the evaluators'. If a reviewer doesn't support opinions with evidence, the readers must take the reviewer's word for it and depend solely on the reviewer's reputation and authority. However, most of us are skeptical and won't take "trust me" as adequate evidence of the value of something.

Read the following article from *Consumer Reports.* The two main criteria are stated. What are they? The lesser criteria for judging each ingredient in the meal are implied: the frozen eggs were too salty, implying that there is a proper level of saltiness in fresh eggs that was exceeded. What other examples of implied criteria do you find?

Note that the article does make recommendations as well but that the major emphasis is on evaluating freshly prepared and frozen breakfasts.

Following the article are some further questions about the way it was written.

READINGS

Frozen Breakfasts

Consumer Reports

Given the choice of sleeping late or cooking breakfast, many people forgo the food and choose the snooze. But the folks who dream up convenience foods have something to nourish you even after those extra 40 winks: frozen breakfasts you pop into the oven.

These A.M. versions of TV dinners are sold under the *Swanson* label. We bought and tested three. One breakfast consists of two scrambled eggs, a sausage, and hash-brown potatoes. Another has two slices of French toast and two sausages. The third has three pancakes and two sausages.

The frozen breakfasts cost about twice as much as comparable, freshly made breakfasts. Fresh eggs, sausage, and hash-brown potatoes cost about 43 cents to prepare. CU shoppers paid an average of 84 cents for the frozen counterpart of that meal. Homemade French toast with sausages costs about 40 cents. The average price of the frozen variety was 74 cents. Pancakes with sausages cost about 36 cents to fix at home; it's 75 cents for the frozen breakfast.

The extra money is the price of convenience, of course. To cook a *Swanson* breakfast, all you do is roll out of bed, take the package from the freezer, and put the paperboard container in a *cold* oven. Turn the oven on and go take your shower. In 20 to 25 minutes, you have breakfast. (If you use a microwave oven, there's no time for a shower. The breakfasts cook in less than *four* minutes.)

Nutrition is one thing

The serving size of each frozen breakfast is probably about the size you'd make if you were cooking from scratch—unless you're a big eater. And the frozen meals compared fairly well, nutritionally, with fresh breakfasts made with the same basic ingredients.

Their protein content averaged from 26 to 29 percent of the National

Consumer Reports is a magazine published by Consumers Union, an independent organization that investigates and tests products and publishes the results. The magazine accepts no advertising and refuses to let advertisements for products use its name. Many people won't buy anything before they check it with *CR*.

Academy of Sciences/National Research Council's Recommended Daily Allowance (RDA) for a man. The homemade counterparts contain about the same percentage of protein. The carbohydrate content was comparable to that of homemade breakfasts, too.

The frozen breakfasts had about the same number of calories as comparable fresh breakfasts. The frozen egg breakfast had 454; the fresh, 415. The frozen pancakes had 481, the fresh, 472. The biggest calorie gap was between frozen and fresh French toast—327 for the frozen breakfast, 440 for the fresh.

Many of the calories come from the fat content in these meals, and much of that fat is saturated. Americans consume too much fat, in the opinion of many nutritionists. But these frozen breakfasts don't contain any more fat than the same breakfasts made from scratch.

Many Americans also consume too much sodium. And the frozen breakfasts contained a generous supply of the mineral. But their fresh counterparts contain even more: The freshly made pancake breakfast has 1015 milligrams of sodium, compared to 716 milligrams for the frozen; the fresh French toast has 655 milligrams, versus 538 for the frozen; the fresh egg breakfast has 707 milligrams, as against 665 milligrams for the *Swanson* egg breakfast.

Taste is another

Some people's taste buds may not wake up when the alarm clock rings. But, for wide-awake people, we did an informal taste test. CU staffers were served homemade breakfasts and *Swanson* breakfasts (cooked in a regular gas oven) without being told which was which. The conclusions:

• The fresh eggs won. The *Swanson* eggs were characterized as too salty and slightly stale-tasting. The texture was oddly heavy and spongy.

• The frozen hash-brown potatoes were deemed only slightly inferior to the fresh. The primary drawback to the frozen hash-brown patty was its chewiness.

• Our panelists had no distinct preference for either French toast. The frozen toast looked appetizing, they said. But it was chewy and, perhaps, a bit dry. It had a spicy aroma and flavor, probably from the sausage.

• The fresh pancakes came out ahead of the frozen. The frozen ones, according to the panelists, had an artificial, doughy aroma. The flavor was doughy and sweet. Like the French toast, the pancakes picked up flavor from the sausage—this time a pork, rather than a spice, flavor. The texture of the pancakes was soft, slightly chewy, and sometimes a bit too dry around the edges.

• Sausage was the best-liked component of the frozen breakfasts. In fact, the taste testers seemed to prefer the *Swanson* sausage to the freshly cooked.

Although it looked pale brown and steamy, the flavor and aroma were meaty and spicy. The texture was slightly dry and chewy. There was only a trace of greasiness.

We also cooked the frozen breakfasts in a microwave oven and fed them to the same CU staffers. Our tasters had about the same opinion of the breakfasts—except that they thought the *Swanson* eggs from the microwave were a bit better than those from the gas oven.

Recommendations

If you're not overly fussy about the taste or the price, you might consider a *Swanson* frozen breakfast an acceptable way to start the day. If so, try the French toast with sausages first. It tasted better than the other frozen affairs. It was also lowest in calories. Its fat and sodium content were comparatively low, too.

Discussion Questions: "Frozen Breakfasts"

1. How does the writer begin the essay? Does the beginning help the reader understand the writer's main point?
2. What is the main idea of the essay? Where is the evaluation presented?
3. What criteria are used to evaluate these breakfasts?
4. Who was the essay written for (the audience)? How can you tell? What accommodations for audience do you find in the essay?
5. What organizational plan did the writer use? Jot a rough outline.
6. What specific details are used to support the evaluation? Are there enough details to convince a reader that the idea is valid?

The next readings present a famous speech by Dr. Martin Luther King, Jr., and an evaluation of that speech by columnist Garry Wills. Read the speech first and try to determine in your own mind what makes it good (if you believe that it is). That is, try to measure it against certain standards that you might hold for speeches on important topics.

Next, read Mr. Willis' assessment of the speech. What criteria does he use to judge the speech? How does he substantiate his judgment? Does his evaluation meet your criteria, or were they completely separate criteria? Does he convince you that he is right even though you hadn't looked at the speech the way he had?

I Have A Dream

Martin Luther King, Jr.

Five score years ago, a great American, in whose symbolic shadow we stand, signed the Emancipation Proclamation. This momentous decree came as a great beacon light of hope to millions of Negro slaves who had been seared in the flames of withering injustice. It came as a joyous daybreak to end the long night of captivity.

But one hundred years later, we must face the tragic fact that the Negro is still not free. One hundred years later, the life of the Negro is still sadly crippled by the manacles of segregation and the chains of discrimination. One hundred years later, the Negro lives on a lonely island of poverty in the midst of a vast ocean of material prosperity. One hundred years later, the Negro is still languishing in the corners of American society and finds himself an exile in his own land. So we have come here today to dramatize an appalling condition.

In a sense we have come to our nation's capital to cash a check. When the architects of our republic wrote the magnificent words of the Constitution and the Declaration of Independence, they were signing a promissory note to which every American was to fall heir. This note was a promise that all men would be guaranteed the unalienable rights of life, liberty, and the pursuit of happiness.

It is obvious today that America has defaulted on this promissory note insofar as her citizens of color are concerned. Instead of honoring this sacred obligation, America has given the Negro people a bad check; a check which has come back marked "insufficient funds." But we refuse to believe that the bank of justice is bankrupt. We refuse to believe that there are insufficient funds in the great vaults of opportunity of this nation. So we have come to cash this check—a check that will give us upon demand the riches of freedom and the security of justice. We have also come to this hallowed spot to remind America of the fierce urgency of *now.* This is no time to engage in the luxury of cooling off or to take the tranquilizing drugs of gradualism. *Now* is the time to make real the promises of Democracy. *Now* is the time to rise from the dark and desolate valley of segregation to the sunlit path of racial justice. *Now* is the time to open the doors of opportunity to all of God's children. *Now* is the time to lift our nation from the

---

Martin Luther King, Jr. led the civil rights movement in the 1950s and 1960s in his role as president of the Southern Christian Leadership Conference until he was assassinated in 1968. One of the best speakers in American history, King delivered this speech in front of the Lincoln Memorial to over 200,000 people who had gathered as part of the March on Washington for Jobs and Freedom, August 28, 1963. He was awarded the Nobel Peace Prize in 1964.

quicksands of racial injustice to the solid rock of brotherhood.

It would be fatal for the nation to overlook the urgency of the moment and to underestimate the determination of the Negro. This sweltering summer of the Negro's legitimate discontent will not pass until there is an invigorating autumn of freedom and equality. 1963 is not an end, but a beginning. Those who hope that the Negro needed to blow off steam and will now be content will have a rude awakening if the nation returns to business as usual. There will be neither rest nor tranquillity in America until the Negro is granted his citizenship rights. The whirlwinds of revolt will continue to shake the foundations of our nation until the bright day of justice emerges.

But there is something that I must say to my people who stand on the warm threshold which leads into the palace of justice. In the process of gaining our rightful place we must not be guilty of wrongful deeds. Let us not seek to satisfy our thirst for freedom by drinking from the cup of bitterness and hatred. We must forever conduct our struggle on the high plane of dignity and discipline. We must not allow our creative protest to degenerate into physical violence. Again and again we must rise to the majestic heights of meeting physical force with soul force. The marvelous new militancy which has engulfed the Negro community must not lead us to a distrust of all white people, for many of our white brothers, as evidenced by their presence here today, have come to realize that their destiny is tied up with our destiny and their freedom is inextricably bound to our freedom. We cannot walk alone.

And as we talk, we must make the pledge that we shall march ahead. We cannot turn back. There are those who are asking the devotees of civil rights, "When will you be satisfied?" We can never be satisfied as long as the Negro is the victim of the unspeakable horrors of police brutality. We can never be satisfied as long as our bodies, heavy with the fatigue of travel, cannot gain lodging in the motels of the highways and the hotels of the cities. We cannot be satisfied as long as the Negro's basic mobility is from a smaller ghetto to a larger one. We can never be satisfied as long as a Negro in Mississippi cannot vote and a Negro in New York believes he has nothing for which to vote. No, no, we are not satisfied, and we will not be satisfied until justice rolls down like waters and righteousness like a mighty stream.

I am not unmindful that some of you have come here out of great trials and tribulations. Some of you have come fresh from narrow jail cells. Some of you have come from areas where your quest for freedom left you battered by the storms of persecution and staggered by the winds of police brutality. You have been the veterans of creative suffering. Continue to work with the faith that unearned suffering is redemptive.

Go back to Mississippi, go back to Alabama, go back to South Carolina, go back to Georgia, go back to Louisiana, go back to the slums and ghettos of our northern cities, knowing that somehow this situation can and will be changed. Let us not wallow in the valley of despair.

I say to you today, my friends, that in spite of the difficulties and frustrations of the moment I still have a dream. It is a dream deeply rooted in the American dream.

I have a dream that one day this nation will rise up and live out the true meaning of its creed: "We hold these truths to be self-evident; that all men are created equal."

I have a dream that one day on the red hills of Georgia the sons of former slaves and the sons of former slaveowners will be able to sit down together at the table of brotherhood.

I have a dream that one day even the state of Mississippi, a desert state sweltering with the heat of injustice and oppression, will be transformed into an oasis of freedom and justice.

I have a dream that my four little children will one day live in a nation where they will not be judged by the color of their skin but by the content of their character.

I have a dream today.

I have a dream that one day the state of Alabama, whose governor's lips are presently dripping with the words of interposition and nullification, will be transformed into a situation where little black boys and black girls will be able to join hands with little white boys and white girls and walk together as sisters and brothers.

I have a dream today.

I have a dream that one day every valley shall be exalted, every hill and mountain shall be made low, the rough places will be made plain, and the crooked places will be made straight, and the glory of the Lord shall be revealed, and all flesh shall see it together.

This is our hope. This is the faith with which I return to the South. With this faith we will be able to hew out of the mountain of despair a stone of hope. With this faith we will be able to transform the jangling discords of our nation into a beautiful symphony of brotherhood. With this faith we will be able to work together, to pray together, to struggle together, to go to jail together, to stand up for freedom together, knowing that we will be free one day.

This will be the day when all of God's children will be able to sing with new meaning

My country, 'tis of thee,
Sweet land of liberty,
   Of thee I sing:
Land where my fathers died,
Land of the pilgrims' pride,

From every mountain-side
  Let freedom ring.

And if America is to be a great nation this must become true. So let freedom ring from the prodigious hilltops of New Hampshire. Let freedom ring from the mighty mountains of New York. Let freedom ring from the heightening Alleghenies of Pennsylvania!
  Let freedom ring from the snowcapped Rockies of Colorado!
  Let freedom ring from the curvaceous peaks of California!
  But not only that; let freedom ring from Stone Mountain of Georgia!
  Let freedom ring from Lookout Mountain of Tennessee!
  Let freedom ring from every hill and molehill of Mississippi. From every mountainside, let freedom ring.
  When we let freedom ring, when we let it ring from every village and every hamlet, from every state and every city, we will be able to speed up that day when all of God's children, black men and white men, Jews and Gentiles, Protestants and Catholics, will be able to join hands and sing in the words of the old Negro spiritual, "Free at last! free at last! thank God almighty, we are free at last!"

Your Evaluation of "I Have a Dream"

1. What criteria do you believe should be used to evaluate a speech on an important issue?
2. Apply your criteria to Dr. King's speech.

A Dream Peculiarly American

By Gary Wills

Martin Luther King Jr. was the greatest orator of modern times. Where Churchill growled, Dr. King sang. No one has been able to replace him in this respect, as in so many others. Jesse Jackson's use of alliterative slogans is a kind of disco version of the old Baptist sermon. But Dr. King raised that form to a level of political artistry unmatched since Lincoln's second inaugural address.

Dr. King's greatest speech was the one whose 20th anniversary we now celebrate, his "I have a dream" speech. The magic of the man's delivery makes us hear his every rhythm, each inflection, when we look at the mere words on a page. But Dr. King's vocal skill can distract us from a realization of the speech's literary genius, simply as a text.

The main achievement of the speech is to create a geography of the spirit, fusing two great image systems, that of the Bible and that of America's frontier. The Psalms and the prophets chart an interior landscape that echoes the outer world's—valleys of despair, green pastures of repose, the rock of refuge, the rivers of righteousness, the mountains of eternity.

Dr. King points his auditors to-

ward "the high plain of dignity and discipline," to "the majestic heights" of non-violence. He asks them to "hew out of the mountain of despair a stone of hope."

This part of the speech sweeps up to the grand scriptural vision of exalted valleys and humbled mountains. But then Dr. King looks at America's real geography of repression, "the motels and the highways, and the hotels of the city . . . the narrow jails." Yet he says that even "the red hills of Georgia" can be transformed. "Even the state of Mississippi . . . sweltering in the heat of oppression, will be transformed into an oasis of freedom and justice."

To prove that this is possible, Dr. King merges the scriptural vision with America's dream, expressed in the song "America." Taking off from the end of the song's first stanza ("From every mountainside let freedom ring"), he takes us from height to height, westward across the country, opening new vistas of hope, pursuing the free frontier dream.

"Let freedom ring from the prodigious hilltops of New Hampshire . . . from the heightening Alleghenies of Pennsylvania . . . from the snow-capped Rockies of Colorado. . . ."

Then, having called up all of America's historical yearning outward for freedom, Dr. King swings that vision back around, brings it to bear on the geography of oppres-

---

Garry Wills is a nationally syndicated columnist who has a Ph.D. from Yale University. In this column Wills analyzes the strength of the speech by Martin Luther King, Jr.

sion. The American dream will only be fulfilled if we find the spiritual frontier wherever, in our midst, is want and oppression: "So let freedom ring from Stone Mountain in Georgia . . . from Lookout Mountain in Tennessee . . . from every hill and molehill of Mississippi, from every mountainside."

Dr. King's genius was his ability to evoke the best in us, to remind us what America means, to link that with the longer hopes of historical peoples, with the whole religious literature of liberation. He was the patriot rebel and the orthodox dissenter. He said in his speech that his dream was "deeply rooted in the American dream." We can see, now, how reversible that formula is—that America's finest aspirations, if they are to be achieved, must be rooted in his dream.

Garry Wills' Evaluation of "I Have a Dream"

1. What criteria does Wills use?
2. How does he support his evaluation of Dr. King's speech?
3. Give your reaction to his choice of criteria and evaluation.

The next two essays are evaluations but not in the sense of reviews. They make value judgments about societies and governments based on criteria which they state or imply. As you read the essays, try to determine what criteria the writers are using. Evaluate their conclusions yourself. Do you agree with their assessment of the situation?

Excerpt from *The Grapes of Wrath*

John Steinbeck

The spring is beautiful in California. Valleys in which the fruit blossoms are fragrant pink and white waters in a shallow sea. Then the first tendrils of the grapes, swelling from the old gnarled vines, cascade down to cover the trunks. The full green hills are round and soft as breasts. And on the level vegetable lands are the mile-long rows of pale green lettuce and the spindly little cauliflowers, the gray-green unearthly artichoke plants.

And then the leaves break out on the trees, and the petals drop from the fruit trees and carpet the earth with pink and white. The centers of the blossoms swell and grow and color: cherries and apples, peaches and pears, figs which close the flower in the fruit. All California quickens with produce, and the fruit grows heavy, and the limbs bend gradually under the fruit so that little crutches must be placed under them to support the weight.

Behind the fruitfulness are men of understanding and knowledge and skill, men who experiment with seed, endlessly developing the techniques for greater crops of plants whose roots will resist the million enemies of the earth: the molds, the insects, the rusts, the blights. These men work carefully and endlessly to perfect the seed, the roots. And there are the men of chemistry who spray the trees against pests, who sulphur the grapes, who cut out disease and rots, mildews and sicknesses. Doctors of preventive medicine, men at the borders who look for fruit flies, for Japanese beetle, men who quarantine the sick trees and root them out and burn them, men of knowledge. The men who graft the young trees, the little vines, are the cleverest of all, for theirs is a surgeon's job, as tender and delicate; and these men must have surgeons' hands and surgeons' hearts to slit the bark, to place the grafts, to bind the wounds and cover them from the air. These are great men.

Along the rows, the cultivators move, tearing the spring grass and turning it under to make a fertile earth, breaking the ground to hold the water up near the surface, ridging the ground in little pools for the irrigation, destroying the weed roots that may drink the water away from the trees.

The Nobel Prize–winning author John Steinbeck wrote *The Grapes of Wrath* in 1939 and was awarded the Pulitzer Prize for it in 1940. Though he wrote over a dozen popular novels, many people still consider *The Grapes of Wrath* his masterpiece. Written during the Great Depression of the 1930s, the novel followed a migrant family, the Joads, in their quest for work and a home in California. Interspersed with the story are chapters such as the following, which are more expository in nature, and discuss conditions in the country as a whole.

And all the time the fruit swells and the flowers break out in long clusters on the vines. And in the growing year the warmth grows and leaves turn dark green. The prunes lengthen like little green bird's eggs, and the limbs sag down against the crutches under the weight. And the hard little pears take shape, and the beginning of the fuzz comes out on the peaches. Grape blossoms shed their tiny petals and the hard little beads become green buttons, and the buttons grow heavy. The men who work in the fields, the owners of the little orchards, watch and calculate. The year is heavy with produce. And men are proud, for of their knowledge they can make the year heavy. They have transformed the world with their knowledge. The short, lean wheat has been made big and productive. Little sour apples have grown large and sweet, and that old grape that grew among the trees and fed the birds its tiny fruit has mothered a thousand varieties, red and black, green and pale pink, purple and yellow; and each variety with its own flavor. The men who work in the experimental farms have made new fruits: nectarines and forty kinds of plums, walnuts with paper shells. And always they work, selecting, grafting, changing, driving themselves, driving the earth to produce.

And first the cherries ripen. Cent and a half a pound. Hell, we can't pick 'em for that. Black cherries and red cherries, full and sweet, and the birds eat half of each cherry and the yellowjackets buzz into the holes the birds made. And on the ground the seeds drop and dry with black shreds hanging from them.

The purple prunes soften and sweeten. My God, we can't pick them and dry and sulphur them. We can't pay wages, no matter what wages. And the purple prunes carpet the ground. And first the skins wrinkle a little and swarms of flies come to feast, and the valley is filled with the odor of sweet decay. The meat turns dark and the crop shrivels on the ground.

And the pears grow yellow and soft. Five dollars a ton. Five dollars for forty fifty-pound boxes; trees pruned and sprayed, orchards cultivated—pick the fruit, put it in boxes, load the trucks, deliver the fruit to the cannery—forty boxes for five dollars. We can't do it. And the yellow fruit falls heavily to the ground and splashes on the ground. The yellowjackets dig into the soft meat, and there is a smell of ferment and rot.

Then the grapes—we can't make good wine. People can't buy good wine. Rip the grapes from the vines, good grapes, rotten grapes, wasp-stung grapes. Press stems, press dirt and rot.

But there's mildew and formic acid in the vats.

Add sulphur and tannic acid.

The smell from the ferment is not the rich odor of wine, but the smell of decay and chemicals.

Oh, well. It has alcohol in it, anyway. They can get drunk.

The little farmers watched debt creep up on them like the tide. They sprayed the trees and sold no crop, they pruned and grafted and could not pick the crop. And the men of knowledge have worked, have considered, and the fruit is rotting on the ground, and the decaying mash in the wine vats is poisoning the air. And taste the wine—no grape flavor at all, just sulphur and tannic acid and alcohol.

This little orchard will be a part of a great holding next year, for the debt will have choked the owner.

This vineyard will belong to the bank. Only the great owners can survive, for they own the canneries too. And four pears peeled and cut in half, cooked and canned, still cost fifteen cents. And the canned pears do not spoil. They will last for years.

The decay spreads over the State, and the sweet smell is a great sorrow on the land. Men who can graft the trees and make the seed fertile and big can find no way to let the hungry people eat their produce. Men who have created new fruits in the world cannot create a system whereby their fruits may be eaten. And the failure hangs over the State like a great sorrow.

The works of the roots of the vines, of the trees, must be destroyed to keep up the price, and this is the saddest, bitterest thing of all. Carloads of oranges dumped on the ground. The people came for miles to take the fruit, but this could not be. How would they buy oranges at twenty cents a dozen if they could drive out and pick them up? And men with hoses squirt kerosene on the oranges, and they are angry at the crime, angry at the people who have come to take the fruit. A million people hungry, needing the fruit—and kerosene sprayed over the golden mountains.

And the smell of rot fills the country.

Burn coffee for fuel in the ships. Burn corn to keep warm, it makes a hot fire. Dump potatoes in the rivers and place guards along the banks to keep the hungry people from fishing them out. Slaughter the pigs and bury them, and let the putrescence drip down into the earth.

There is a crime here that goes beyond denunciation. There is a sorrow here that weeping cannot symbolize. There is a failure here that topples all our success. The fertile earth, the straight tree rows, the sturdy trunks, and the ripe fruit. And children dying of pellagra must die because a profit cannot be taken from an orange. And coroners must fill in the certificates—died of malnutrition—because the food must rot, must be forced to rot.

The people come with nets to fish for potatoes in the river, and the guards hold them back; they come in rattling cars to get the dumped oranges, but the kerosene is sprayed. And they stand still and watch the potatoes float by, listen to the screaming pigs being killed in a ditch and covered with quicklime, watch the mountains of oranges slop down to a putrefying ooze; and in the eyes of the people there is the failure; and in the eyes of the hungry there is a growing wrath. In the souls of the people the grapes of wrath are filling and growing heavy, growing heavy for the vintage.

Discussion Questions: *The Grapes of Wrath*

1. What is the effect of the beginning? What words create the sense of fertility and production?

2. Where does the reader begin to understand Steinbeck's main idea?

3. What shift in tone and word choice did you notice in the second half of the chapter? Did that shift help you to realize the author's main idea?

4. Find examples of parallel structure, that is, sentences that begin with the same words or with the same word order, such as "Burn coffee for fuel. . . . Burn corn to keep warm. . . ." What effect do such structures have?

5. What does Steinbeck's final metaphor (or comparison) mean: "the grapes of wrath are filling and growing heavy, growing heavy for the vintage?"

6. What is being evaluated? List the value-laden words which Steinbeck uses first to praise the producers of food and then to condemn those that prevent its use by the people.

7. Did Steinbeck provide enough examples (evidence) to convince you that his evaluation was correct?

The Japanese Model

Adam Smith

"Do you remember," said my visitor, "the stories about Usa?"

My visitor was an old friend, an American who lives in the Far East, where he drums up business for his American firm. As for Usa, it is a town on the main southernmost Japanese island, Kyushu.

"The story used to be," said my visitor, "that because Japanese goods were so cheap and shoddy, they were all sent to Usa before they were exported to be stamped MADE IN USA, so that people would think they had been made in the United States."

"I remember," I said, "That's like the story about how the Japanese filched the plans for a battleship but got them just wrong enough so that when the ship was launched it turned upside down."

"Well," said the Far East hand, "you haven't heard stories like that for twenty-five years. Detroit is reeling from Japanese imports, and you see joggers wearing earphones and carrying little Japanese tape decks not much larger than cigarette packs. I have to go meet some of my Japanese associates in New York now. They think New York is charming—and so *cheap*, they keep saying. Such *bargains*."

The Far East hand left with me a book that is a huge best seller in Japan. It was written by a Harvard professor, Ezra Vogel, and its English-language edition has sold a respectable twenty-five thousand copies. But in Japan it is a runaway success: four hundred fifty-five thousand copies sold. The title is *Japan as No. 1: Lessons for America.* "The very title," said Edwin Reischauer, a former ambassador to Japan, "will blow the minds of many Americans. Japan today has a more smoothly functioning society [than ours] and an economy that is running rings around ours." One Japanese official has said that the United States has now taken the place of Japan's prewar colonies. The United States supplies the raw materials—the coal, the grain and soy beans, the timber—to this superior modern industrial machine, and it gets back the machine's superior industrial products.

Japan's economic performance has been well documented in Vogel's book. In 1952, Japan's gross national product was one third that of France. By the late 1970s, it was larger than those of France and Britain combined, and half as large as that of the United States. Japan is the leading automobile manufacturer. Of the world's twenty-two largest and most modern steel plants, fourteen are in Japan and none are in the United States.

Adam Smith, a pseudonym for George J. W. Gordon, writes articles on economics for *Esquire* magazine and other publications. He has published four popular books on economics and is also a novelist.

Health? Japan has the world's lowest infant mortality rate. In 1967 the life expectancy of the average Japanese passed that of the average American, and in 1977 Japan's life expectancy rate passed Sweden's to become the highest in the world.

Education? About 90 percent of all Japanese graduate from high school, and they generally spend sixty more days a year in high school than do their American counterparts.

Crime? In Japan the cities are safe, and the Japanese carry large amounts of cash and don't even worry bout it. Americans are accustomed to annual increases in the crime rate; in Japan, the crime rate is going *down.*

Labor? The Japanese visitors are shocked again. Professor Vogel says that the American factory seems almost like an armed camp to them: "Foremen stand guard to make sure workers do not slack off. Workers grumble at foremen, and foremen are cross with workers. In the Japanese factory, employees seem to work even without the foreman watching."

What are the Japanese doing right? And how have they done it on a crowded group of islands, without enough coal and oil, without significant natural resources, without adequate farmland?

The rather chilling answer is that they have done it by a social process— by a kind of group behavior modification. An average Japanese who goes to work for a company is there for life. He works throughout the day in an atmosphere in which consensus is always the goal. If, as his career progresses, he needs retraining, the company will retrain him, so he need not get involved in the protection of rights that American unions strive for. The company's goals are his. The people he sees socially are from the company.

The government works the same way, striving for consensus within itself and for consensus with business. Elite bureaucrats, their ties reinforced by social contacts in the geisha houses and on the golf course, form an elaborate old-boy network and move in lockstep through the age ranks.

And all this starts very early. Children are taught the value of cooperation, says Vogel, "however annoying they may find group pressures." The group pressure helps to explain the low crime rate. The policeman is part of the group: his little kiosk also contains the neighborhood bulletin board. The criminal, in fact, is encouraged to turn himself in. Even Japanese gangs exist in a consensus 5with the police.

The whole design of group activity is a conscious one. After World War II, the Japanese decided what they needed to survive, and they followed their decision. They even learned golf and baseball with the same sense of purpose that they applied to business and government. Americans win arguments: the Japanese win agreements. Americans try for victory: the Japanese try for consensus.

Nobody can deny Japan its success. What is so chilling is the implication of that success: Japan works and America doesn't. The Japanese leaped from feudalism to a modern corporate society without the intervening four hundred years of individualism that have characterized Western Europe and the United States. Our individualism was all very well in its time, but that was when energy was plentiful and the world was agricultural. But now we live in a postagrarian world, and individualism doesn't work anymore: "Our institutional practices promote adversary relations and litigation, divisiveness threatens our society," warns Vogel.

What we ought to do, he argues, is to borrow some of the models that have worked for the Japanese: more group direction, more "central leadership oriented to a modern economic order," more cooperation between business and government.

You can see why this is at once so provocative and so chilling. Should we all gather behind the banners of IBM and General Motors? When William H. Whyte Jr. wrote *The Organization Man,* the phenomenon he documented was considered alarming. Do we really want five hundred highly trained bureaucrats, a close-knit group from elite universities, to establish our goals and run our government? Our experience with the best and the brightest was not totally happy. Should we teach youngsters not to win, just to tie?

Japanophiles point out that America, too, had groups: New England town meetings, farmers' granges, professional guilds. But in our mobile society, group solidarity has become attenuated. We have lost a sense of community.

This is not the direction we are going in. Americans complain that their government is too big and directs them too much. They are more and more suspicious of big business. They distrust, the polls show, all of their institutions.

There isn't any doubt that we are losing ground in the world, and that we have forgotten what safe cities and a sense of community feel like. Is the group model what it takes to survive? Could we adopt it? More to the point, is it the way we want to live?

Discussion Questions: "The Japanese Model"

1. Smith begins the essay by substantiating a point—what is it?
2. What details does he use to support that idea?
3. Where does he begin to evaluate the worth (or value) of Japan's method of success?
4. What one word is a tip-off of Smith's attitude toward Japanese business values? How many times does he repeat the word?
5. Why does Smith end with a series of questions? Does the reader know what answers Smith would give? How would you answer Smith's questions?

ASSIGNMENT 7: THE EVALUATIVE ESSAY

Write an evaluation of a movie, concert, play, book, or sports event for someone of your own age and interests. Remember that your judgment should be based on clearly defined criteria. Your aim is to let the reader decide whether he, too, would enjoy the work, so you have to give him something more specific than just your opinion. (In the case of a sports event, which is nonrepeatable, your evaluation will let the reader know what he missed. For example, just how good was the last game of the World Series?) Discuss criteria to evaluate these events or works of art with your classmates.

1. What criteria could you use to evaluate a movie? List some.
2. What determines whether a concert is good?
3. How do you judge a play?
4. How do you decide if book is good?
5. What criteria could you use to evaluate a sports event?

In this example, what basic writing principle did the writer forget?

MOVIE: *WHERE THE BUFFALO ROAM*

The film *Where the Buffalo Roam* was very entertaining, to say the least. The lead role was played by Bill Murray (formerly of "Saturday Night Live"), who definitely was a good choice to play an underground writer. The movie was very entertaining and was made up of many funny scenes showing the many adventures of Gonzo, who seemed to cause chaos wherever he went. His lawyer and closest friend is Laslo, played by Peter Boyle. Lazlo is just as "off the wall" as Gonzo and the two of them find that they keep getting deeper and deeper in trouble. Most of the movie is shown in flashbacks from the late sixties and early seventies, when Gonzo was fighting the law, establishment, and Nixon in his literature. I would recommend this movie to anyone who is in a crazy mood and wants to laugh their head off. On a scale of one to ten I give *Where the Buffalo Roam* a big nine.

This paragraph illustrates what happens when you *tell* someone a movie is good rather than *showing* them. We need examples of the funny scenes and the problem situations so that we can judge whether the movie is funny or not; we just don't like to take someone else's word for it. In other words, the writer must remember to *substantiate* the evaluation.

Look now at the next student example. What did this student do that the other writer did not? List the criteria the student used to evaluate this movie *and* the evidence (examples, details) used to substantiate the evaluation.

STUDENT ESSAY

AN AMERICAN WEREWOLF IN LONDON

Many werewolf movies have been made in the past few years. One of the best was *An American Werewolf in London* because it was more than just the average werewolf movie. Aside from excellent special effects and music, it also contained humor, which is rare in horror movies.

The main attraction of this movie was its special effects. It was a very bloody movie. When people got shot, you saw blood gushing from the wounds, and when the werewolf attacked people, you saw it tearing them apart. There was also an incredibly convincing accident near the end of the movie where buses crashed into cars, and people went through windshields and got run over by cars.

When David, the werewolf, would change, he didn't look like the werewolves of the old movies. He didn't walk upright, and he wore no clothes. He actually changed into a huge wolf, and you saw him change.

Another horrible special effect occurred when Jack, David's friend who was killed by the same werewolf as the one that bit David, would come back and tell David to kill himself so that he could die in peace. Each time he would pop up, he would be more putrified.

The music in this movie was not the typical organ music you hear in most horror movies. All of the songs pertained to the moon. For example, the movie started out with "Blue Moon," and throughout the movie there were other songs of that nature.

Humor played an important role in that it broke the tension in many places. Once, when Jack popped in to tell David to kill himself, he said, "Did you ever talk to dead people? They're boring." There were many other "one-liners" such as that throughout the movie.

Another funny incident was when David, after a night of killing people as a werewolf, woke up naked in the zoo. First he stole a child's balloons, then a woman's coat. Scenes like this helped the movie move along and provided some comic relief.

I would not recommend this movie for the squeamish. This movie is for those who don't mind a lot of blood and gore. The excellent combination of special effects, music, and humor make *An American Werewolf in London* the perfect movie for horror fans.

Discussion Questions: *An American Werewolf in London*

1. List the criteria used by the author to evaluate this movie.
2. What details were used to substantiate the author's evaluation?

3. Were the criteria chosen appropriate (in your opinion)?
4. Were more details needed to substantiate the writer's opinions?

WRITING ACTIVITY

Beginning the Assignment

1. What will you evaluate?
2. What criteria will you use?
3. What details support your evaluation for each criterion?

Writing a Draft

As you write a draft, check to be sure that you are "showing" the readers rather than "telling" them. You have to give them enough examples as evidence for them to be able to say, "Oh, I see what you mean." Just giving them your opinion of a movie or concert is not good enough; let them experience enough of it through your words so that they can make a judgment. For example, instances of scenes from a movie, lines of dialogue, or description of photography are incorporated into a film review so readers can understand the reviewer's opinion.

Revising Your Writing

Answer these questions about your own paper, or exchange papers and respond to a classmate's paper:

1. Are the criteria for evaluation clearly stated or implied so that the standards being used are evident to the reader? List the criteria used.
2. Were the criteria chosen appropriate for the subject being evaluated? Explain.
3. What authority or credentials did the writer have for evaluating the subject?
4. Are there enough specific details to show you, the reader, that the judgment was fairly arrived at? If not, where does the writer need to add more details?

ASSIGNMENT 8: THE EDITORIAL OPINION

Choose an issue such as gun control, abortion, capital punishment, euthanasia, or some other controversial issue.

Read at least one article on each side of the issue and then write a newspaper editorial that states your opinion or evaluation of the issue. You may wish to focus on a particular case (such as the insanity defense of John W. Hinckley, who attempted to assassinate President Reagan) rather than on the larger issue of insanity defenses in general. The criteria you are using to judge the issue should be clearly stated or implied in your editorial.

Prepare a bibliography of sources you used to provide background on the subject. For a guide to bibliographical form, see Appendix A.

Two student and two professional examples follow. Read them and be prepared to discuss their strong and weak points. What evidence (substantiation) does each use to support the writer's opinion? Where does each writer define the issue or clarify a particular point of view?

STUDENT EDITORIALS

AN EDITORIAL: KEEP NUCLEAR POWER PLANTS

Though all of us were concerned when the Three Mile Island nuclear power plant malfunctioned and had to be shut down a few years back, that is not sufficient reason to stop building other nuclear generating plants or to abandon those that we have. Let's take the safety issue. No one in the United States has been hurt by any accident in a nuclear plant, and the odds that one will be hurt in any given year are one in 300 million. Getting into a car is much more dangerous. If anything, TMI has made the industry safe because it pointed to the need for better trained personnel and for a closer watch on safety procedures.

Safe waste disposal is another problem but not an insurmountable one. Scientists have a plan already for embedding waste in glass (which is inert, can't rust, and won't leak), and then burying it. The generating plants themselves give off less radiation than people get from other sources such as x-rays or television sets.

But the biggest reason for continuing nuclear power plants is the clean, inexpensive, and uninterruptible production of electricity. Nuclear plants don't cause acid rain as do fossil fuel plants. Such rain is destroying the lakes and wildlife in much of the eastern forest area. Nuclear plants cost more to build but less to run, and their use lessens our dependence on Arab oil, which is good both for our pocketbooks and for our national security.

We feel that to abandon nuclear generating plants now is to turn our backs on a really efficient way to combat the energy shortage and to keep us in bondage to Arab oil interests. We can't afford to do either one.

AN EDITORIAL:
CAN WE AFFORD TO TAKE THE CHANCE ON NUCLEAR POWER?

The accident of Three Mile Island has focused the country's attention once more on nuclear generating plants and their safety. It is true that a major accident was averted, but the consequences of such a disaster would have been enormous: three to four thousand dead, fifty thousand deaths later from radiation-induced cancer, contamination of land, water, and air. Even the level of radiation emissions from TMI may have been enough to cause malformations in new animal livestock and babies born shortly after the event. One doctor feels that one thousand new cases of leukemia will result in twenty years. Can we accept this accident and take the chance that even more serious ones will occur?

Nuclear reactors are being built twenty-four miles from New York City, twelve miles from Gary, Indiana, ten miles from Philadelphia, and five miles from Trenton, New Jersey. Can we expose the entire populations of great urban centers to possible nuclear accidents?

TMI was not the only near-disaster. Brown's Ferry in Alabama and the Fermi Reactor in Detroit both suffered partial core meltdowns and narrowly averted the release of deadly radiation.

What of our alternatives? Little has been done to spur research and development of solar, thermal, and wind power, which are clean and potentially useful sources of energy. Even though that is true, hundreds of small solar installations are currently in effect and thousands more are planned. If we spent money on research into these alternatives, we might find we could do without nuclear power plants.

We feel that to endanger the lives of millions is not worth the energy produced by nuclear plants, and we should do all we can to investigate alternative power sources to that of nuclear power.

Discussion Questions: "Keep Nuclear Power Plants" and "Can We Afford to Take the Chance on Nuclear Power?"

1. For the essay that supports the building of nuclear power plants, discuss the criteria used, the evidence brought to bear, and the essay's strongest and weakest arguments.
2. Do the same for the essay that opposes nuclear power plants.
3. Which essay do you find more effective? Why?

Evaluation

PROFESSIONAL EDITORIALS

An Editorial: Death Penalty is Right

Miami Herald

When he signed death warrants for John Spenkelink and Willie Darden, Gov. Bob Graham fulfilled the most awesome responsibility that a state confers upon its governor. In years past, this newspaper would have said that he was wrong, that the concept of capital punishment was wrong. But today, after prolonged soulsearching and impassioned debate within our Editorial Board, we conclude that the governor was right.

Capital punishment is a question of conscience. No question pierces more thoroughly the heart of the relationship between the individual and the state. No question is as irresolvable by the usual means of proof, because the "proof" exists, finally, only in one's view of whether the state has the right to demand that those who commit heinous murder must forfeit their own lives.

To this question of conscience, which we have debated fully and fervidly, we must answer yes. The states *does* have the right—indeed, the duty—to say to the individual citizen on behalf of all other citizens: "When you murder with deliberation and malice, you shatter the bond that prevents society from becoming a jungle. And that is a transgression that society cannot condone or forgive."

Its opponents argue that capital punishment amounts to murder by the state. If one accepts that view, it therefore follows that the state, in exacting capital punishment, flouts the very sacredness of human life upon which Western civilization is premised.

We respect the wellspring of conscience from which that argument flows, but we cannot drink from it. That cup is tainted by a fundamental illogic. It cheats the victim, and weakens the civilizing bond of law, by implicitly stating that the victim's life is worth less than the life of his murderer.

Human life *is* sacred. And because it is, the society that truly values human life asserts that valuation by imposing on murderers the most extraordinary penalty possible: death. If respect for life and for society's reverence for life is to continue, the inevitability of society's maximum penalty must be clearly understood by all who would wantonly take the life of another.

That is not to say that we accept the theory that capital punishment deters heinous crime. We do not. The evidence of capital punishment's deterrent effect is tenuous at best. Moreover, the deterrence argument is both intellectually specious and irrelevant to the sole purpose of capital punishment.

If executing one murderer deters

another murder, that effect is incidental. The state does not execute condemned murderers to make them object lessons for others. The state executes murderers because they have violated the cardinal rule that the people, through their Legislature and their courts, have decreed to be inviolable.

Opponents argue that capital punishment is inherently discriminatory because those condemned to death in the past were too often poor, too often black. That argument, to society's shame, is true—*as applied to the past.* But the conditions that obtained in the past, especially in the segregated South, no longer obtain. The U.S. Supreme court rectified them in 1972 and 1976.

In those years the High Court struck down some states' death-penalty laws and upheld others' in decisions that imposed uniform standards on them all. No black man ever again will be sentenced to death by a Jim Crow judge upon conviction by a Jim Crow jury. Florida's law complies with the Supreme court standards, which make death-penalty statutes as fair as any that man has devised.

The fundamental question, then, remains not whether capital punishment is a deterrent, not whether it is fair, but whether a civilized society can justify this ultimate sanction. And that question is, and always will be, answerable only in one's conscience.

Our answer, derived with great difficulty, comes from an institutional conscience cleared by the process of argument and thought. Our answer is yes.

An Editorial: Who Gets the Chair?

The New York Times

"There will be less brutality in our society if it is made clear we value human life." So said Governor Graham of Florida as he decreed that John Spenkelink, a drifter who murdered a fellow drifter, and Willie Jasper Darden, Jr., who killed a merchant during a holdup, should be executed this morning.

Whether one or both in fact die, the Governor's dictum is not supportable. No one can say with certainty that killing deters killing. Even in symbolic terms, the Governor's words are a kind of gallows humor. What else can "less brutality" mean when used to describe the reactivation of the electric chair after a 15-year lapse? What else can "value human life" mean when a state with 132 people on Death Row, more than any other, starts to clear out the inventory? And as for "made clear," the only thing being clarified is that society values some lives more than others.

It would be easier to defend capital punishment if at least it were applied consistently—if the rich or the notable went to the chair. But that rarely happens, as is newly evident from the violence on the streets of San Francisco. A jury has found Dan White guilty only of manslaughter for gunning down a mayor and a city supervisor. Drifters, even those who get religion, get fried; former county officials, "filled with remorse," get seven years, eight months.

Why is there not more remorse about this "system" of capital punishment? One reason is that all its faces are hooded. There is a division of labor and no person or agency—be it prosecutor, jury, judge, governor, state, nation or hangman—need accept responsibility. And from all this diversity of laws, juries and defendants emerges a pattern of who among guilty murderers is condemned: they are all poor.

We abhor capital punishment because we believe it is wrong for the state so to take life; because it is applied capriciously even among the clearly guilty; because even juries make mistakes; and because we think that, far from deterring, it creates a tolerance for killing. But no argument against capital punishment is more damning than to find out who is condemned.

The way to value human life, Governor Graham, is to do so.

Discussion Questions: "Death Penalty is Right" and "Who Gets the Chair?"

1. For the essay that supports the death penalty, discuss the criteria used, the evidence brought to bear, and the essay's strongest and weakest arguments.
2. Do the same for the essay that opposes the death penalty.
3. Which essay do you find more effective? Why?

WRITING ACTIVITY

Beginning the Assignment

1. Briefly summarize an article on one side of the issue.
2. Briefly summarize an article opposed to the opinion above.
3. Which argument is more convincing to you? Why? List points you want to mention in your own editorial.

Writing a Draft

Editorials are brief, yet a reader has to understand the content of the opinion. What opening sentence can you construct to get to the heart of the matter quickly?

Each paragraph could center on one of your main points and its supporting evidence. Make a brief outline of your main ideas and the supporting details.

Write a conclusion which makes your opinion of the issue clear to your reader.

Revising Your Writing

Evaluations should be grounded in facts. Though in a brief editorial, writers cannot cite all the sources they have read to substantiate their points, as they would do in a more comprehensive report or term paper, the editorial should depend on a thorough background. That knowledge should be evident in at least a few references in the writing.

Check your rough draft to see that specific support for your opinion has been given, or exchange papers in pairs or in groups within your class and have other readers respond to your evidence. Is it sufficient or does more need to be provided? If so, where?

Ask yourself or the other readers to state your editorial position in a sentence or two. If this can't be done, your editorial may be too general or unfocused. Go back to the main points you wish to make, and try to state each one clearly in a sentence.

MASTERY ASSIGNMENTS

1. Write an evaluation of a *type* of movie: horror films, science fiction, fantasy types like *Star Wars,* Clint Eastwood films, teenage exploitation films, "summer" films, the big "blockbuster" films, and the like. What audience does the type appeal to? What are the usual ingredients? How well done are these films? Are there clear differences among the individual films that make up the genre?

2. Do the same sort of evaluation of soap operas, situation comedies, or TV commercials for shampoo, soda pop, detergent, or the like.

3. Evaluate a speech made by a prominent public figure. Try to determine what criteria apply to your evaluation of the speech (which would range from "Was it successful with the audience?" to "Did it educate the audience?") Cite specific parts of the speech to substantiate your opinion.

4. Evaluate a new life-style in comparison to a more traditional way of living or doing things.

CHAPTER 6

Writing to Persuade: Recommending

This purpose has at its base the idea that someone will think or act differently about a subject after being persuaded by a writer. Newspaper columnists, friends, parents, and many others offer us their recommendations. As members of a free society, we are exhorted to vote for people at all levels of government, and as consumers we are bombarded with persuasive appeals to spend our money. It is important that we know how to recommend something to someone *and* that we know what ways others use to persuade us to do something.

There are two basic forms of reasoning that all of us follow in everyday life and that are used by others to persuade us to do something: induction and deduction.

Induction is often called "the scientific method" because scientists conduct a series of trials or experiments before they can draw a conclusion about the subject they are investigating. If, for example, they are testing a new antibiotic to cure pneumonia, they will experiment with the drug in the lab, in animal tests, and in human volunteers before they will be able to say with any degree of certainty that the drug is safe and effective. Induction therefore proceeds like this:

Test 1
_____

Test 2
_____

Test 3
_____

Test 4
_____
- -
Generalization

How many tests or experiments are required depends on how important
it is that the generalization be valid. The more tests, generally the more
assurance that the conclusion will be correct. Would you want to take an
antibiotic after only 10 trials on animals or human volunteers? Probably
not, because you would feel that 10 trials are not sufficient. On the other
hand, if you had a friend who once was late for a date, how many additional
instances of his or her being late would it take for you to conclude (or gen-
eralize) that this person is chronically late? Most of us would probably make
that generalization after only three or four instances. A writer using the
inductive process has to judge whether she has provided enough instances
to substantiate her case to the reader's satisfaction. *Note here* that induction
does not result in absolute proof. No matter how often an antibiotic has
been deemed safe and effective in trials, there may be side effects which
occur in certain individuals. And, no matter how often your friend has been
late, there is always the chance that the next time he or she will be on time.
But inductive reasoning *can* establish probability. Other examples of inductive reasoning include the way an allergist proceeds to find the cause
of your itching or sneezing. The infamous "scratch tests" are an inductive
way of determining if you are allergic to a substance by using needles to
deposit small amounts of known allergens under the skin and then by ob-
serving the skin to note any reactions. Induction is used any time a person
observes or records a number of instances before arriving at a generalization
about those instances.

Deduction, the other major form of reasoning, is often a companion to
induction but also is used by itself to persuade. Deductive reasoning follows a three-part logical "proof" known as a syllogism. The three parts are
a major premise, which is an assumption generally accepted as true by the
reader; a minor premise, which often needs to be further substantiated (hence
the need for trials or experiments of induction); and a conclusion, which
follows from the two premises. Following are two examples of syllogisms.

Major premise: A substance which causes a skin reaction on
(an assumption   Mary's skin is responsible for Mary's allergic
commonly agreed   symptoms.
on)

Minor premise:	Strawberries cause a reaction on Mary's skin.
(a statement which can be substanti- ated)	
Conclusion:	Strawberries are responsible for Mary's al- lergic symptoms.
Major premise:	A student who has a 3.00 grade-point average in high school and 1,000 on the S.A.T. exams will be successful at Metropolitan University.
Minor premise:	George has a 3.00 average and a 1,000 S.A.T. score.
Conclusion:	George will be successful at Metropolitan University.

This last syllogism illustrates a problem for users of deductive argu- ments: the major premise may be faulty or so open to other influences as not to be reliable. Though colleges do admit people based on the logic above, we all know students like George who fail and students without George's grade-point average and S.A.T. scores who prove to be successful. A healthy dose of skepticism of major premises used in arguments is a good pre- ventative of being misled.

Actually in most arguments, the writer does *not* produce the whole syl- logism but rather makes a statement which contains *hidden* premises. Can you find the hidden premise in this statement: "The man the detective questioned would not look him in the eye, so he must be the bank robber the police were looking for." Underlying that statement is a major premise: People who don't look a questioner in the eye are guilty of wrongdoing. This assumption should not simply be accepted; there are many possible reasons for someone not to look directly at a detective. Another example of the use of hidden premises often occurs during political campaigns: "Senator X was seen talking to a corrupt labor leader. We can have only honest candidates for office. Don't vote for Senator X." This statement as- sumes that because Senator X talks with someone, that the senator agrees with the corrupt person or is dishonest or corrupt herself. That is a big assumption which no voter should accept without substantiation. Good de- ductive reasoning should be based on reasonable and commonly accepted major premises and on minor premises that can be supported inductively. In this chapter, Thomas Jefferson's *Declaration of Independence* provides a classic example of a deductive argument.

Aside from the failure to examine basic premises or to provide enough evidence to support a premise (sometimes called hasty generalization), there are two other common barriers to good reasoning. One is arguing by attacking an opponent personally (*ad hominem*) when such an attack is irrelevant to the issue: "Don't vote for Senator Y; he is bald and has false teeth," or "Governor Z's daughter was once convicted of shoplifting." Senator Y's personal appearance should have nothing to do with his competence for office, and Governor Z cannot be held responsible for his daughter's acts.

Another barrier to good reasoning is arguing that something caused something else to happen simply because the events occurred one after the other (*post hoc ergo propter hoc*): "I lost my job because I saw a black cat this morning," or "Your baby will have a birthmark because you were frightened by a mouse." Whether you lose a job or have a baby with a birthmark will depend on causes that should be able to be substantiated by evidence and not simply tied to events that are coincidences.

When you are on the receiving end of advertising, political rhetoric, or other attempts to persuade, remember to examine the assumptions on which the argument is based, look at the evidence needed to support any claims, and watch out for the common barriers to good reasoning. Similarly, when you as a writer attempt to persuade someone else, try to observe the principles of logic and reasoning.

Recommending almost always requires writers to explain, substantiate, and evaluate before they can recommend anything. That is, it involves all four circles of our model, shown in Figure 6.1.

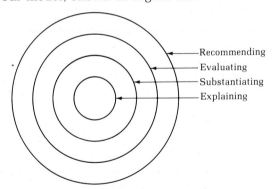

Figure 6.1
Relationship of Four Writing Purposes

The writer trying to recommend an idea or action to someone must take into account the audience's needs even more than writers trying to explain, substantiate, and evaluate. Because the purpose of this type of essay is to get agreement from someone else, that person's needs must be met in order to win his or her approval of the writer's recommendation.

How can a writer convince someone to believe as he or she does? In a nutshell, the answer is by careful explanations and marshaling of evidence so that the reader feels the weight of the argument favors the writer's point of view.

Below is a plan with many options which can be used to analyze others' arguments and to write your own recommending essays. Please note that no plan suits every writer or every subject, but if you consider the points on the plan as you read or write recommendations, you will be better able to analyze and write persuasive arguments.

Sample Plan for Recommending Essays

A. Introduction

   Option 1: Establish common ground with the reader by pointing out shared beliefs, attitudes, or experiences.

   Option 2: Cite a case study, a fact, or an incident you witnessed or read about to get your reader to think about the issue from a fresh perspective.

   Option 3: Explain the background of the issue or problem so that the reader will know something of its history or origin.

   Option 4: Explain how you developed your interest or knowledge of the subject so that your recommendation will seem credible.

B. Main Points

   1. State the criteria for solving the problem. For example, suppose you were arguing that the campus parking system is inadequate. What are the desirable features of a good parking system? Possibilities include: (a) it must be cheap, (b) it must provide enough space for cars, and (c) it must be administered fairly.

   2. State your thesis, that is, your position on the issue.

   3. Support your position with evidence: facts, statements of authority, case studies, and so on. Choose sources that will be convincing to your reader, which entails knowing your reader's probable assumptions and beliefs.

   4. If you need to, counter the arguments of your reader, but be respectful and logical. Point out why other alternatives would not work as well as your solution.

   Note: The order of these points is highly variable. Some writers may choose to refute (counter) the arguments of the reader first in order to open the mind to a new solution to a problem. Also, criteria for a solution are not always directly stated but may be implied in the thesis or elsewhere.

C. Conclusion

> *Option 1:* Restate your main point. You may wish to summarize the points you have made in support of the main idea.

> *Option 2:* You may wish to use an incident or other evidence here to dramatize the benefit of accepting your position or the danger of rejecting it.

Using this plan, read the following essay by an educator and identify the plan he used for his essay of recommendation. Following the essay are specific questions for you to answer.

READINGS

How the S.A.T.'S Are Used— and Sometimes Abused

James W. Wickenden

Recent charges by Ralph Nader against the Educational Testing Service and the passage last year of a "truth-in-testing" law in New York State have focused national attention on the use of standardized tests in college admissions. Despite the continuing controversy, few admission officers have been asked for comments. Yet, as the primary users of test scores, we are in the best position to explain their function in the admission process— how they are used and, on occasion, abused—at those institutions where the scores are considered in the decision-making process.

Each year more than 2 million students enter American colleges and universities, and over a million college applicants take the Scholastic Aptitude Test. The College Board commissioned the Educational Testing Service to build and administer the test. Scores on the S.A.T. range from 200 to 800; the mean scores in 1979 were 427 on the Verbal section and 467 on the Math.

While believing that standardized tests can make a constructive and positive contribution to the admission process, I also believe that some of the recent criticism of the tests is justified. Several issues relating to the use of test scores in the admission process deserve mention.

To begin with, I have serious reservations about those colleges and universities that tie admission to only two variables—grade-point averages and S.A.T. scores. Such a policy not only ignores critically important information about the personal characteristics and non-academic talents of the applicants but also assumes a degree of accuracy in predicting academic success that the S.A.T.'s have not demonstrated. While a correlation indeed does exist between test performance and grades in the first year of college, the relationship is far from perfect. Last year, for example, Princeton offered a place in the Class of 1983 to a young woman with a Verbal score of 300, some 350 points below the mean score for other accepted applicants. Because she was the valedictorian of her high school class and had been in this country only five years, we decided to disregard her S.A.T. perfor-

---

James Wickenden, Director of Admissions at Princeton University, wrote this article for *The Chronicle of Higher Education,* a newspaper for academics.

mance. At the end of her first year she had three A's, three B's, and two C's. Yet a college with an S.A.T. "floor" might not have accepted her.

Secondly, the S.A.T.'s place a premium on speed. Therefore, students who are careful, thoughtful, and considered in their judgments may be penalized as they wrestle with the subtleties of complex questions.

I am also concerned about the effects the tests can have on the self-esteem of those who take them. Students who score at the national mean on the Verbal portion of the S.A.T. may think of themselves as "only a 430," and they may question their intellectual abilities. What needs to be emphasized—and what the Educational Testing Service has stated all along—is that the S.A.T.'s are not intended to measure adaptability, motivation, creativity, native talent, or the capacity to succeed in a particular occupation. Instead, they are designed simply to measure *developed ability.* This measurement is used by admission officers to make a reasoned prediction of a student's academic performance in the first year of college, but it must be used with sensitivity and with an understanding of the background of the applicant.

The debate over standardized tests might be less strident if the colleges and universities conducted validation studies to show the extent of correlation between test scores and college grades and then made their findings accessible to the public. Currently, the results of such studies appear in academic journals, which are read primarily by psychometricians, psychologists, sociologists, and educators. It might be helpful to applicants if they knew how students with various S.A.T. scores had performed at the kinds of institutions to which they were thinking of applying.

Finally, I am concerned that many who work in admissions and spend a good portion of the year interpreting test scores may have little or no training in tests and measurements.

Despite these concerns, I nevertheless am a staunch advocate of the responsible use of standardized tests in the admission process.

Although critics of the Educational Testing Service claim otherwise, I firmly believe that the services provided by that organization have helped talented minority-group and disadvantaged applicants gain admission to selective colleges. Those black, Hispanic, and native American applicants who participate in the minority-search program offered by E.T.S. and who perform well on the S.A.T.'s receive literally hundreds of letters from colleges across the country seeking them as applicants. I am persuaded that the S.A.T. has opened more doors than it has closed for minority-group and disadvantaged students.

If the S.A.T.'s were abolished, admission officers would have no alternative except to rely on grades, rank in class, and evaluations by teachers and counselors; these vary tremendously in quality from school to school.

Generally, the reports that come from college-preparatory independent schools and from affluent suburban schools, where the counselor-student ratio may be 1 to 50, are far more comprehensive and informative than those from inner-city schools, where the counselor-student ratio may be 1 to 500. A first-rate performance on the S.A.T.'s, however, can offset the less informative report that often comes from schools with understaffed counseling services. One high school in New York City, for example, has only two counselors for a senior class of approximately 800—yet last year Princeton accepted 22 of its applicants. Most of those applicants had not only excellent grades but also superb test scores. Good grades alone would not have been sufficient to warrant admission, since at selective colleges the majority of the applicants rank in the top 10 to 15 percent of their secondary school classes and thus have very similar transcripts.

Without the S.A.T.'s, some institutions might revert to earlier practices and develop their own admission tests. In all likelihood such tests would be inferior in quality to those painstakingly developed by E.T.S.

Moreover, they would be likely to vary substantially in quality and content from institution to institution, and they would require students interested in several institutions to submit to a range of tests (if schedules could be worked out) or to limit the number of schools to which they could apply.

Given the above, what would I recommend?

First, that colleges and universities that tie admission decisions to an arbitrarily determined level of performance on the S.A.T.'s reconsider that policy.

Second, that colleges and universities with flexible admission policies insure that the admission officers interpreting test scores are adequately trained in tests and measurements. Moreover, those colleges should conduct annual studies to determine which of the variables in the admission process are the best predictors of academic success.

Third, that E.T.S. continue to improve and refine its procedures, free from the kind of legislative interference that could have the effect of making the tests less valid and more expensive, and could reduce the number of times they are administered (currently six times a year).

While E.T.S. and the College Board should continue to advise admission officers on the proper use and interpretation of the tests, to inform students about how the tests are constructed and scored, and to educate the public on the effectiveness and limitations of the tests, I prefer to see service of this nature come as a response to pressure from the users of the tests rather than from legislative initiatives. Frankly, I am concerned about the overreaction of some politicians to those critics who are reluctant to acknowledge the extent to which the tests are valid, and the contributions they have made to opening up educational opportunities for the less affluent.

Discussion Questions: "How the S.A.T.'s Are Used . . ."

1. How does the writer begin the essay? Does the beginning help the reader understand the writer's main point?
2. What is the main idea of the essay? Write down the focus sentence(s) that contain(s) the main idea.
3. Who was the essay written for (the audience)? How can you tell? What accommodations for audience do you find in the essay?
4. List each argument *against* the S.A.T.'s and the evidence Wickenden uses to support his points. Is there enough evidence?
5. List each argument *for* the S.A.T.'s and the evidence used to support each. Is there enough evidence?
6. What recommendations does he make? Do they seem logical in light of his earlier discussion?

The Declaration of Independence

**IN CONGRESS, JULY 4, 1776
THE UNANIMOUS DECLARATION OF THE
THIRTEEN UNITED STATES OF AMERICA**

Thomas Jefferson

When in the Course of human events it becomes necessary for one people to dissolve the political bands which have connected them with another, and to assume among the powers of the earth, the separate and equal station to which the Laws of Nature and of Nature's God entitle them, a decent respect to the opinions of mankind requires that they should declare the causes which impel them to the separation.

We hold these truths to be self-evident, that all men are created equal, that they are endowed by their Creator with certain unalienable Rights, that among these are Life, Liberty and the pursuit of Happiness. That to secure these rights, Governments are instituted among Men, deriving their just powers from the consent of the governed. That whenever any Form of Government becomes destructive of these ends, it is the Right of the People to alter or to abolish it, and to institute new Government, laying its foundation on such principles and organizing its powers in such form, as to them shall seem most likely to affect their Safety and Happiness. Prudence, indeed, will dictate that Governments long established should not be changed for light and transient causes; and accordingly all experience hath shewn that mankind are more disposed to suffer, while evils are sufferable, than to right themselves by abolishing the forms to which they are accustomed. But when a long train of abuses and usurpations, pursuing invariably the same Object evinces a design to reduce them under absolute Despotism, it is their right, it is their duty, to throw off such Government, and to provide new Guards for their future security. Such has been the patient sufferance of these Colonies; and such is now the necessity which constrains them to alter their former Systems of Government. The history of the present King of Great Britain is a history of repeated injuries and usurpations, all having in direct object the establishment of an absolute Tyranny over these States. To prove this, let Facts be submitted to a candid world.

He has refused his Assent to Laws, the most wholesome and necessary for the public good.

Thomas Jefferson, the third president of the United States, was the main author of the *Declaration of Independence*. Jefferson attempted to explain the reasons for the colonies' separation from Great Britain in such a persuasive way that the message would unite the colonies behind the war for independence.

He has forbidden his Governors to pass laws of immediate and pressing importance, unless suspended in their operation till his Assent should be obtained; and when so suspended, he has utterly neglected to attend to them.

He has refused to pass other Laws for the accommodation of large districts of people, unless those people would relinquish the right of Representation in the Legislature, a right inestimable to them and formidable to tyrants only.

He has called together legislative bodies at places unusual, uncomfortable, and distant from the depository of their Public Records, for the sole purpose of fatiguing them into compliance with his measures.

He has dissolved Representative Houses repeatedly, for opposing with manly firmness his invasions on the rights of the people.

He has refused for a long time, after such dissolutions, to cause others to be elected; whereby the Legislative Powers, incapable of Annihilation, have returned to the People at large for their exercise; the State remaining in the mean time exposed to all the dangers of invasion from without, and convulsions within.

He has endeavored to prevent the population of these States; for that purpose obstructing the Laws for Naturalization of Foreigners; refusing to pass others to encourage their migration hither, and raising the conditions of new Appropriations of Lands.

He has obstructed the Administration of Justice, by refusing his Assent to Laws for establishing Judiciary Powers.

He has made Judges dependent on his Will alone, for the tenure of their offices, and the amount and payment of their salaries.

He has erected a multitude of New Offices, and sent hither swarms of Officers to harass our people, and eat out their substance.

He has kept among us, in times of peace, Standing Armies without the Consent of our legislatures.

He has affected to render the Military independent of and superior to the Civil Power.

He has combined with others to subject us to a jurisdiction foreign to our constitution, and unacknowledged by our laws; giving his Assent to their Acts of pretended Legislation; For quartering large bodies of armed troops among us; For protecting them, by a mock Trial, from punishment for any Murders which they should commit on the Inhabitants of these States; For cutting off our Trade with all parts of the world; For imposing Taxes on us without our Consent; For depriving us in many cases, of the benefits of Trial by Jury; For transporting us beyond Seas to be tried for pretended offenses; for abolishing the free System of English Laws in a neighboring Province, establishing therein an Arbitrary government, and enlarging its Boundaries so as to render it at once an example and fit instrument for introducing the same absolute rule into these Colonies; For taking away our Charters, abolishing our most valuable Laws and altering fundamentally the Forms of our Governments; For suspending our own Legislatures, and declaring themselves invested with power to legislate for us in all cases whatsoever.

He has abdicated Government here, by declaring us out of his Protection and waging War against us.

He has plundered our seas, ravaged our Coasts, burnt our towns, and destroyed the lives of our people.

He is at this time transporting large Armies of foreign Mercenaries to complete the works of death, desolation and tyranny, already begun with circumstances of Cruelty & Perfidy scarcely paralleled in the most barbarous ages, and totally unworthy the Head of a civilized nation.

He has constrained our fellow Citizens taken Captive on the high Seas to bear Arms against their Country, to become the executioners of their friends and Brethren, or to fall themselves by their Hands.

He has excited domestic insurrections amongst us, and has endeavored to bring on the inhabitants of our frontiers, the merciless Indian Savages, whose known rule of warfare, is an undistinguished destruction of all ages, sexes, and conditions.

In every stage of these Oppressions We have Petitioned for Redress in the most humble terms; Our repeated Petitions have been answered only by repeated injury. A Prince, whose character is thus marked by every act which may define a Tyrant, is unfit to be the ruler of a free people.

Nor have We been wanting in attention to our British brethren. We have warned them from time to time of attempts by their legislature to extend an unwarrantable jurisdiction over us. We have reminded them of the circumstances of our emigration and settlement here. We have appealed to their native justice and magnanimity, and we have conjured them by the ties of our common kindred to disavow these usurpations, which would inevitably interrupt our connections and correspondence. They too have been deaf to the voice of justice and of consanguinity. We must, therefore, acquiesce in the necessity, which denounces our Separation, and hold them, as we hold the rest of mankind, Enemies in War, in Peace Friends.

WE, THEREFORE, the Representatives of the UNITED STATES OF AMERICA, in General Congress, Assembled, appealing to the Supreme Judge of the world for the rectitude of our intentions, do, in the Name, and by authority of the good People of these Colonies, solemnly publish and declare, That these United Colonies are, and of Right ought to be FREE AND INDEPENDENT STATES; that they are Absolved from all Allegiance to the British Crown, and that all political connection between them and the State of Great Britain, is and ought to be totally dissolved; and that as Free and Independent States, they have full Power to levy War, conclude Peace, contract Alliances, establish

Commerce, and to do all other Acts and Things which Independent States may of right do. And for the support of this Declaration, with a firm reliance on the protection of Divine Providence, we mutually pledge to each other our Lives, our Fortunes, and our sacred Honor.

Discussion Questions: "The Declaration of Independence"

1. This classic argument explains, substantiates, evaluates, and recommends.
   a. What does Jefferson explain are the colonists' basic assumptions about the rights of men and governments?
   b. What substantiates their claim that the present government of Great Britain under the king has become "destructive of these ends?"
   c. What evaluation of the king and of the legislature (Parliament) does the Declaration make?
   d. What course of action (recommendation) does the essay then say is necessary?
2. The Declaration had two audiences: the powers in Great Britain and the American colonists themselves (since the Continental Congress had to announce the action it had taken). Can you find evidence in the essay of these two prospective readers?
3. What is the effect of repeating "he" in the several paragraphs which substantiate the colonists' claims?
4. What is the tone (or attitude taken toward the subject) of the first paragraph? Why do you think that the Declaration begins this way rather than with angrier words?
5. The Declaration follows the classic deductive argument. See if you can find the three major parts:
   a. A major premise on which (it is hoped) everyone can agree.
   b. A minor premise which needs to be proved by observation or other facts.
   c. A conclusion logically derived from the major and minor premises.
6. Try rewriting the first two paragraphs of the Declaration into more modern language. Do you find your version *more* or *less* effective? Why?

The Time Factor

Gloria Steinem

Planning ahead is a measure of class. The rich and even the middle class plan for future generations, but the poor can plan ahead only a few weeks or days.

I remember finding this calm insight in some sociological text and feeling instant recognition. Yes, of course, our sense of time was partly a function of power, or the lack of it. It rang true even in the entirely economic sense the writer had in mind. "The guys who own the factories hand them down to their sons and great-grandsons," I remember a boy in my high school saying bitterly. "On this side of town, we just plan for Saturday night."

But it also seemed equally true of most of the women I knew—including myself—regardless of the class we supposedly belonged to. Though I had left my factory-working neighborhood, gone to college, become a journalist, and thus was middle class, I still felt that I couldn't plan ahead. I had to be flexible—first, so that I could be ready to get on a plane for any writing assignment (even though the male writers I knew launched into books and other long-term projects on their own), and then so that I could adapt to the career and priorities of an eventual husband and children (even though I was leading a rewarding life without either). Among the results of this uncertainty were a stunning lack of career planning and such smaller penalties as no savings, no insurance, and an apartment that lacked basic pieces of furniture.

On the other hand, I had friends who were married to men whose long-term career plans were compatible with their own, yet they still lived their lives in day-to-day response to any possible needs of their husbands and children. Moreover, the one male colleague who shared or even understood this sense of powerlessness was a successful black journalist and literary critic who admitted that even after twenty years he planned only one assignment at a time. He couldn't forget his dependence on the approval of white editors.

Clearly there is more to this fear of the future than a conventional definition of class could explain. There is also caste: the unchangeable marks of sex and race that bring a whole constellation of cultural injunctions against power, even the limited power of controlling one's own life.

We haven't yet examined time-sense and future planning as functions of

Gloria Steinem is one of the best-known women writers today. Her articles appear in *New York* magazine and *Ms* magazine, both of which she helped found. She is active politically in the cause of peace, civil rights, and women's rights. This essay is from her 1983 book *Outrageous Acts and Everyday Rebellions.*

discrimination, but we have begun to struggle with them, consciously or not. As a movement, women have become painfully conscious of too much reaction and living from one emergency to the next, with too little initiative and planned action of our own; hence many of our losses to a much smaller but more entrenched and consistent right wing.

Though the cultural habit of living in the present and glazing over the future goes deep, we've begun to challenge the cultural punishment awaiting the "pushy" and "selfish" women (and the "uppity" minority men) who try to break through it and control their own lives.

Even so, feminist writers and theorists tend to avoid the future by lavishing all our analytical abilities on what's wrong with the present, or on revisions of history and critiques of the influential male thinkers of the past. The big, original, and certainly courageous books of this wave of feminism have been more diagnostic than prescriptive. We need pragmatic planners and visionary futurists, but can we think of even one feminist five-year-plan? Perhaps the closest we have come is visionary architecture or feminist science fiction, but they generally avoid the practical steps of how to get from here to there.

Obviously, many of us need to extend our time-sense—to have the courage to plan for the future, even while most of us are struggling to keep our heads above water in the present. But this does not mean a flat-out imitation of the culturally masculine habit of planning ahead, living in the future, and thus living a deferred life. It doesn't mean the traditional sacrifice of spontaneous action, or a sensitive awareness of the present, that comes from long years of career education with little intrusion of reality, from corporate pressure to work now for the sake of a reward after retirement, or, least logical of all, from patriarchal religions that expect obedience now in return for a reward after death.

In fact, the ability to live in the present, to tolerate uncertainty, and to remain open, spontaneous, and flexible are all culturally female qualities that many men need and have been denied. As usual, both halves of the polarized masculine-feminine division need to learn from each other's experiences. If men spent more time raising small children, for instance, they would be forced to develop more patience and flexibility. If women had more power in the planning of natural resources and other long-term processes—or even in the planning of our own careers and reproductive lives—we would have to develop more sense of the future and of cause and effect.

An obsession with reacting to the present, feminine-style, or on controlling and living in the future, masculine-style, are both wasteful of time.

And time is all there is.

Discussion Questions: "The Time Factor"

1. Steinem begins with a generalization about planning. To whom does this generalization apply? To whom does she extend this generalization? Why?

2. What is the main idea of the essay? Write down the focus sentence(s) that contain(s) the main idea?

3. For whom was the essay written? Who is referred to as "us" and "our"?

4. What evidence from her own life and others' experience does Steinem use to support her main idea? Is this evidence sufficient for you to believe?

5. What argument does she make that inability to plan is a function of discrimination against women and/or minority groups? Do you agree?

6. The ninth paragraph warns against some counterproductive ways of planning. What are they? Is there enough support for you to understand what Steinem means?

7. What recommendations does Steinem make about the way men and women should perceive time? Is she persuasive to you? Why or why not?

8. What do you think of the last line? Is it effective as an ending? Why or why not?

The Technology of Medicine

Lewis Thomas

Technology assessment has become a routine exercise for the scientific enterprises on which the country is obliged to spend vast sums for its needs. Brainy committees are continually evaluating the effectiveness and cost of doing various things in space, defense, energy, transportation, and the like, to give advice about prudent investments for the future.

Somehow medicine, for all the $80-odd billion that it is said to cost the nation, has not yet come in for much of this analytical treatment. It seems taken for granted that the technology of medicine simply exists, take it or leave it, and the only major technologic problem which policy-makers are interested in is how to deliver today's kind of health care, with equity, to all the people.

When, as is bound to happen sooner or later, the analysts get around to the technology of medicine itself, they will have to face the problem of measuring the relative cost and effectiveness of all the things that are done in the management of disease. They make their living at this kind of thing, and I wish them well, but I imagine they will have a bewildering time. For one thing, our methods of managing disease are constantly changing—partly under the influence of new bits of information brought in from all corners of biologic science. At the same time, a great many things are done that are not so closely related to science, some not related at all.

In fact, there are three quite different levels of technology in medicine, so unlike each other as to seem altogether different undertakings. Practitioners of medicine and the analysts will be in trouble if they are not kept separate.

1. First of all, there is a large body of what might be termed "nontechnology," impossible to measure in terms of its capacity to alter either the natural course of disease or its eventual outcome. A great deal of money is spent on this. It is valued highly by the professionals as well as the patients. It consists of what is sometimes called "supportive therapy." It tides patients over through diseases that are not, by and large, understood. It is what is meant by the phrases "caring for" and "standing by." It is indispensable. It is not, however, a technology in any real sense, since it does not involve measures directed at the underlying mechanism of disease.

It includes the large part of any good doctor's time that is taken up with simply providing reassurance, explaining to patients who fear that they have

Lewis Thomas is a physician, a professor of medicine, and Director of the Memorial Sloan Kettering Cancer Center in New York. His writing blends the disciplines of science and the humanities, and his books are popular with laypersons and physicians alike. This essay is from his first collection of essays, *Lives of a Cell* (1974).

contracted one or another lethal disease that they are, in fact, quite healthy.

It is what physicians used to be engaged in at the bedside of patients with diphtheria, meningitis, poliomyelitis, lobar pneumonia, and all the rest of the infectious diseases that have since come under control.

It is what physicians must now do for patients with intractable cancer, severe rheumatoid arthritis, multiple sclerosis, stroke, and advanced cirrhosis. One can think of at least twenty major diseases that require this kind of supportive medical care because of the absence of an effective technology. I would include a large amount of what is called mental disease, and most varieties of cancer, in this category.

The cost of this nontechnology is very high, and getting higher all the time. It requires not only a great deal of time but also very hard effort and skill on the part of physicians; only the very best of doctors are good at coping with this kind of defeat. It also involves long periods of hospitalization, lots of nursing, lots of involvement of nonmedical professionals in and out of the hospital. It represents, in short, a substantial segment of today's expenditures for health.

2. At the next level up is a kind of technology best termed "halfway technology." This represents the kinds of things that must be done after the fact, in efforts to compensate for the incapacitating effects of certain diseases whose course one is unable to do very much about. It is a technology designed to make up for disease, or to postpone death.

The outstanding examples in recent years are the transplantations of hearts, kidneys, livers, and other organs, and the equally spectacular inventions of artificial organs. In the public mind, this kind of technology has come to seem like the equivalent of the high technologies of the physical sciences. The media tend to present each new procedure as though it represented a breakthrough and therapeutic triumph, instead of the makeshift that it really is.

In fact, this level of technology is, by its nature, at the same time highly sophisticated and profoundly primitive. It is the kind of thing that one must continue to do until there is a genuine understanding of the mechanisms involved in disease. In chronic glomerulonephritis, for example, a much clearer insight will be needed into the events leading to the destruction of glomeruli by the immunologic reactants that now appear to govern this disease, before one will know how to intervene intelligently to prevent the process, or turn it round. But when this level of understanding has been reached, the technology of kidney replacement will not be much needed and should no longer pose the huge problems of logistics, cost, and ethics that it poses today.

An extremely complex and costly technology for the management of coronary heart disease has evolved—involving specialized ambulances and hospital units, all kinds of electronic gadgetry, and whole platoons of new professional personnel—to deal with the end results of coronary thrombosis. Almost everything offered today for the treatment of heart disease is at this level of technology, with the transplanted and artificial hearts as ultimate examples. When enough has been learned to know what really goes wrong in heart disease, one ought to be in a position to figure out ways to prevent or reverse the process, and when this happens the current elaborate technology will probably be set to one side.

Much of what is done in the treatment of cancer, by surgery, irradiation, and chemotherapy, represents halfway technology, in the sense that these measures are directed at the existence of already established cancer cells, but not at the mechanisms by which cells become neoplastic.

It is a characteristic of this kind of technology that it costs an enormous amount of money and requires a continuing expansion of hospital facilities. There is no end to the need for new, highly trained people to run the enterprise. And there is really no way out of this, at the present state of knowledge. If the installation of specialized coronary-care units can result in the extension of life for only a few patients with coronary disease (and there is no question that this technology is effective in a few cases), it seems to me an inevitable fact of life that as many of these as can be will be put together, and as much money as can be found will be spent. I do not see that anyone has much choice in this. The only thing that can move medicine away from this level of technology is new information, and the only imaginable source of this information is research.

3. The third type of technology is the kind that is so effective that it seems to attract the least public notice; it has come to be taken for granted. This is the genuinely decisive technology of modern medicine, exemplified best by modern methods for immunization against diphtheria, pertussis, and the childhood virus diseases, and the contemporary use of antibiotics and chemotherapy for bacterial infections. The capacity to deal effectively with syphilis and tuberculosis represents a milestone in human endeavor, even though full use of this potential has not yet been made. And there are, of course, other examples: the treatment of endocrinologic disorders with appropriate hormones, the prevention of hemolytic disease of the newborn, the treatment and prevention of various nutritional disorders, and perhaps just around the corner the management of Parkinsonism and sickle-cell anemia. There are other examples, and everyone will have his favorite candidates for the list, but the truth is that there are nothing like as many as the public has been led to believe.

The point to be made about this kind of technology—the real high technology of medicine—is that it comes as the result of a genuine understanding of disease mechanisms, and when it becomes available, it is relatively inexpensive, relatively simple, and relatively easy to deliver.

Offhand, I cannot think of any important human disease for which medicine possesses the outright capacity to prevent or cure where the cost of the technology is itself a major problem. The price is never as high as the cost of managing the same diseases during the earlier stages of no-technology or halfway technology. If a case of typhoid fever had to be managed today by the best methods of 1935, it would run to a staggering expense. At, say, around fifty days of hospitalization, requiring the most demanding kind of nursing care, with the obsessive concern for details of diet that characterized the therapy of that time, with daily laboratory monitoring, and, on occasion, surgical intervention for abdominal catastrophe, I should think $10,000 would be a conservative estimate for the illness, as contrasted with today's cost of a bottle of chloramphenicol and a day or two of fever. The halfway technology that was evolving for poliomyelitis in the early 1950s, just before the emergence of the basic research that made the vaccine possible, provides another illustration of the point. Do you remember Sister Kenny, and the cost of those institutes for rehabilitation, with all those ceremonially applied hot fomentations, and the debates about whether the affected limbs should be totally immobilized or kept in passive motion as frequently as possible, and the masses of statistically tormented data mobilized to support one view or the other? It is the cost of that kind of technology, and its relative effectiveness, that must be compared with the cost and effectiveness of the vaccine.

Pulmonary tuberculosis had similar episodes in its history. There was a sudden enthusiasm for the surgical removal of infected lung tissue in the early 1950s, and elaborate plans were being made for new and expensive installations for major pulmonary surgery in tuberculosis hospitals, and then INH and streptomycin came along and the hospitals themselves were closed up.

It is when physicians are bogged down by their incomplete technologies, by the innumerable things they are obliged to do in medicine when they lack a clear understanding of disease mechanisms, that the deficiencies of the health-care system are most conspicuous. If I were a policymaker, interested in saving money for health care over the long haul, I would regard it as an act of high prudence to give high priority to a lot more basic research in biologic science. This is the only way to get the full mileage that biology owes to the science of medicine, even though it seems, as used to be said in the days when the phrase still had some meaning, like asking for the moon.

Discussion Questions: "The Technology of Medicine"

1. What classification of technology does Lewis explain?
2. What explanation does he offer for each classification?
3. What does Thomas evaluate as he classifies?
4. Where do you find Thomas' recommendation?
5. What do you think of Thomas' recommendation in light of his evidence?
6. Are there any clues as to Thomas' audience? Has he made any assumptions about the reader's age or background that he shouldn't have?

On the Rim of Belonging

Alma Bagu

Sitting in a classroom with about 33 English-speaking kids and staring at words on a blackboard that to me were as foreign as Egyptian hieroglyphics is one of my early recollections of school. The teacher had come up to my desk and bent over, putting her face close to mine.

"My name is Mrs. Newman," she said, as if the exaggerated mouthing of her words would make me understand their meaning. I nodded "yes" because I felt that was what she wanted me to do. But she just threw up her hands in a gesture of despair, and touched her fingers to her head to signify to the class I was dense, whereupon all 33 classmates fell into gales of laughter. From that day on, school became an ordeal I was forced to endure.

In the early grades I attended a special class for Spanish-speaking children who spoke no English. I did well in this class and learned the simple phrases I was taught, but when I was in my regular class, I would not participate in oral discussions nor answer questions because I was painfully self-conscious of my heavy Spanish accent.

Most of the time the Puerto Rican children stuck together because we felt more at ease with each other. "Spic" was a word with which I was very familiar. The other children at school rarely called us by our names. They just said, "hey, spic," and clucked like hens, making fun of our language.

People in school seemed annoyed when we spoke Spanish among ourselves. It was if our teachers had taken upon themselves the task of straining out every drop of Puerto Rican culture we possessed to mold us into what they thought we should be. Some teachers would lecture us on how rude we were to speak a "strange" language in the presence of those who could not understand it. (This concern for propriety never made much sense to me, since the white English-speaking children didn't associate with us anyway. But I have to admit, I got a kick out of making the English-speaking children feel as uncomfortable around me as they made me feel around them.) Some teachers handed out punishments to those who spoke Spanish in school ("I must speak English in school" written five hundred times). Some Puerto Rican kids who found difficulty with English were considered retarded and placed in C.R.M.D. classes.

Alma Bagu, a writer working in New York City, contributed the following article to *The Center Forum*, published by The Center for Urban Education.

Literature was constantly being given us to bring home to our parents. Some of the literature insisted that our parents speak English in the home. Other pamphlets contained menus that the boards of health and education felt we should have. They warned of the perils of all-starch diets. For some reason they believed we ate nothing but rice and beans for breakfast, lunch, and dinner.

My mother read all the pamphlets, for they were printed in Spanish as well as English, and then tore them up and threw them away with the trash. "I feed my children well," she would say, and go right on speaking Spanish at home. Now, as an adult, I am grateful to her for not conforming and keeping our culture alive, at least in our home. But as a child I felt ashamed; I wanted my mother to be like the English-speaking mothers, who went to P.T.A. meetings and accompanied our class on trips.

I never tried to achieve scholastic success for fear of being laughed at for even trying. By the time I went to high school, I was completely fed up with education. I was part of a Puerto Rican clique. The only others treated worse than us, I felt, were the Negroes, a feeling that gave us a sense of superiority over them. We did our best to aggravate our teachers and white classmates, and there was among us an unspoken pact to speak English only when necessary.

I dropped out of school at 16, and later, when I had my own children, I wanted them to speak only English in order to avoid the same problems I had. For the sake of making things easier for my children when they went to school, I abandoned so many of the beautiful customs of my culture. I made little *Americanos* of them so they would not feel like aliens in the classroom. I finished the job on my children that my teachers started on me. I denied my offsprings some of my most beautiful memories. As a child I would ask for my mother's blessing as I left the house. *"Benedicion,"* I would say. *"Dios te bendiga,"* she would always answer. God bless you. The candles of appeasement to the saints and friendly spirits, which belonged to the religion my mother brought with her from Puerto Rico, no longer burn. The rebelliousness and desire to be known as a Puerto Rican— whether out of pride or a feeling that I couldn't make it in a white American society—was gone. Because I wanted my children to be accepted by the *Americanos,* I closed the door on my own heritage.

The irony of the whole thing was that my children weren't accepted anyway. One day my daughter came home from school, her hazel eyes brimming over with tears that spilled onto her tan cheeks. "I'm not a dirty spic," she cried. And my son reported to me that he was the second dirtiest kid in his class. "The dirtiest one is a colored boy. I'm darkest after him." His classmates, he said, were always asking what he was. I had taught him to say he was an American. But even his teacher, he said, wouldn't accept that answer. His olive complexion had made him different, and being Puerto Rican had set him apart.

Faced with the fear that the school system would make drop-outs of my children too, I moved from a fairly good neighborhood to one that was well populated with Puerto Ricans—in other words a "ghetto"—where my children would be—and were—accepted for what they are.

Discussion Questions: "On the Rim of Belonging"

1. Why does the writer begin with a narrative incident from her own experience?
2. What other recollections of her school years reinforced her feeling of being an outsider?
3. What are her solutions? Are they reasonable in light of the evidence she presented? Can you think of another alternative solution to the problem?

ASSIGNMENT 9: THE RECOMMENDATION

Set up criteria for judging something that you buy (jeans, peanut butter, stereo equipment, toothpaste, etc.), and evaluate several brands of that product to determine which one(s) should be recommended to a friend.

Read the following student examples. As before, be prepared to analyze their effectiveness or ineffectiveness. Questions following each example direct your attention to features of the essays.

STUDENT ESSAYS

FILM PROCESSING

There are many processing labs where people can take their film. However, not all of these labs offer the same quality. In this report, the three labs specifically mentioned are Fotomat, Kodak, and Quality Color. The latter two labs I have had direct experience with by working in a camera shop. It must be understood that pictures are a product which one buys from the processing lab. Therefore, care must be taken to get the most quality for the money. This report will hopefully take some of the mystery out of these different labs.

At these three labs there are two important differences already present. The first is in what each lab will print. Kodak and Quality Color print and charge the customer only for those prints which do come out. Fotomat, like many other labs, prints everything. Although places like this usually will refund money for the prints if the customer is not pleased, the lab is actually banking on the fact that many people will not bother returning the poor prints. The other major difference is cost. Kodak, for example, charges at least three or four dollars more to develop a roll of twenty-four exposure prints than does either Fotomat or Quality Color. In fact, Kodak is significantly higher on all of their services. The reason for this will be discussed in detail later on. From here on in I will often times refer to the cheaper processing labs, such as Fotomat and Quality Color, as economy labs.

From working in a camera store, I have observed two ways in which a customer can often times be misled by these so-called economy labs. One mistake often made is encouraged by processors which advertise that they use Kodak paper. Many people then begin to think that good pictures are synonymous with Kodak paper. This is not the case. The truth of the matter is that the processing itself is what really makes the difference. I also found out that processors which push the fact that they use Kodak paper often confuse the customer into thinking that they are getting Kodak processing. Many times I have seen people come into the store and ask for what they think is Kodak processing, when they are really getting Kodak paper with economy lab processing. I try to explain the difference to them so they can decide for themselves which lab to use.

Much has been said about Kodak processing. The truth is that they have the largest color processing lab in the country, which is located in Rochester, New York. From my experiences with my employer, whose family has been in the photo business for over fifty years, and with customers themselves, I have yet to hear of a commercial lab which does a better service than Kodak. Why is Kodak processing a better quality than say Fotomat and why should I pay the extra money? There are several reasons why

The first reason is that Kodak only processes their own film. This may be a surprise but every roll of film is unique in its color tints and its tendencies. Labs, including economy labs, will usually process almost every common brand of film. By doing this, they can never get the optimum quality out of any one brand of film. This comment is also true for other film. For instance, Agfa film is best developed when an Agfa lab does the work. The only problem is that there are no Agfa labs in this country.

There is an important advantage to Kodak's size, which concerns the chemicals needed to process the film. Since Kodak processes such an enormous quantity of film, the customer can always be assured that the chemicals will always be fresh. Most of the economy labs do a much smaller volume than Kodak does. The customer can never be sure if the chemicals are going to be as fresh as they should be. Film inspection is also a major factor. At Kodak, every roll of film is inspected before it leaves the plant. Very few rolls are neglected. Quality Color, I know for a fact, only spot-checks their film. This means that if any dirt should get into one of the machines, even if it's only a speck, several rolls of film can be damaged before someone realizes it. I have no doubt that many other economy labs follow the same practice because it is one easy way to keep costs down.

In our store, we did two comparison tests between Kodak and Quality Color, our economy lab. In the first test, we shot two rolls of film identically, using two identical cameras. We sent out one roll to each lab for developing. When the rolls came back, we sent a couple of prints back to be duplicated. After repeating this procedure a third time, we were ready to compare results. The prints sent to Kodak were pretty consistent in quality. The three prints agreed to probably around 5 percent of each other. The economy prints were much more inconsistent. The first batch almost matched the Kodak prints for both color and sharpness. However, the second and third batches showed significant deviation. Although it's a fact that a picture can never be reproduced exactly, the test showed how one lab can get consistently closer to the original than the other. It also must be kept in mind that our store feels that our economy lab is superior to the other two economy labs which we have had in the past. We also feel that our lab is superior to Fotomat. Although this is only an opinion, the point is that our economy lab is not a ripoff, and for the money, we feel that they do a good job. In the second test, we took two prints from Kodak and the two corresponding economy prints and mounted them to a board. We placed the board in our window in direct sunlight. After approximately three weeks, we took them out of the window and compared them. The end result showed that the economy prints faded at least twice as fast as the Kodak prints. Although nobody is going to put their pictures to that kind of punishment, and even under normal conditions any print will fade, the economy lab's faded faster. The test really showed Kodak's superiority in that respect.

There are many custom labs throughout the country which do relatively small amounts of finishing with very good quality. These labs generally will do all types of work and are for the most part more expensive even than Kodak. Most of us, however, send our work to commercial labs. There are those who are very happy with economy labs such as Fotomat. There is nothing wrong with the people who feel that way. If, however, people are unhappy or suspicious of the quality of economy labs, I recommend that they at least try Kodak or a custom lab. A lot of people come into our store to have their film processed. Of all the finishing we take in, approximately eight out of ten bags are for Kodak processing. The facts just explained are the reasons why.

Discussion Questions: "Film Processing"

1. How does the writer begin the essay? Does the beginning help the reader accept the writer's background and experience? Does the writer seem credible to you?
2. What is the main idea of the essay? Write down the focus sentence(s) that contain(s) the main idea.
3. What is the function of the second and third paragraphs? What does the writer want the reader to understand?
4. What main points does the writer make about Kodak in the fourth, fifth, and sixth paragraphs? Are these convincing to you?
5. The seventh paragraph concerns an experiment done at the camera store where the writer works. Was this information helpful to the evaluation?
6. How well does the conclusion follow the support given in the essay?

COMPARISON: JENSEN R406, PIONEER KP-7500, SONY XR-50

Car stereos in recent years have advanced in leaps and bounds. Today the market is flooded with numerous brands offering various features. Having owned four car stereos myself and having helped many other people select and install their own stereos, I feel I know more about this subject than do many other people. In this paper I will examine three quality units: the Pioneer KP-7500 at $229, the Jensen 406 at $239, and the Sony XR-50 at $244.

One of the more important aspects of a car stereo is the convenience that it offers. Naturally, the easier a stereo is to operate, the less you are distracted from driving. Pushbutton tuning is a very useful convenience feature. It eliminates the need for fooling with dials to select a radio station. Both the Jensen and Pioneer units have pushbutton tuning. Another useful feature is auto-reverse. Auto-reverse automatically plays the other side of a tape once the first side has been played through. Again the Pioneer and Jensen units offer this feature. The Sony set has auto-eject and power-off-eject. Auto-eject ejects the tape when one side is played through. Power-off-eject ejects the tape when the power is turned off via the ignition switch. This feature reduces the possibility of forgetting to eject a tape before turning your car off resulting in your tape getting fouled in the tape deck.

Probably the most important area of comparison is sound quality. One of the newest innovations in stereo equipment is metal tapes which offer superior sound quality. The Sony SR-50 and the Pioneer KP-7500 have metal tape capability while the Jensen R406 does not. Stereos reproduce sound so logically that the more sound and the better the sound that can be reproduced, the better the unit is. The range of sounds a stereo is capable of reproducing is measured in its frequency response. A rating of 50 to 12,000 hertz (Hz) is considered full range and a rating of 30 to 15,000 Hz is considered the ultimate in sound reproduction. The Jensen R406 has the best frequency response for its radio section carrying a rating of 30 to 15,000 Hz (ultimate) while the Sony XR-50 and the Pioneer KP-7500 have ratings of 50 to 12,000 Hz (full range). The Jensen has the best FM frequency response but its tape response (50 to 12,000 Hz) does not match. In this area the Sony system is at the top of the list with a rating of 32 to 14,000 Hz. The Pioneer has a rating of 50 to 12,000 Hz for its tape section. Stereo separation, the ability of the unit to play the material intended for the right side through the right speaker, is another area to consider when buying a car stereo. In this rating the higher the number, the better the separation. The best stereo separation of the three units was found in the Pioneer KP-7500 with a rating of 45 decibels (dB). The Jensen and the Sony are equal to each other with ratings of 30 dB and 35 dB, respectively.

When choosing a stereo, each buyer must decide what features he or she wants and proceed along those lines. The features I look for are auto-reverse, high tape frequency response, and high stereo separation. On these grounds my choice of the three units mentioned would have to be the Pioneer KP-7500. This unit has a slightly lower frequency response than the Jensen R406, but it has a much greater stereo separation.

Discussion Questions: "Jensen R406, Pioneer KP-7500, Sony XR-50"

1. How does the writer begin the essay? Does the beginning help the reader understand the writer's main point?

2. What is the main idea of the essay? Write down the focus sentence(s) that contain(s) the main idea.
3. Who was the essay written for (the audience)? How can you tell? What accommodations for audience do you find in the essay?
4. What criteria did the writer use to evaluate the subject? List criteria and jot down the main supporting details for each criteria.
5. Are there enough details to convince a reader that the evaluation is correct?
6. Does the conclusion follow logically from the evidence given? Would you agree with his recommendation?

GETTING THE MOST FOR YOUR CABLE TV DOLLAR

The age of cable television is upon us. Everyday more and more people are paying to see quality entertainment without commercial interruption. Local residents have three choices of cable entertainment services. They can subscribe to: Home Box Office (HBO), Showtime, or Prism. As a subscriber of the latter two and a friend of a subscriber of the former, I am quite familiar with these three services. All three services cost about the same (twenty dollars per month) and offer the same selection of recent movies each month. After examining the three services individually, however, some distinct differences can be found in the program content and the program schedule which clearly make Prism the best choice.

Home Box Office's program schedule consists entirely of recent movies and entertainment specials starring celebrities like Diana Ross and Bette Midler. HBO does offer a twenty-four hour-a-day viewing schedule on the weekends. Throughout the week, however, HBO is only on the air during the evening hours. Because of such a limited amount of air time a particular movie or special is usually shown only once a day. If subscribers are not at home at the time a program is offered or want to watch something else at the same time, they will miss the program on Home Box Office.

Showtime's program content is more varied than HBO's but not better. Like HBO, Showtime offers the latest movies and specials. Showtime occasionally offers some older movie classics such as *Singin' in the Rain* and *Citizen Kane* as well. The weakest spots in Showtime's schedule are its self-produced "comedy" series such as "Bizarre" and "Laff-a-thon." These so-called humorous programs are poorly produced and horrendously unfunny. They are geared toward the uneducated mind and usually rely on sexual slurs and profanity to extract laughs from the audience. Even though Showtime offers a twenty-four-hour schedule every day of the week, the movies and specials are rarely shown more than once a day. The rest of the air time is taken up by those ridiculous "comedy" shows, which obviously cost less to produce and make more money for

Showtime than the films and specials which must be bought from the major studios.

Prism, in comparison, offers the biggest selection of home entertainment available to the cable subscriber. Prism's content consists of the most recent movies, movie classics, and specials plus a whole lot more. The "plus" of Prism's programming is its sports coverage. Each season, Prism offers quite a number of home Phillies and Flyers games which are not telecast on regular channels because of local "blackouts." Since Prism is on the air twenty-four hours every day and does not need to rely on its own "comedy" productions to fill time, Prism shows its programs as many as three times each day. In other words, it is virtually impossible to miss something you want to watch because it is offered at various times of the day and night.

In these inflationary times, it is not easy to get the most for your money. This is especially true in the area of entertainment. With movie prices averaging four dollars, concert and sporting event prices averaging fifteen dollars, it is easy to see why a lot of people are opting for cable television. For roughly twenty dollars a month, cable subscribers can get top-notch entertainment right in their own homes. If you decide to get "hooked up" to a cable television service, subscribing to Prism is the best way to get the most out of your entertainment dollar. Prism offers something to please everyone and a convenient schedule to meet everyone's needs. One of the definitions of a "prism" is something that is multicolored, brilliant and dazzling." Prism subscribers will soon find out that Prism actually does live up to its meaning.

Discussion Questions: "Getting the Most for Your Cable TV Dollar"

1. How does the writer begin the essay? Does the beginning help the reader understand the writer's main point?
2. What is the main idea of the essay? Write down the focus sentence(s) that contain(s) the main idea.
3. For whom was the essay written (the audience)? How can you tell? What accommodations for audience do you find in the essay?
4. Briefly outline the body of the essay. How did the writer decide to organize the discussion? Did the writer compare the three services on same basis?
5. What specific details are used to evaluate each service? Are there enough details to convince a reader that the idea is valid? Where would you add examples or other details?
6. How does the writer end the essay? Does the ending help the reader understand the writer's main idea?

WRITING ACTIVITY

Beginning the Assignment

1. What product will you investigate?
2. What makes you a believable evaluator of this product?
3. What criteria will you use to evaluate the product?
4. What does your audience want to know about this product?
5. Which brand names are you using? Why?
6. What details do you note about each brand?
7. Which one(s) will you recommend? Why?

Writing a Draft

As you are writing, care should be taken to evaluate each brand on the same basis *and* in the same order. If readers read about price, record of repair, and quality of function for one brand of dishwasher, for example, they will expect to see the same criteria presented in the *same order* for the next brand. Switching criteria is not fair and changing the order creates confusion. An outline to follow will help you stay on track.

Revising Your Writing

Exchange your draft with a classmate and read each other's as if you were in the market for the type of product that he or she is recommending. Ask yourself the following questions:

1. Do I have any questions about the criteria being used to evaluate the product?
2. Did the writer compare the various brand names fairly by evaluating each one according to the same criteria?
3. Was there enough evidence of quality given to support the writer's evaluation?
4. Do I agree with the writer's recommendation? Would I buy the product recommended? Why or why not?

Share your reactions with your classmate and help proofread for any sentence structure faults or mechanical errors as well.

ASSIGNMENT 10: THE PROBLEM/SOLUTION ESSAY

What do you think should be done about *one* of these campus problems?

1. The parking situation
2. The vandalism and/or litter problem
3. Student involvement in student government or other activities
4. Other problem

You will discuss these topics in small groups first to share ideas. Then you will be asked to write a letter to an administrator or dean, analyzing the situation and proposing a solution.

Below is a letter a student wrote about problems during preregistration. What do you think of her suggestions?

STUDENT ESSAY

PROBLEM LETTER

Dear Sir:

There are a few problems dealing with preregistration that I feel the administration should be aware of. Also, I feel that I may have some solutions to these problems that would better help the students with the preregistration process.

First of all, there are some problems dealing with advisors. Many times I have heard students complain that their advisors are not available, are not helpful in picking out classes, and that some advisors (through no fault of their own) are not familiar with the college in which they are advising. I feel that advisors should have a certain number of hours that they must be in their offices, prior to preregistration. For example, the advisors could be told that they must spend a minimum of three or four hours a day in their office the week prior to preregistration. Also, I feel that the advisors should be screened, by the administration, each term, as to their knowledge of the college in which they are advising. This way the administration will be able to make sure that advisors have read their advisor's handbook and know what they are talking about when they advise students. Advisors should advise in the college with which they are most familiar. If this is not possible, because of the faculty–student body ratio, then the previous suggestion would handle the problem just as efficiently.

There is also the problem of notification of closed classes. I feel that the students sometimes have a hard time finding out about up-to-date class closings because they are listed on only two sheets of paper on the whole campus. Perhaps it would be a good idea to broadcast closed listings on the television set in Lares Building, the center for student activities. Also, I think it would be a good idea to post closed classes on the bulletin board in Lares or put a list outside the Student Activities Office. You will notice that all three areas suggested are in Lares. This is a prime choice for posting lists because it is where the majority of students congregate at one time or another during the day.

The final problems deal with the preregistration office itself. A large number of students I have talked to can only go to preregister during common break, when the personnel of that office have their lunch break. Also, when students do go to the office to preregister, they are faced with a long waiting line. I feel that it is reasonable to ask these employees to take their lunch break an hour prior to common break or an hour after. In solving the problem of long lines, I would suggest that perhaps the office secretaries, faculty members, or representatives from the administration could volunteer to work in the preregistration office when it gets very crowded.

Thank you for listening to my suggestions. With these solutions I feel that many of the annoyances that students face at this time of preregistration can be avoided.

> Sincerely,

Discussion Questions: Problem Letter

1. How does the writer begin the letter? Does the beginning help the reader understand the writer's main point?
2. What is the main idea of the essay? Write down the focus sentence(s) that contain(s) the main idea.
3. What accommodations for audience do you find in the essay?
4. a. List each problem and the solutions proposed.
   b. Is any more evidence needed to explain these points? If so, where and what kind?
5. If you received this letter, how would you react to the writer's suggestions? Explain.

WRITING ACTIVITY

Beginning the Assignment

1. What is especially important about the audience for this assignment?
2. Which problem will you choose? Define and explain what it is with evidence as needed.
3. What possible solutions are there?
4. What are the possible consequences and implications of each solution?
5. Which solution do you favor, and why?

Writing a Draft

Offering recommendations to solve problems is not only a matter of getting all the facts straight and presenting them in a clear manner. Often *how* you recommend something to someone will determine whether the recommendation will be accepted. Having knowledge of the subject is important and will improve your credibility, but tact and paying attention to what the reader is like and what he or she needs to know are also crucial.

Write your draft with your reader in mind. Are you approaching the person in a reasonable, businesslike way instead of angrily or arrogantly? Give the decision maker some evidence of the problem so that he or she knows that you know some of the background. Consider some of the implications of your solution to the problem so that the solution seems feasible. Discuss alternatives to the solution you chose and why those alternatives may not solve the problem as well as your solution does.

Revising Your Writing

Read your draft or exchange it with other members of your class.

1. What sentences, phrases, or words show the writer's accommodation to the audience?
2. Is the problem clearly defined? Will the reader agree from the evidence presented that a problem exists? If not, what more should be explained?
3. What solutions are proposed?

4. What consequences are there to these solutions? Are they adequately explained? If not, what should be explained further?
5. Is the recommendation a reasonable and feasible solution to the problem? Explain.

MASTERY ASSIGNMENTS

1. Write a letter to a local official on some current issue about which you have strong feelings. Include your ideas or recommendations for solving the problem.
2. Try to help a friend solve a problem. Evaluate the situation, explore alternatives, and make a recommendation based on your assessment of the situation.
3. Write a letter to your parents asking them for something (a car, a summer in Europe, a change in colleges). Explain what you want and your reasons for wanting it. Be sure to give as much evidence as you can to substantiate your request.
4. A local real estate company wants citizens of your township or city to submit a 300- to 500-word essay entitled "Why a Prospective Home Buyer Should Buy Here" for inclusion in a brochure of homes for sale to go to an executive transfer relocating service. You need to go beyond "it's a nice place to live" and offer evidence of good services, good schools, and good quality of life in your area.

APPENDIX A

The Research Assignment

In the future you will often be asked to do research for a written assignment which will be called either a research paper or a term paper. What does this mean? Generally, it means that your instructor wants you to read widely and in depth on a topic, be able to synthesize or explain what you have read, and then present your knowledge clearly and logically while acknowledging the sources you have used. Also, you may sometimes want to use an outside source very briefly in a paper which is not formally designated a research assignment. If so, you will still need to know how to quote the source in the context of your paper and how to handle the footnote and bibliography entries.

Most college students have already written research assignments sometime in their previous schooling, but they may not have been taught *how* to do it, or the lessons they were taught may not have seemed very practical when it came to the task at hand. The aim of this appendix is to give you some practical advice on how to write research assignments. It will enable you to build on what you already know and will give suggestions to make the task easier. Because the research assignment is still basically like any other writing assignment, we will begin with the basic principles of writing as described in Chapter 1, but this time focus specifically on the research assignment. Following are some suggested topics and some principles to guide you in writing such a paper.

SUGGESTIONS FOR RESEARCH ASSIGNMENTS

1. Write a position paper to send to your congressman or senator to get him or her to vote a certain way on a current issue. You will need to identify an issue now under consideration, analyze it, and set forth your recommendation in clear fashion.

2. Choose an older relative of yours—living or dead—and determine the year in which he or she was the same age you are now. Explore *one* aspect of life led in that year:

World politics	Medicine
Domestic economy	Art
Environment	Music
Transportation	Other cultural activities

   If the person is alive, you may wish to interview him or her.

   Then compare life in that time with the life in your time (remember to limit it to one aspect). Evaluate the differences: Were the "good old days" better than today?

3. Investigate an issue related to another course you are taking. Reach a conclusion based on your research. (Some possibilities include vitamin C and its effectiveness in preventing disease, the influence of heredity or environment on personality development or intelligence, or the influence of preschool education on later academic success.)

4. Choose a writer you admire and investigate what literary critics have thought of his or her work by reading reviews or journal articles. Decide whether you agree with the critics' evaluations. You will need to limit the number of works by one author.

BASIC PRINCIPLES FOR WRITING RESEARCH PAPERS

A. Think About the Writing Assignment or Situation

Sometimes, instructors will select the topic on which you will write. If this is the case, look carefully at the topic and ask:

1. What does the assignment ask me to do?
2. Who will read this paper?
3. What does he or she want me to accomplish?

The answers to these questions will lead into the thinking that you will need to do before starting the paper.

For example, is the topic one that requires simply finding a large amount of information and presenting it? A paper for a health class on "The Effects of Heroin on the Human Body'' would be of this type. Such a paper is intended to supply information and requires very little, if any, interpretation. In the scheme of our four purposes, it would fit most neatly under *explaining.*

Or a topic may ask you to present an opinion and back it up with evidence that you have gathered through research. Examples of this type would be "Capital Punishment Should (or Should Not) Be Abolished" and "A Nuclear Weapons Freeze Should (or Should Not) be U.S. Policy." Of the four purposes we have discussed, this type of topic involves *substantiating* most heavily.

Another possibility is that you are asked to interpret evidence or to evaluate a subject. In this case, you would need to present the evidence, determine criteria for judging the subject, and then make a judgment. Topics of this sort include: "Is the character of Sophie in *Sophie's Choice* a heroine?" or "Which of the three movies in the *Star Wars* trilogy is the best?" The purpose of these topics is *evaluation.*

Finally, an assigned topic may ask you to analyze a problem and suggest ways to solve the problem. For example, "What should be done about Social Security?" "What steps should be taken to improve public education in the United States?" These topics involve *recommending* most heavily.

But what if your topic is not assigned? An instructor may simply require a paper based on some aspect of the course. What do you do then? Since it is easier to do a better job if you are at least somewhat interested in a topic, choose that part of the course that you are taking which interests you the most. If it is a history class, would you like to find out more about the politics, the culture of a country, the role of women, the technology of the time, or the role of religion? If you can select an aspect of the course that is interesting to you, you are well on your way to writing a good paper. Try to talk over ideas with a friend, a parent, or the course instructor. Don't forget brainstorming as a possible way to develop leads. Start writing about the course, and see what subjects keep popping up. Other suggestions for developing a topic follow.

B. Get Started by Playing with Ideas

The question-asking techniques studied in Chapter 1 are very useful in preparing to do a research assignment. Jotting down questions about the subject may help you to discover what you already know and what still needs to be investigated. You may also get some ideas on how to approach a subject because answering one of the questions may provide a direction for further inquiry.

For example, let's say that your history professor has asked you to do a paper on unions. You could ask yourself questions such as these:

Who were the first union leaders?
What were the first unions?
Where were they started?
When did unions appear?
Why did people feel that unions were necessary?
How did unions overcome their obstacles?

What other kinds of questions might be asked about unions?
Now write down questions you could ask about your proposed or assigned topic.

C. Be Specific

1. *Finding Information*

   A research paper will be strong only if it has enough specific details. For this you have to read widely on the topic and take careful notes of facts, opinions, statistics, and other information. Methods of doing research vary widely from individual to individual and from subject to subject, but here are some suggestions.

   a. Get an idea of the scope of the material you will be using. Go to the card catalog in your library, and look at the cards in the subject section of the catalog for your topic. You may need to try some alternative subject listings in order to find material on your topic. Make a list of all books on the topic and copy their call numbers so that you can find them easily if you decide to use them. The list can be put on individual 3 by 5 or 4 by 6 cards (some prefer cards because they can be used later to make up the bibliography). Or you can write them all on paper. Though library cataloging systems differ somewhat, most catalog subject cards look like this:

	HISTORY, MODERN—20th CENTURY	
Call number	D421 .C26 1969	Cantor, Norman F The age of protest: dissent and rebellion in the twentieth century, by Norman F. Cantor. New York, Hawthorn Books [1969] xv, 368p. illus. 24cm.
Subject card		Bibliographical references included in "Notes" (p.[337]–345)	A list of sources that might prove useful
Indicates Subjects covered in book		1. History, Modern—20th century. 2. Dissenters. I. Title.

Books are also cataloged under authors and titles. If you know an author's name or a title of a book, you can look it up in the card catalog to get its call number. Following are examples of author and title cards:

Author card

D421	Cantor, Norman F
.C26	The age of protest: dissent and rebellion
1969	in the twentieth century, by Norman F. Cantor.

    New York, Hawthorn Books [1969]
        xv, 368p.   illus.   24cm.

    Bibliographical references included in
    "Notes" (p.[377]–345)

        1. History, Modern—20th century.   2.
    Dissenters.   I. Title.

Title card

        The age of protest

D421	Cantor, Norman F
.C26	The age of protest: dissent and rebellion
1969	in the twentieth century, by Norman F. Cantor.

    New York, Hawthorn Books [1969]
        xv, 368p.   illus.   24cm.

    Bibliographical references included in
    "Notes" (p.[337]–345)

        1. History, Modern—20th century.   2.
    Dissenters.   I. Title.

Whether your library is arranged by the Dewey Decimal System or by the Library of Congress system, the number in the upper left of the card tells where to find the book. Consult the library guide (usually located near the catalog) or ask the librarian to show you where the books are shelved.

b. After you have seen what books are available, check a journal or magazine index to see if there are articles on your topic. It can truly be said that there is an index for every subject! Some of the more commonly used indexes are:

(1) For current topics of interest such as gun control, abortion, nuclear disarmament, and pollution control:

(a) *The Reader's Guide to Periodical Literature.* Indexes most general-interest magazines, such as *Time* and *Newsweek*.

Sample entry:

Catching customers with sweepstakes.
F. Peterson and J. Kesselmann-Turkel.il.Fortune 105:84–5+ F 8 '82

Translation:

An article in *Fortune* magazine on using sweepstakes contests to get new customers. It is illustrated (il.), and appears in volume 105 on pages 84 and 85, plus more in the back pages of the magazine. The date is February 8, 1982.

(b) *The New York Times Index.*

Indexes articles appearing in this newspaper, which most libraries carry on microfilm or microfiche.

Sample entry for the January 1–15, 1983 index:

Plutonium
Supreme Court agrees to review ruling that overturned $10 million damage award in death of Kerr-MeGee Corp. plutonium plant worker Karen G. Silkwood, who was contaminated with plutonium; a Silkwood Portrait (S), Ja 11,II,9:1

Translation:

The article also contains a short description of Miss Silkwood (S) and is found in the January 11 edition in the second section (or B section) on page 9, column 1.

(c) *Poole's Index to Periodical Literature, 1802–1907.* For common periodicals in the nineteenth century.

For topics of interest to sociologists, psychologists, economists, or humanists, such as the effects of early education on the development of children:

Social Sciences Index

Sample entry:

Human needs and job satisfaction: a multi-dimensional approach. T. F. Cawsey and others. bibl Hum Relat 35:704–14 S'82

Translation:

This article in *Human Relations* has a bibliography (bibl.) on this subject and is found in volume 35 on pages 704–14 in the September 1982 issue.

(3) For topics of interest to scientists and technicians:

Applied Science and Technology Index

Sample entry:

> Archaeological geology in the eastern Mediterranean [Symposium, Cincinnati] Geology 11:49–53 Ja '83

Translation

> This article from a symposium is printed in the journal *Geology*, volume 11, January 1983, on pages 49–53.

(4) For topics in the arts:

    (a) *Art Index*

        Sample entry:

> More than a hotel [Fragrant Hill Motel, Peking]. T. Hoving. col il Connoisseur 213:68–81 F '83 ["col il" is "colored illustration"]

    (b) *Music Index*

    (c) *Dramatic Index, 1909–1953*

(5) For students of sociology or psychology:

    (a) *Sociological Abstracts*

        Sample entry:

> 84N8988 Bynum, Jack E.(Oklahoma State U, Stillwater 74078), Teaching Undergraduate Sociology, *Teaching Sociology*, 1982, 10, 1, Oct 51–54

    (b) *Psychological Abstracts*

        Sample entry:

> 6806 Small, Arnold C.; Hallenbeck, Albert R. & Haley, Robert L. (George Mason U) The effect of emotional state on student ratings of instructors.
> *Teaching of Psychology*, 1982 (Dec), Vol. 9(4), 205–208

(6) For business topics:

Business Periodicals Index

Sample entry:

> Computer-aided engineering use gains. W. B. Scott. il *Aviat. Week Space Technol.* 117:81–3 N 22 '82

(7) For topics affecting education:

Education Index

Sample Entry:

> Learning cycles in the general chemistry laboratory. D. M. Whisnant. J Coll Sci Teach 12:434–5 My '83

(8) For topics on humanities and literature:

Humanities Index

Sample entry:

> Mark Twain's changing perspective on the past. J. W. Gargano. South Atlan Q 80:454–65 Aut '81 ["Aut" is "Autumn"]

(9) For topics about literature:

Modern Language Association (MLA) Index

Sample entry:

  Orwell. 9297 Katz, Wendy R.

"Imperialism and Patriotism: Orwell's Dilemma in 1940." *MSLC* 3 (1979):99–105.

Translation:

  This article is found in *Modernist Studies: Literature and Culture 1920–1940.*

Check with your librarian for other indexes. Also, don't overlook encyclopedias, atlases, dictionaries, biographical dictionaries, reviews, and digests. Depending on your topic, many of these could serve as a source of information. Most reference works have a key to their most commonly used abbreviations. If any puzzle you, ask the reference librarian. Once you have a list of articles, find out which journals your library has by consulting the reference or periodicals librarian. If your library does not have the journals you need, ask if there is an interlibrary loan arrangement with other libraries through which you might obtain the information you need, or try to find another library in your area that might have these periodicals. If your library does have them, ask where they are shelved or where the microfilm or microfiche is kept. Then locate the journal and read the article.

EXERCISE 1. Write down the sources that you have located for your proposed topic. Include books, periodicals, and any other reference material.

2. *Note Taking*

Once you have found information, you need to read and take notes for use in the paper. A time-honored method of note taking is one that uses individual cards for each piece of information or each direct quote. Although no law says that you *have* to take notes that way, notes on cards do offer several advantages:

a. Individual pieces of information or quotes are easily arranged and rearranged if they are on separate cards. That advantage does help when it comes time to make a rough plan for your paper.

b. Keeping track of where the information was found and on what page it is located is made easier if each card contains only one piece of information.

c. Full information on each source can be recorded once on a bibliography card and then just a short title put on each separate information card, together with the appropriate page number.

Let's look at some sample bibliography and information cards.

Bibliography Cards

Book	**Article**
Hoffman, Lois Wladis, and Ivan F. Nye, eds. *Working Mothers*. San Francisco: Jossey-Bass, 1974.	Grossman, Allyson Sherman. "More than Half of All Children Have Working Mothers." *Monthly Labor Review*, 105 (Feb. 1982), 41–43. Note need for inclusive pages.

Information Cards

Hoffman, p. 142 "Having household responsibilities has been found to contribute to self-esteem in the children of working-mother families."	Grossman, p. 41 "In March 1981, 31.8 million youngsters below age 18—54 percent of the nation's total—had mothers who were either employed or looking for work."

If you keep careful track of all sources, your task will be easier when it comes time to prepare the footnotes and the bibliography of the finished paper. You don't want to forget a page number, date, or publisher's name and have to go back to the library to look it up. (It wouldn't be the first time this has happened to anyone, but it is irritating and time consuming.)

One other observation on note taking: It is very difficult to decide as you take notes what you will use and what you will not use. Take down *any* relevant information, but be prepared not to use much of it in your final paper. A good guess is that about half of your information will be discarded, *but you won't know which half until you begin to write.* After you focus your ideas more clearly, you will know what information you will use. But the proces of reading widely will help you to get to this stage of the assignment.

EXERCISE 2. Begin taking notes on the sources you have found.

EXERCISE 3. Select three quotations from sources you are using for your paper and write paraphrases of those quotations. Your instructor may ask you to turn in the exact quotes along with your paraphrases.

D. Focus Your Ideas

Now that you have read widely on a particular topic, you have to decide just what it is that you wish to write about. Think of a point you want to prove or an idea you wish someone to understand. Formulate a sentence that includes the subject you are discussing *and* an attitude word or opinion word about the subject that will provide the direction for your paper. For example.:

1. Ultrasound is a relatively new technique that is proving to be *very helpful* in diagnosing disease.
2. Though research scientists present conflicting studies, vitamin C supplements may be *beneficial* to one's health.
3. Television commercials during children's programs *promote bad nutrition* and *poor eating habits.*
4. Early childhood education has a lasting *positive* effect on children's later performance in school.
5. Color imagery in Stephen Crane's "The Open Boat" *contributes* to the theme of man's *helplessness.*
6. Thomas Jefferson was a *more effective* president than was George Washington.

EXERCISE 1. For each of the following topics, think of some "fact and attitude" sentences which could serve as focus sentences for a research paper.

a. Gun control
b. Hazardous waste disposal dumps
c. Control of nuclear power plants
d. Soap operas
e. College athletic programs
f. Computer science education
g. U.S. trade agreements with the USSR or the People's Republic of China
h. Causes of the Vietnam war
i. The increasing divorce rate
j. Roles of women in American society

EXERCISE 2. Write a focus sentence based on your proposed or assigned topic. You may wish to have your instructor read it to see if you have a clear statement of your main idea.

E. Select Details That Fit the Focus

1. *Subpoints*

Once you have a main-idea sentence, you will begin to put together ideas for your paper. Look at the material you have gathered on note cards with an eye to deciding where in the paper you will use the material. You may wish to make a formal outline, or just to list the main subpoints of your argument or explanation. Let us look at a formal outline and a more informal list for a student paper on the vitamin C controversy. (The paper is presented later in its entirety.)

Outline

    I. Introduction
       A. Frequency of colds
       B. Popular remedy for colds—vitamin C
   II. The controversy over vitamin C
       A. The position of Linus Pauling
       B. Scientists' reactions to Pauling's position
       C. Results of others' studies
          1. Vitamin C and colds
          2. Vitamin C and cancer
  III. The function of vitamin C in the body
       A. Places where it is found in the body
       B. Dosages needed to maintain health
       C. Hazards of possible overdosage
  IV. Conclusion

Informal List

Begin with introduction on colds and how some people are taking vitamin C for them.

Discuss controversy over vitamin C by mentioning Pauling and his detractors.

Go on to discuss other studies besides Pauling's on effect of vitamin C on colds and cancer.

Discuss what *is known* about vitamin C and the body, including dosages and problems of abuse.

Conclude that it is probably OK to take vitamin C supplements.

EXERCISE 1. Try to think of three to five subdivisions of your topic or focus sentence that you want to develop. (If you have trouble with this step, you may not have enough information to sustain a research paper or your topic may be too limited to develop in a several-page paper.)

2. *Use of Evidence and Quotations*

Once you have selected the main points of your explanation or argument, you will need to choose the evidence or data you will use to support these points. You will then try to work this material into the paper as you write a rough draft.

When you quote evidence from a source word for word, use quotation marks: "The effect of vitamin C in decreasing general morbidity during the common cold appears to be minimal." Or you may paraphrase (put the information in your own words): The American Medical Association says that vitamin C does not have much effect on the progress of the common cold. Paraphrases do not require quotation marks, but do require a source citation.

Caution: Either quote *or* paraphrase. Don't combine quoted material with your own words in the same sentence. It confuses the reader. ③ Also, you *must* list the source for any information that is not common knowledge. "Common knowledge" includes the number of feet in a yard, the length of a football field, the capital of a state or country, or any such information that almost anyone would already know. The source of any other information should be cited in parentheses or by a footnote or endnote. ④ When in doubt, list the source! On the other hand, avoid the "cut and paste" term paper, in which you string together a number of quotes with "and then he said," or "next, Dr. Peabody remarked."

⑤ Your quotes and evidence should back up points that *you are* making, that is, serve as examples that what you are saying is true. ⑥ Never use a quote without first introducing it and letting the reader know its context or commenting on it afterward. The following section of a term paper illustrates how quotes and paraphrase can be worked into the text of a paper to support a point the writer wants to make.

Edith Jones Wharton was a modern woman born into the confines of Victorian New York society. As her definitive biographer, R. W. B. Lewis, describes her: *intro* "She was clothes-conscious and money-conscious, but she was also addicted to books and ideas and the world of imagination. There was, indeed, no one like her in her New York generation. A growing awareness of the fact deepened her sense of loneliness and gave her an air of unpredictability" (35). She was hurt by the fact that women of her class were expected to be only ornamental and were criticized for any ambition. Indeed, when her first engagement was broken [by the gentleman's mother, whose motive was probably to prevent her son from coming into his inheritance when he married (Lewis 46)], Edith Jones Wharton had to endure the following public declaration of her difference in the Newport *Daily News*: "The only reason assigned for the breaking of the engagement hitherto existing between Harry Stevens and Miss Edith Jones is an alleged preponderance of intellectuality on the part of the intended bride. Miss Jones is an ambitious authoress, and it is said that, in the eyes of Mr. Stevens, ambition is a grievous fault'' (Lewis 45).

As you work on a rough draft, you will be faced with selecting and discarding evidence. Don't be too discouraged if, as mentioned earlier, you have to throw away much of what you found in books and articles. One or two pieces of evidence as support for a point is enough, and the extra must simply be cast aside.

On the other hand, you may experience the opposite problem. More evidence may be needed to back up your idea, in which case you will have to return to the original sources or look for new ones to find supporting evidence.

F/G. Keep the Focus Clear/Connect Related Parts

Just as these principles are important in an essay, they are important in a term paper. In fact, because of a term paper's length, it is easier to become disorganized in a research assignment.

One way to help yourself is to check the topic sentences of your paragraphs to see if they are explaining or expanding your focus and are not introducing an irrelevant point. Check each piece of evidence to be sure that it supports a point you are making and that it is not just a marvelous quote you couldn't resist, even though it doesn't fit anywhere. Make sure that your topic sentences lead the reader from your last paragraph to the next one by using transitional devices such as "Another point to consider is . . ." or "A second reason for the colonies' break with England was. . . ." Remember that a reader needs to be led from point to point and that transitions act as bridges from one paragraph to the next.

At this point, look at the following student paper to see how he handled his information on vitamin C. Note main subdivisions, transitions between sections, use of evidence, documentation techniques, and format of the body of the paper.

THE VITAMIN C CONTROVERSY

If you are like most Americans, you suffer through three colds every year—each lasting three to ten days. The average American misses seven days of work each year with a cold. Colds are estimated to cost our society more than $19 billion annually in labor lost. Hundreds of millions of dollars are spent each year for medicines to clear our heads and ease our pains. Doctors agree, however, that no practical cure has yet been found for this disease, which occurs more often than all others combined.

Since 1970, tens of millions of Americans have been taking a product that they believe can remedy colds—vitamin C (ascorbic acid). They gulp orange juice, consume citrus fruits, and take synthetic vitamins by the handful. Americans take more than 28 million pounds of supplemental vitamin C pills annually. It is a $100-million-a-year industry (Ponte 94). But the claims about vitamin C extend far beyond improved resistance to colds. Its possible benefits are diverse and far-reaching. Vitamin C has been claimed to lower cholesterol levels, control bleeding, moderate our sleeping habits, break heroin addiction, improve mental health, enhance the healing of wounds of burn patients, control excessive menstrual bleeding, improve the absorption of iron, help to cure cancer, and even to control the aging process (Wang 54).

But how substantiated are these claims? How much vitamin C do we really need in our diets? As I am a student of science, this topic, which has many scientists and doctors on both sides of the vitamin C controversy, is of particular interest to me. It demonstrates how medical science is advanced through men who are willing to test new ideas, through controversy, and through the interpretation of research and studies.

The man who leads the vitamin C controversy is Dr. Linus Pauling—one of the greatest scientists of the twentieth century. He is the only person in history to win two unshared Nobel Prizes. He is the winner of two top American scientific prizes, the author or coauthor of more than four hundred papers, and a major contributor to the understanding of chemical bonding, proteins, antibodies, serological reactions, hemoglobin, and the hereditary hemolytic anemias (Pogash 88). In 1970 he published the best-selling book *Vitamin C and the Common Cold,* in which he claimed that by ingesting 1,000 milligrams (mg) daily—instead of the 60-mg daily minimum then recommended by the National Research Council—a person would catch 45 percent fewer colds and suffer 60 percent fewer days of illness. Pauling wrote that if enough people took such huge doses of vitamin C, the common cold could be eradicated within decades (Ponte 94–95).

Even though Pauling was a great scientist, many of his peers were appalled to see him make sweeping claims about a field outside his expertise. Pauling admitted that he had not done much laboratory research in the field of vitamin C. However, he claimed to be the first person ever to look over the mass of published material with an open mind, without bias.

His proposals caused great controversy. Within days of publication of his book his views were attacked and he was accused of abdicating the role of objective scientist for that of vitamin C salesman. The National Academy of Sciences refused to publish one of his papers on vitamin C, and *Science* refused to publish another. The *Journal of the American Medical Association* (JAMA) refused to publish Pauling's review on the grounds that the material had appeared elsewhere. JAMA did publish two studies contradicting Pauling's claims, and, in response to questions from the public, the association issued the statement, "The effect of vitamin C in decreasing general morbidity during the common cold appears to be minimal" (Pogash 90).

C

One such skeptic was Dr. Terance W. Anderson of the University of Toronto. Expecting to prove Pauling wrong, Anderson and fellow researchers carried out a carefully controlled test during the winter of 1971–72. Five hundred patients were given placebos daily and five hundred patients were given the real thing– 1,000 mg of vitamin C daily. The second group was also given 4,000 mg during the first three days of illness. The results surprised Dr. Anderson and his colleagues. Twenty-six percent of the volunteers taking vitamin C were free of illness throughout the winter, compared to only 18 percent of those taking placebos. Those taking vitamin C experienced 30 percent fewer total days off work. To Anderson, these results were impressive (Ponte 95).

II C₁

However, the findings remain ambiguous. Two follow-up studies done by Anderson only partially confirmed his initial results. Other studies have tended to prove Pauling wrong altogether. In one study of 868 Navaho Indian children, for example, in which half the children received 1,000 mg of ascorbic acid and half received a placebo, those taking the vitamin actually had longer illnesses and more illnesses than those with low levels of vitamin C in their blood. This demonstrates how difficult it is to get an answer as to how effective vitamin C really is in treating and preventing colds (Wang 53).

II C 11

The verdict is also out on vitamin C and its effect on cancer. Pauling's more recent contention that vitamin C can prolong the lives of cancer patients is based primarily on a Scottish hospital study in which Dr. Ewan Cammeron treated one hundred terminally ill cancer victims with ten grams of vitamin C daily. He compared their progress and survival rate with that of one thousand control patients and found that the ascorbate-treated patients lived an average of three hundred days longer.

II C₂

Dr. Charles Moertel of the Mayo Clinic did not believe that the study was valid because Dr. Cammeron compared the vitamin C patients with a control group of former case histories, not with a group of patients currently in the hospital. Therefore, Moertel did a similar study of patients with advanced forms of cancer. He found that vitamin C had no therapeutic effect.

II Cₐ

Pauling retorted that the Mayo Clnic did not test the value of vitamin C because 87 percent of the cancer patients had received chemotherapy, which Pauling has long maintained damages the body's immune system and thus hampers the effects of vitamin C. This led the clinic to do a second study of patients who are not receiving chemotherapy. The results of the study have not yet been tabulated (Pogash 90).

III A

The truths about vitamin C are hard to come by. There are, however, some things which can be said with certainty. Vitamin C is concentrated in certain parts of our bodies. It is in the adrenal glands, which supply adrenalin when we are angry, afraid, or otherwise under stress. The body also concentrates vitamin C in the white blood cells, our defense against infection and germ invasion, and in the liver, the organ that cleans poisons out of our blood. Vitamin C is also richly supplied to our brains. Vitamin C plays an important part in our body's immune system. Recent research indicates that vitamin C may enhance the body's production of interferon, prostaglandins, T-lymphocytes, and immuno-globulins—weapons in the body's self-defense system. The difference between quick recovery and prolonged sickness or death might depend on how much C the body has available when germs or viruses invade it (Ponte 95).

So how much vitamin C do we really need for our bodies to be their healthiest? To maintain itself, the human body normally stores about a month's supply of vitamin C. This amounts to roughly 1,500 mg. But illness or stress can substantially decrease the body's vitamin C reserves. Cigarette smoking also robs the body of vitamin C, since the chemicals in cigarette smoke interact with ascorbic acid to remove it from the blood (Wang 50–53). The National Research Council sets the Recommended Dietary Allowance of vitamin C at 50 mg daily for an average adult, 80 mg for a pregnant woman, and 100 mg for a nursing mother. This is quite sufficient to prevent scurvy, a disease common in past centuries to sailors who lived at sea for months without fruits and vegetables. However, Pauling believes that millions of people are suffering today from "sub-clinical scurvy." That is, they may be getting enough vitamin C to prevent scurvy in its grossest form, but their bodies lack the vitamin C to ward off colds and to fight infections.

Scurvy is rare among animals because virtually every animal manufactures its own vitamin C. A few living things cannot make their own—among them is man. To determine exactly how much vitamin C our bodies need, according to Pauling, we should study how much animals produce on their own. One such study of rats suggests that if a laboratory rat were the size of a 150-pound person, its body would be making between 1,800 and 4,100 mg of vitamin C on quiet days and close to 10,000 mg when ill or under stress. While it may be imprecise to compare humans with rats—which have a metabolism far more active than ours—findings from other studies of mammals which produce vitamin C has led Pauling to conclude that a normal person requires somewhere between 1,000 and 2,000 mg of supplemental vitamin C daily, and 10,000 mg or more at times of illness or stress (Ponte 96–97).

Despite all the possible good that vitamin C can do, many doctors caution against taking it by the handful. Large doses of ascorbic acid can act as a diuretic and laxative. Others who have a tendency to form kidney stones are advised to keep their intake below 4,000 mg a day, since ascorbic acid breaks down into oxalate, which is excreted in the urine via the kidneys, where it may accumulate and cause blockages. Overdoses theoretically could lead to demineralization of the bones (Wang 53). Also, vitamin C can interact with prescription drugs and produce false results in blood tests. Doctors also caution against shocking the body by suddenly taking large doses of vitamins. When starting to take vitamins, increases in doses should be gradual. This is also true when a person stops taking vitamins (Ponte 97).

Certainly, there are many questions that need to be answered about vitamin C and its effect on the nation's health. The contradictory studies and tests form a very difficult puzzle for scientists and doctors. However, there is no doubt that the solution to this puzzle is forthcoming. The answers will be difficult to obtain because there are a great many variables involved when testing people who are sick. But through careful, thorough, and repetitive research, we will someday have a clear picture as to just how important vitamin C is. Of course, this will take time. In the meantime, for those who are believers, there are very few risks involved in taking vitamin C supplements. The possible risks have been noted earlier, but they are minimal. It is important to note that the body cannot store vitamin C for a long period of time. It is water soluble and is soon excreted from the body. This makes vitamin C generally safe to take. Even if it is someday proven that Dr. Pauling is totally wrong and vitamin C is of little medical value, I believe that at this time it is beneficial for the believer in vitamin C to take supplements. Vitamin C is relatively cheap, relatively safe, and can have a positive effect on a person's state of mind.

Works Cited

Pogash, Carol. "The Great Gadfly," *Science Digest* June 1981: 88–110.
Ponte, Lowell. "The Facts About Vitamin C." *Readers Digest* Oct. 1980: 94–97.
Wang, Julie. "Vitamin C: Dr. Pauling Was Right." *New York* 9 April 1979: 51–54.

Many instructors may wish you to entitle your bibliography page "Works Cited," to show just what material you have documented, but there are other alternatives. Ask your instructor what kind of bibliography you should provide.

A note here on documentation techniques. The student paper just presented follows the most recent Modern Language Association format, but other forms of documentation may be preferred by your instructor in English or another course for which you are to prepare a research assignment. *Always check* with your professor for the preferred form!

MLA Documentation

The Modern Language Association now recommends citing sources in parentheses directly after each quote or paraphrase from a source. A footnote (at the bottom of the page) or endnote (on the last page of the paper) is used only if some explanation of the source or information about it is necessary. The material in parentheses then directs the reader to the list of works cited at the end of the paper. Therefore, only the author's last name and page reference of the quote or paraphrase are usually necessary.

If you are using more than one book by an author, use a short title after the name and before the page reference (Wharton, *Ethan* 10). If more than one author wrote the book or article, use *both* their names in the parentheses (Flower and Hayes 221). If you use the author's name in the text before the quote or paraphrase, only the page reference is required in the parentheses following the quote. *Remember* that you are trying to help the reader to find the citation of the source by directing her to your bibliography. Include the information in parentheses that she would need to find the full reference in your list of Works Cited.

Note that the parentheses are placed after the quote but before the end punctuation for the sentence and that there is no comma between author and page (Wang 53), nor a "p." for page. If your paper were to use a long quotation (over fifty words), you would *indent* and single-space the quote. The parentheses with the author's name and page number then go *after* the end punctuation. Because long quotes have already been set off from the text, *no* quotation marks are necessary around the long quotation.

If your instructor asks you to use footnotes or endnotes (the older form of documentation), you will number each quote and paraphrase consecutively through the paper, placing the number one-half space above the line just after the quotation marks or any end punctuation. The note containing the information about the source of the quote then goes at the end of the paper (endnote) or at the bottom of each page (footnote). Endnotes make it more difficult for the reader to read each quote and then check the source, but much easier for the typist. Footnotes are just the reverse.

For such notes you will need to provide the author, title, place of publication, publisher, date, and page number of a book. Articles require the author, title, journal name, volume number, date, and page number. Following are some examples:

Sample Forms for Earlier Method of Documenting Sources in Footnotes or Endnotes

[1]Granville Hicks, *The Great Tradition* (New York: Macmillan, 1935), pp. 295–296. [reference for a book]

[2]J. D. Williams and Scott D. Alden, "Motivation in the Composition Class," *Research in the Teaching of English,* 17, No. 2 (1983), 101. [reference for an article]

[Article with two authors from a journal. Note volume number (17) and absence of "p." or "pp." for pages. Omit "p." or "pp." only when there is a volume number. If the month is given for a periodical, omit the number of the issue after the volume number: 15 (June 1982), 75.]

[3]Alan Lightman, "If Birds Can Fly, Why Can't I?" *Science 83,* Oct. 1983, p. 22.

[Article from a monthly magazine.]

[4]Hicks, p. 297.

[Second reference: Note that *op. cit.* is no longer used.]

[5]Hicks, p. 298.
[Note that *ibid.* is also no longer used.]

If an author has written two of the works you are using, use his name and the short title of the work cited in the note:

[11]Lewis, *Main Street,* p. 10.
[12]Lewis, *Babbitt,* p. 105.

If no author is given (as in some magazines or newspapers), use the title as the first entry and alphabetize using the title in the bibliography:

[8]"Improving Detection," *USA Today,* June 1982, p. 14.

A bibliography called "Works Cited" (those sources you quoted or paraphrased in the paper) is an alphabetical list placed on a separate page of the paper. As noted in the student paper on vitamin C, the author's last name is typed flush with the left-hand margin and if a second line is required, it is indented five spaces:

Pogash, Carol. "The Great Gadfly." *Science Digest* June 1981: 88–110.

Note, too, that all the page numbers for an article are given but none for a book, and no p. is used before the number for either article or book.

Hicks, Granville. *The Great Tradition.* New York: Macmillan, 1935.

Items are double-spaced throughout.

APA Documentation

A third popular format for documenting sources is that of the American Psychological Association (APA), which is used in the social and behavioral sciences. As in the MLA style followed by the student paper discussed above, the APA puts the source of information in parentheses after the quotation or paraphrase, but there are some differences:

1. APA uses author's last name and date of publication, but never the title. It denotes page numbers with a "p." End punctuation goes after parentheses. *Examples:* "Cigarette smoking also robs the body of vitamin C, since the chemicals in cigarette smoke interact with ascorbic acid to remove it from the blood" (Wang, 1979, p. 50).

or

Wang (1979) reports that "cigarette smoking also robs the body of vitamin C, since the chemicals in cigarette smoke interact with ascorbic acid to remove it from the blood" (p. 50).

2. In the APA style, "long" quotations are defined as those over four lines of typed text and are double-spaced (not single-spaced as in MLA style). They are introduced by the author's name and date in parentheses in a complete sentence which ends in a colon. *Example:*

Wang (1979) has found the following information:

The page number goes in parentheses following the long quotation.

As in the MLA style, if the author's name is cited in the text, the date and page number are all that need be cited in parentheses. If the date is given with the author's name, then only the page number is left to appear after the quote or paraphrase. An APA list of works usually called References is set up in substantially the same way as the MLA (but note small differences).

1. A work is alphabetized by the author's last name *but* only the initial of the first name is used. The name is followed by the publication date.

2. The second line is indented only three spaces instead of five. *Example:*

Wang, J. (1979). Vitamin C: Dr. Pauling was right. *New York,* pp. 51–54.

(Note that contrary to MLA style, there are no quotation marks around the article title.) However, APA retains p. or pp. for articles in newspapers or magazines but not in journals.

3. If a volume number is given for a journal, it goes after the journal title and *before* the page numbers. It is also underlined. Note that no pp. abbreviation is used for journal articles. *Example:*

Williams, J. D. and Alden, S. D. (1983). Motivation in the composition class. Research in the Teaching of English, 17 (1), 101–120.

EXERCISE 1. Prepare five parenthentical notes or traditional footnotes (as your instructor directs) from the sources you have used for your research paper.

EXERCISE 2. Prepare a list of Works Cited page for the five sources used in the notes prepared for Exercise 1 above.

H. Write an Ending

Endings for term papers, which must draw together the many points raised in the long paper, generally range in length from a long paragraph to a page or two. Endings summarize points made, point to questions still to be solved, or try to give the reader some idea of the importance of the topic discussed. See the ending of the sample paper on vitamin C for an example.

EXERCISE 1. Read the endings of several articles in this text. Could any be improved? Which ones? What good features do you see in any of the endings?

I. Rethink, Reorganize, Rewrite

A term paper must go through several drafts before it will all fit together and make sense. If you have been working on a paper as you have been applying these principles, you may now have a rough draft.

Strategy 1: Gain some distance from it. Let it sit for a day or two at least and then reread it. As you read, mark places that seem fuzzy or weak. Go back and make things clearer (where explanations were fuzzy) and add more support (where support was weak).

Strategy 2: Ask others to read it and mark those places they find confusing or do not find convincing. Then revise those sections.

Strategy 3: Check the first sentence of every paragraph to see if you have provided a bridge between what you last said and what you are about to say.

Strategy 4: Examine carefully your introduction and conclusion because those are the parts that readers will notice most. Does the introduction give some kind of framework or context to the paper? That is, does it tell the reader what the paper will be about, provide enough background to understand the point you will be making, and indicate a clear idea of your direction? Does the conclusion let readers see where they have been and the importance of the material that they have read? Give readers a summary of your ideas and/or their importance. You don't want them to ask, "So what?" Follow the U.S. Army's prescription for report writing:

> Tell 'em what you're going to tell 'em.
> Tell 'em.
> Tell 'em what you told 'em.

And one might add:

> Tell 'em *why* you told 'em or what they might do about what you told 'em.

A Brief Guide to Usage

MINI-LESSON 1: FRAGMENTS, RUN-ONS, AND COMMA SPLICES

1. Any group of words that does not contain a subject or a verb is not a complete sentence but a fragment.

Swimming in the pool
John after the football game
Over in the next room

Hint: Always look for the verb *first.* If you are not sure, use "he or she" or "they" in front of the word to make a sentence.

The Buick never started on cold mornings.
   he *never,* they *never* = no verb
   she *started,* they *started* = verb

To be a complete verb, words ending in *ing* must have a helper such as *is* or *are.*

She *was walking* down the street,
   (complete verb)

carrying a large bucket of paint.
(incomplete verb)

Then try to find the subject by asking "who?" or "what?" before the verb.

The college student found a part-time job.

   verb = *found*
   Who found? *The college student* (or just *student* = subject)

2. If a group of words with a subject *and* a verb is a dependent or subordinate clause, it cannot stand alone. Compare:

The party was over.	*After* the party was over,
He had a flat tire.	*Because* he had a flat tire,
The concert was successful.	*Since* the concert was successful,
She had met him before.	*That* she had met him before,

The only difference between the pairs is the italicized word of the second pair. This word is a *dependent clause beginner* (you may know it as a subordinator) because it signals a dependent clause. Get to know these common clause beginners:

that	after	so that
which	although	unless
who	because	until
whose	before	when
what	if	where
since	while	

3. There are only *three* ways to punctuate two related sentences correctly.

a. C _____ . C _____ .

b. C _____ ,   and _____ .

                 but _____ .

                 or _____ .

                 nor _____ .

                 for _____ .

                 (so, yet) _____ .

You *must* use the comma before the conjunction in this compound sentence.

c. (1) C _____ ; _____ .

(2) C _____ ; however, _____ .

moreover, _____ .

in addition, _____ .

on the other hand, _____ .

for example, _____ .

also, _____ .

then, _____ .

Note the following examples:

a. She had a cold. She decided to play tennis anyway.
b. She had a cold, but she decided to play tennis anyway.
c. (1) She had a cold; she decided to play tennis anyway.
   (2) She had a cold; however, she decided to play tennis anyway.

Note: If you change the sentences above by eliminating a subject or creating a dependent clause, the punctuation changes.

Although she had a cold, she decided to play tennis anyway.
    (dependent clause)   (independent clause)
She had a cold but decided to play tennis anyway.
    (independent clause with two verbs)
(See Mini-lesson 2 for further help.)

Exercises

Revise these sentences.

1. Many of Ernest Hemingway's novels have similar subjects, two of the most frequent are love and war.
2. Something missing from the performance.
3. Mr. Gordon's business meetings were usually well attended however on the day after Thanksgiving many members of the department were absent, they were on vacation.
4. Howard's new bicycle came today he's out front. Showing off for the neighbors.

5. Many Americans who are concerned about the pollution of their drinking water they fear a shortage of uncontaminated water.
6. The cat, a clean, intelligent, domestic animal.
7. When a person must get to work or school on snowy winter mornings and the car won't start one explanation the battery.
8. The quarterback dropped back to pass the ball, unfortunately, slipped from his grip into the hands of a rushing lineman.
9. Ms. Towers wished to avoid traffic moreover she liked driving early in the morning when the air was fresh.
10. Many students are unsure about the course of study they have chosen, moreover, they are not certain about the job market for their skills once they graduate.

MINI-LESSON 2: PUNCTUATION I— COMMAS AND SEMICOLONS

1. There are certain, definite places where commas are used:

a. Between two complete sentences joined by *and, but, or, for, nor* (*so, yet*).

> The student tried to register for a course,
> *but* the class was already filled.

b. To separate an introduction from the main sentence.

> When I crave chocolate, nothing else will satisfy me.
> Yes, she is here with me.
> After he left the football field, the other team scored two touchdowns.
> Paul, will you buy me a Coke?
> In the morning after a long, hard night, the officer's face looked drawn and tired.
> Before diving, the wise person checks the depth of the water and the condition of the bottom.
> For example, George could not read a newspaper.

Please note where the main sentence starts. *One exception:* If a short prepositional phrase (under five words) comes before the main sentence and there is no confusion in meaning, no comma is necessary: During the night he heard many noises.

c. To separate words in a series.

> Steve bought a hat, gloves, and boots.
> He rowed across the lake, fished for awhile, and rowed back to prepare breakfast.
> The short, plump woman walked her large German shepherd.

d. To separate places and dates.

> Abington, Pennsylvania, is a suburb of Philadelphia.
> December 7, 1941, is a date many Americans remember.

2. There are some judgment situations, requiring thought and care.

a. Interrupters are words or phrases which come in the middle of a sentence and interrupt the flow. They are usually extra and could be left out of the sentence. Such words are set off by commas.

> He is, moreover, a thief.
> A good student, generally speaking, pays attention in class.
> Mrs. Martin, our next-door neighbor, is a lawyer for the federal government.

but

b. If the word or phrase does not really interrupt but gives necessary information, no commas are used.

> The box that was on the shelf has disappeared.
> Their daughter Susan just graduated from high school.
> The woman who wanted change seemed to be in a hurry.

Hint: Do not put a comma before the word *that*.

3. Semicolons are strong commas and can be used only in a few places:

a. Between two complete sentences when *and, but, or, nor, for* (*so, yet*) are not used.
> The student tried to register for a course; however, the class was already filled.
> Mary was a skater; George was a track star.

b. To function as a strong separator when the sentence already contains many commas.
> He had in his hand, a pistol; in his boot, a knife; in his belt, a sword; in his eyes, a gleam of hatred.

Note: Semicolons connect only items of equal rank.

Exercises

Punctuate the following sentences correctly.

1. No I do not believe I have met you before however I am happy to know you now.
2. Before beginning to write the student gathered her materials turned off the stereo and shut the door.
3. Beginning college can be bewildering and frustrating for some students so they should seek help from an advisor or counselor.
4. People in business find that writing clearly speaking confidently and organizing their time efficiently are three essential skills.
5. Looking across the wheat field at the gathering storm the couple was terrified to see what they thought was a tornado.
6. A young film director who wants to make a popular low-budget film should probably make a horror movie.
7. Categories for the school flower show include fresh and dried flowers in arrangements sculptures made from fruit and vegetables whole plants grown from seed and pictures made with parts of plants.
8. People present at the reading of the will were Mary Green the dead man's widow Sarah and Lois Green his daughters Art Johnson his doctor Susan Blake his lawyer and Laura Green Michaels his sister.
9. My only grandmother who lives in La Crosse Wisconsin was born on February 2 1895.
10. The wind began to ripple the still water of the lake the chill in the air said autumn was coming.

MINI-LESSON 3: PUNCTUATION II— OTHER PUNCTUATION MARKS

Quotation Marks

1. Any directly quoted statement is enclosed in quotation marks and is usually introduced by a comma or a colon. Note the position of the punctuation in the following examples:

Mary said, "It is snowing again."

"Not again!" exclaimed Sam. "We must have three feet of snow on the ground already."
"Let's turn on the radio," Mary said, "to see what the weatherman says."
Mary and Sam turned on Accuweather and heard the following report: "Cloudy today with periods of snow likely. High today 10 above zero with winds from the north at 10 to 20 mph."

Note that in these examples, most punctuation goes *inside* the quotation marks. Below are some examples showing how to punctuate some other kinds of sentences.

"May I go?" he asked. (Quote asks a question.)
Did she say, "I know her"? (Whole sentence asks a question, but the quote does not.)
"I wish to lodge a complaint," the customer said; "The radio still does not work."

Caution: Do *not* use quotation marks for indirect quotations:

The judge said that she would sentence the prisoner tomorrow.

2. There are some miscellaneous uses for quotation marks:

a. To enclose titles of short works such as poems, short stories, essays, and song.
One of the early Beatles' hits was "I Want to Hold You Hand."
b. To enclose words used in a special sense or words being defined.
"Morale" means spirit or emotional state, while "moral" has to do with abiding by rules of conduct.

Note: Single quotation marks indicate a quote within a quote:
The speaker shouted, "Thomas Jefferson was right when he said 'Life, Liberty, and the Pursuit of Happiness' were 'unalienable rights.'"

Apostrophes, Colons, Dashes, and Parentheses

1. Know the rules for using the apostrophe to form the possessive of a noun:

a journey of one day = a one day's journey
a vacation of one week = a week's vacation   } *Singular:* Add 's.
a hat of a man = a man's hat

a journey of two days = a two
   days' journey
a vacation of three weeks = a three
   weeks' vacation
the hats of the men = the men's
   hats

Plural: Look at the plural form of the word first. If it ends in s, add the '. If it doesn't end in s, add 's.

Do not use the apostrophe with pronouns to form the possessive. They already have possessive forms.

The cook served
my	mine
her	hers
his	his
our	ours
your	yours
their	theirs
its	its
food.

2. A colon is used after a *completed* sentence:

a. Before a list.
   Please get me the following items: paper, ink, stamps, and envelopes.
b. Before a quotation or another sentence or phrase which comments on the first.
   He wondered whether he had the courage: could he die for the cause he believed in?

3. Dashes and parentheses are used sparingly to set off interrupters in certain situations.

a. Dashes are used for a dramatic break in thought:
   Antifreeze, long underwear, and warm gloves—all sold out quickly in the winter of 1977.
b. Parentheses enclose loosely related information or comments:
   Jeanne Smith (1895–1965) saw many changes in transportation in her lifetime.
   Marjorie has seen *King Kong* three times (reason enough to doubt her sanity).

Exercises

Punctuate the following sentences.

1. Where is this mornings paper asked Joan

2. Do you know that mens shirts are on sale asked a KYW announcer
3. The professor announced to the class Read Hawthorne's short story The Minister's Black Veil for Monday
4. After a moment the lottery winner exclaimed How can this be possible
5. Then he asked whether I had seen the long shiny limousine the one driven by the robbers in front of the bank
6. A persons actions and his eyes reveal what he really thinks
7. Joy come here and do the dishes my mother said to my sister
8. A recent report in the newspaper said that an increase in the sales of womens clothes and sportswear for the whole family will aid the garment industry
9. Do you think we did the right oh pardon me
10. I will have a terrible time getting my paper done for history the fact that I only started it last night might have something to do with it

---

MINI-LESSON 4: MAKING PARTS AGREE— NUMBER, ANTECEDENT, AND CASE

1. Subjects and verbs have to agree; that is, they both have to be singular or plural. Don't be misled by words which come between a subject and verb.

John was late.
John, along with his brother, *was* late.
    (besides)
    (like)
    (as well as)
    (in addition to)
    (including)

Two subjects joined by *and* are *plural.*

John and *Jim were* late.

If you are not sure if a verb form is singular or plural, test it using he or she (for one) or they (for two or more).

She swims. They walk.

2. A whole class of words is singular in formal use (though we sometimes use them as plurals in speech).

one	anybody	
each	somebody	
either	everybody	
neither	nobody	
another	anything	is going
anyone	something	
someone	everything	
everyone	nothing	
none		

The following words can be either singular or plural, depending on the sentence:

none	more
any	most
all	some

For example:

Are any of you going to the movies?
Some of the paint was wet.
Some of the children are swinging on the playground swings.

Following are some tricky situations:

Either the cat *or* her *kittens are* hungry.
    (agrees with nearer subject)
There *are* the *people* I was telling you about.
    ("There" is never a subject, and you have to find the subject elsewhere in the sentence.)
The *family is* active in the community.
    (a collective noun used as a unit)
The number of students attending Saturday classes *is* small.
    (a unit)
A number of students *are planning* to go skiing instead.
    (as individuals)

3. Pronouns must agree with the words they refer back to (their antecedents):

George had *his* car fixed.
The *lawyers* filed *their* briefs with the court.

The same pronouns which cause trouble in rule 2 cause trouble here *and* create problems with sexist language. For example, *everyone* is singular and as such takes a singular verb *is;* thus any pronoun used later must be singular in agreement with *everyone.* However, the traditional use of the masculine pronoun *his* to agree with *everyone* is considered offensive to many people.

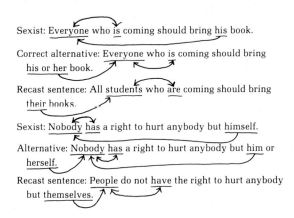

Sexist: Everyone who is coming should bring his book.

Correct alternative: Everyone who is coming should bring his or her book.

Recast sentence: All students who are coming should bring their books.

Sexist: Nobody has a right to hurt anybody but himself.

Alternative: Nobody has a right to hurt anybody but him or herself.

Recast sentence: People do not have the right to hurt anybody but themselves.

(In each of the examples above, note the verb agreements as well.) Of course, if the usage clearly refers to members of one gender, then the correct pronoun choice is one from that gender. For example:

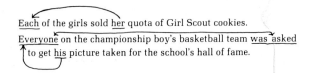

Each of the girls sold her quota of Girl Scout cookies.

Everyone on the championship boy's basketball team was asked to get his picture taken for the school's hall of fame.

Exercises

Correct those verbs which do not agree with their subjects and those pronouns which do not agree with their antecedents. Be sure that verbs agree with their changed pronouns. When necessary, rewrite the sentences.

1. The average person wants the same things, whether they live in the suburbs or the city.
2. The more opportunities a child has, the more proficient they become.

3. In today's impersonal world, friendliness and warmth between friends is even more important.
4. Whenever you need a prescription filled, all you have to do is call the pharmacy, and they will deliver your order.
5. Most department stores will gladly extend credit to its customers.
6. People who shop at Food Fair find that by buying the Food Fair brand vegetables, one can save a few pennies.
7. Neither of the girls feel that they can afford to pay for an evening gown.
8. One of the police officers have found the guilty party.
10. Either the professor or the students in the class seems to have misunderstood what today's assignment was supposed to be.

4. Another kind of agreement problem involves the proper *case* of pronouns. In English we change forms when we use a pronoun as the subject of a sentence or clause or when we use a pronoun as the object of a verb or of a preposition.

I went home. (subject of sentence)
After *I* went home, the party ended. (subject of clause)
The ball hit *me*. (object of the verb *hit*)
The ball was thrown too high for *me* to catch. (object of the preposition *for*)
The committee planned to invite *them* for lunch. (object of the infinitive *to invite,* a verb form)
Preparing *them* for the worst, the cruise director explained the bankruptcy proceedings. (object of the verbal *preparing*)

We also use special forms for showing possession (as mentioned in Mini-Lesson 3). The pronouns and their functions are as follows:

Subjects	Possession	Objects
I	my, mine	me
you	your, yours	you
she, he	her, hers	her, him
it	his, its	it
we	our, ours	us
they	their, theirs	them

Errors occur commonly in these circumstances.
a. When two pronouns are used, always check the use of each pronoun separately.
   Faulty: Between *you and I*, the house is not in good condition.
   Correct: Between *you and me,* the house is not in good condition.

Faulty: *Joe and me* are going to the park later.
Correct: *Joe and I* are going to the park later.

b. The use of *who* versus *whom* is particularly troublesome because so few people use the correct case in speech. The distinction is still pressed in writing, however.

"who" is a subject (I, he, she, we, they)

"whom" is an object (hi<u>m</u>, the<u>m</u>—note *m* ending)

Try substituting a form you know such as "I" or "them" for a *who/whom* construction.

Who called? *I* called.

Whom did he hit? He did hit *them.*

(In this example the sentence has to be put in normal order for the substitution to sound right.)

Be aware, too, that *who* or *whom* always functions in the clause it is part of if the sentence is structured with independent and dependent clauses.

George didn't know (*who* won the NCAA basketball
                              subject

championship in 1985).

Mary told George, (*whom* she had known for years),
                              object of "had known"

that it was Villanova.

George said to (*whoever* would listen), "Why
                              subject of "would listen"

didn't I remember that?"

Mary reminded George that it was Georgetown

to (*whom* he had owed allegiance) since his name
        object of the preposition "to"

and the team's were similar.

Exercises

Correct faulty pronoun use. Some sentences are correct.

1. Susan and her bought matching dresses.
2. My father gave my sisters and me an allowance every Saturday.
3. I have a neighbor whom, believe it or not, collects Cadillacs.
4. Janet and Dave bought ice cream cones for she and I when we went to the park last week.
5. Mr. Johnson and him made an agreement which was accepted by the lawyers and her.

6. We were surprised when the athlete was indicted for using drugs. He had been one to whom everybody referred as an example.
7. Kate asked, "Is it to whom it may concern or to who it may concern?"
8. The dean thanked whoever had been involved in the successful marathon.
9. The salesman gave Joe and I the keys to our new car and the first bill from the finance company.
10. Let's you and I drive over to Ned's house after the game.

MINI-LESSON 5: STREAMLINING SENTENCES

There are three basic ways to get variety in your sentences and eliminate choppiness.

1. *Coordination:* joining two *sentences* together with *and, but, or, nor, for* (use a comma before the joining word); *or* joining two words or phrases together with *and, but, or, nor, for* (no comma needed).

Choppy:	He was a man obsessed by money. He also desired status.
Smoother:	He was a man obsessed by money *and* status.
Choppy:	The old lady stumbled to the door on her cane. She hesitantly opened it.
Smoother:	The old lady stumbled to the door on her cane *and* hesitantly opened it.
Choppy:	He is going to apply for the job. He doesn't stand a chance of getting it.
Smoother:	He is going to apply for the job, *but* he doesn't stand a chance of getting it.

2. *Subordination:* joining two sentences together using a "clause beginner" to make one sentence dependent on the other. The more important of the two ideas should be in the independent clause. Following are some clause beginners:

although	if	that
because	after	while
	when	

For example:

Choppy: Hemingway wrote stories based on his own life. He was skillful enough to make them seem universal.

Smoother: *Although* Hemingway wrote stories based on his own life, he was able to make them seem universal.

Choppy: William Penn founded Philadelphia. He chose the juncture of the Delaware and Schuylkill rivers.

Smoother: William Penn founded Philadelphia, *where* the Delaware and Schuylkill rivers joined.

3. *Modification:* using adjectives, adverbs, and prepositional phrases to combine thoughts and smooth out choppy or wordy sentences.

Choppy: The restaurant was in the valley. It was very rustic. It was the only restaurant there. It was pretty popular. The restaurant served good country cooking.

Smoother: The popular, rustic restaurant, the only one in the valley, served good country cooking.

Another hint for more effective writing: Choose verbs that are active, rather than linking verbs or passive verbs. Note how in the sentences above the only "strong" verb is *served.* All the others are linking verbs (*was*). See Mini-Lesson 6 on reducing wordiness for more help.

Exercises

Rewrite the following sentences to express the ideas as effectively and economically as possible. Be careful to make them complete sentences and to punctuate them properly.

1. Mrs. James will take charge of the United Fund Drive. She is one of the officers of the City National Bank.
2. The teacher gave the student a note. The note was to be given to the person in charge of the school.
3. We watched Andrew through the window of the kitchen. We saw him bury his toys in a hole. The hole was beneath the old oak tree. The oak tree had been planted by his grandfather.
4. Jane wanted to avoid heavy traffic. Jane left home at seven o'clock. Jane wanted to get to work early.
5. Jack ran back to throw a pass. He slipped on a patch of gravel. He fell.

6. The explosion caused a fire. The explosion was loud. People were frightened. The fire lasted awhile. Four alarms were sounded.
7. Window shoppers admired a purse. The purse was made of leather. The leather was studded with pearls. The leather was decorated with other precious stones.
8. Singing in the bathtub relaxes him. He likes to relax by walking in the rain. Sleeping on a firm mattress also soothes him.
9. Ms. Roberts is careful about her appearance. She has an honest record. She is well-liked by our customers. We hired her for many reasons. The main reason is her ability to get along with our customers.
10. The cat is a domestic animal. It is clean. It is intelligent. The cat likes to stay home. It enjoys catching mice. It can be trained to eat at regular hours.

Combine each of the following two groups of sentences using coordination, subordination, and modification. Strive for a balance of longer and shorter sentences.

1. The plane was ready for takeoff in New York.
   It was a 747 jet liner.
   It was bound for Argentina.
   The weather was cold.
   Snow fell on the plane.
   The plane was deiced.
   More snow fell.
   The pilot made a decision.
   He decided to take off.
   He would not wait for more deicing.
   The plane took off.
   The plane lost power.
   The plane hit a few treetops.
   People on the ground were terrified.
   People on board the plane were terrified.
   The plane just made it high enough.
   The plane flew to Argentina.
   The authorities investigated the incident.

2. Many people like horror or disaster films.
   One example of a horror film is *Friday, the 13th.*
   One example of a disaster film is *Earthquake.*
   These films appeal to the audience.
   Psychologists discuss this appeal.
   The appeal is of danger.
   The danger is vicarious, not real.

People feel relief.
People feel safe.
Nothing happens to the people.
They leave the theater.

MINI-LESSON 6: REDUCING WORDINESS

Some students write sentences that are too long and wordy rather than too short. This problem has been called "fog" by Robert Gunning, who has helped many business people write more effectively. Below are some hints to help you control "fog."

1. Say what you mean; don't talk around it:

not	at this point in time	*but*	now
	in this day and age		today
	important essentials		essentials

Avoid redundancy (saying the same thing in different words):

not	each and every	*just*	each

2. Use the active voice rather than the passive voice. It uses fewer words. Compare:

The dog bit the man. (active)
The man was bitten by the dog. (passive)

To make something active, make the *doer* of the action the subject of the sentence. *Exception:* Technical language sometimes needs to be in the passive voice:

The machine *was calibrated* to 0.001 inch.

3. Use strong verbs rather than weak linking verbs. Convert nouns back to verbs.

Wordy:	The board of directors *was* in a *meeting.*
Better:	The board of directors *met.* (The verb does the work of both noun and verb.)
Wordy:	It is Mrs. Jones' judgment that we should buy the company.
Better:	Mrs. Jones *thinks* that we should buy the company.

Exercises

Rewrite these sentences as economically as possible.

1. It is the belief and firm conviction of the writer that we must make some attempt to improve the conditions in which the inmates of the county jail exist during the time that they are waiting for the time to come when they will be called before the bar of justice.
2. There are people in this day and age who prefer paying rent for living quarters to assuming the financial obligation of buying a house in which to reside.
3. In the eventual future it would seem certain that private individuals and firms will get the notion of trying to get in on flights into space.
4. It is requested that each and everyone of you remain seated during the time that the members of the graduating class leave their seats and pass down the aisles to the doors.
5. On account of the fact that an open flame heater uses oxygen, it is possible for such a heater to consume and exhaust all the oxygen that is contained in a closed room. Unfortunately, there are not many who understand this even in this day and age.

MINI-LESSON 7: AVOIDING CONFUSION

Sometimes writers confuse readers by illogical constructions or sentences that could be interpreted a number of ways. Below are some suggestions for making sure that your writing is clear and easily understood.

1. Watch for dangling or misplaced modifiers. In English, words and phrases modify the word or words to which they are closest, so we see humor in the old Pennsylvania Dutch expression, "Throw Momma from the train, a kiss" because it sounds like Momma is being thrown, not the kiss.

Dangling: *By stopping the car suddenly,* the grocery bags slid to the floor. (Who stopped the car? There is no person to do the action in the italicized phrase. Thus it "dangles.")

To fix this sentence, a writer may recast the sentence by converting a phrase into a clause:

> *Revised:* When Martha *stopped the car suddenly,* the grocery bags slid to the floor.

Another possibility is to keep the phrase where it is but provide something for it to modify:

> *Revised:* By *stopping the car suddenly,* Martha caused her grocery bags to topple onto the floor.
> *Dangling:* Arriving *at the top of the mountain,* the view of the valley below was spectacular. (Who arrived? The view?)
> *Revised:* Arriving *at the top of the mountain,* the hikers got a spectacular view of the valley below.

Misplaced modifiers need to be rearranged in a sentence to a position near the words they modify:

> *Misplaced:* I shot an elephant *wearing my pajamas.* (The elephant was wearing pajamas?)
> *Revised:* Wearing *my pajamas,* I shot an elephant.
> *Misplaced:* Hanging *on a hook in the garage,* George saw the garden shears. (This makes George sound as if he has been the victim of an unfortunate incident!)
> *Revised:* George saw the garden shears *hanging on a hook in the garage.*

Be careful where you place modifiers in a sentence because even one word may change your intended meaning. Compare these sentences; only one word changes, but does the meaning of the sentence change?

> Of all the people at the party, Mary likes only George.
> Of all the people at the party, only Mary likes George.

2. Another source of confusion is faulty parallelism. When we write a sequence in a sentence, our readers expect the items in the sequence to have the same grammatical structure. For example, we say "I like walking, swimming, and riding," not "I like to walk, swimming, and to ride." Items in a series are generally easy to proofread for parallelism:

> *Nonparallel:* He decided to try out for the play, auditioning for the Glee Club, and organized an intramural baseball team.
> *Revised:* He decided to try out for the play, audition for the Glee Club, and organize an intramural baseball team.

However, some constructions are not as easily noticed. Note some of the following sentences from Abraham Lincoln's *Gettysburg Address* as good examples of parallel structure:

> Fourscore and seven years ago our fathers brought forth on this continent a new nation, *conceived in liberty*, and *dedicated to the proposition* that all men are created equal.
> But, in a larger sense, *we cannot dedicate, we cannot consecrate, we cannot hallow* this ground.
> The world will little note, nor long *remember, what we say here*, but it can never *forget what they did here*.

Especially troublesome to student writers are the *not only . . . but also* constructions. Remember that whatever structure follows *not only* should also follow *but also:*

> The decorators will *not only paint the walls* but also *stain the woodwork.*

Similar constructions are *both . . . and, either . . . or,* and *neither . . . nor:*

> *Nonparallel:* Sue asked her parents not only for permission to take the trip but also she wanted money for her airline tickets.
>
> *Parallel:* Sue asked her parents not only for permission to take the trip but also for the money to buy the airline tickets.

3. Sometimes pronouns cause confusion if they do not clearly refer to their antecedents—that is, if one pronoun could refer to more than one antecedent:

> *Unclear:* John's father told John that he was supposed to paint the garage doors on Saturday. (It is not clear whether John or his father is supposed to paint the doors.)
>
> *Clearer:* John's father said, "John, you should paint the garage doors on Saturday."
>
> *Clearer:* John's father told John to paint the garage doors on Saturday.
>
> *Unclear:* The family spent their two-week vacation in Bermuda. *This* brought them closer together. (The word *this* doesn't clearly refer to any one idea in the previous sentence. It is implied that the vacation brought them closer together, but a writer should try to make such connections clear.)
>
> *Clearer:* The family spent their two-week vacation in Bermuda. This experience brought them closer together.

Exercises

Revise the following sentences.

1. He almost ate a dozen ears of corn by himself.
2. Strolling along the beach, a sea gull screamed in my ear, shattering the stillness.
3. The zoning board considered the businessowner's petition to change zoning for a new store and whether to allow a neighborhood protest to be lodged.
4. Fred bought a new television set from a department store with a bad antenna.
5. After falling asleep in front of the television set, my family realized how tired I was.
6. Jean asked Rachel if she knew where her car keys were.
7. The professor announced that the class could make up the test which had failed.
8. Bonnie and John were gardening, decided to shop for groceries, and then to relax at home for the rest of the day.
9. A waitress at the nursing home dining room must take people's orders, arranging the food attractively on the trays, and be pleasant throughout the meal.
10. The local high school not only won the girls' and boys' district basketball championship but also two district track crowns.

MINI-LESSON 8: EMPHASIS AND STYLE

In English we are able to emphasize ideas to different degrees by manipulating their placement in a sentence and by elevating or decreasing their importance by how we phrase them. Skilled writers and speakers use these techniques to communicate effectively with their audiences.

1. The position an idea has in a sentence is important. The end is the position of most importance. The beginning is next, and the middle of the sentence gets the least attention from the reader. Compare:

Although you'd never guess it, my grandmother is ninety.
Although my grandmother is ninety, you'd never guess it.

One way to make your sentences more emphatic is to avoid weak beginnings. Compare:

a. There are several people who will not be able to get tickets for the play.
b. Several people will not be able to get tickets for the play.

a. It is unwise to leave your car doors unlocked.
b. Leaving your car doors unlocked is unwise.

Not as common a problem is the weak ending, which also should be avoided. (The preceding sentence was an example!) Compare:

He should be fired, in my opinion.
He should be fired.
In my opinion, he should be fired.

Sometimes writers intentionally reverse a sentence for emphasis:

The million dollar lottery he won!

2. The importance we give an idea can also depend on its grammatical rank in the sentence:

Highest rank: Sentence
                  Independent clause
                  Dependent clause
                  Phrase
Lowest rank: Word

Compare:

The people at the circus laughed at the clown. *He was fat and awkward.* (sentence)
The people at the circus laughed at the clown; *he was fat and awkward.* (independent clause)
The people at the circus laughed at the clown *who was fat and awkward.* (dependent clause)
The people at the circus laughed at the clown *in his fat awkwardness.* (phrase)
The people at the circus laughed at the *fat, awkward* clown. (words)

Compare these versions:

a. We saw Mary Morris at the supermarket today. *She is my husband's cousin.* (sentence)
b. We saw Mary Morris, *my husband's cousin,* at the supermarket today. (phrase)

a. The dancer *who was dressed in gold sequins* dazzled the crowd. (dependent clause)
b. The dancer *in the gold sequins* dazzled the crowd. (phrase)
c. The *gold-sequinned* dancer dazzled the crowd. (word)

a. Sue hopes *that she will graduate this June.* (dependent clause)
b. Sue hopes *to graduate this June.* (infinitive phrase)

a. He admires women *who are intelligent.* (dependent clause)
b. He admires *intelligent* women. (word)

Exercises

1. Improve the emphasis of the italicized phrases by changing their position in the sentence and revising as necessary.

   a. On the corner of 6th and South *is a bookstore* which is old but very complete.
   b. There was *a very important field goal in the last minute of play* which clinched the championship for the home team.
   c. I think that *every student should take a course in reading and study skills* if at all possible.
   d. The cause of the fire was determined to be arson by *the fire chief,* who examined the site of the blaze thoroughly.
   e. It is surprising to me, if I think about it, that so *few people know much about their ancestors* and care so little for their history.

2. Emphasize the following italicized phrases by increasing their grammatical rank and revising as necessary.

   a. The man *convicted of robbing twenty banks* was sentenced to forty years.
   b. The debris on the floor of the hardware store was all that was left *after the flood waters receded.*
   c. *In his first year of teaching,* the professor spent too much time in unnecessary and long-winded explanations.
   d. The manual, *consisting of thirty pages of instructional material,* is written for the beginning computer student.
   e. The *embarrassed* clerk admitted that a mistake had been made.

3. Deemphasize the following italicized ideas by reducing their grammatical rank and making the sentences more concise.

   a. *There are slums in almost any large city.* My hometown has a larger slum area than any other city of its size.

   b. Meeting the demands of constituents is difficult for the legislator. *She is only human.*

   c. *After they turned out the light,* they could see shadowy forms approaching the building from the street.

   d. The Impressionists were a school of painters who did not paint objectively; *the movement began in the late nineteenth century.*

   e. *The stock market has declined recently.* Due to this fact many stocks are now selling at attractively low prices.

3. Style is an elusive concept that often boils down to "It isn't what you say, it's the way you say it." The techniques discussed so far (position and grammatical rank) are part of a writer's style. So is sentence variety. Readers certainly get tired reading many long sentences with strings of clauses and phrases (one reason for the modern reader's difficulty in reading turn-of-the-century writer Henry James). Similarly, readers get impatient with many short, choppy sentences. The ideal is a mixture to provide enough complexity (the long) and enough breaks (the short).

Exercise

Revise the passage below to improve the mixture of long and short sentences.

One of the most difficult things college students have to do is to choose a major, which at most schools they must do sometime in the sophomore year. Some students choose a subject they like, while other students pick a major that will lead to a lucrative career whether they like the course of study or not. Most counselors agree that students should take an introductory course in a subject being considered by students for their majors if only to see that the students are suited to that subject as a course of study. No major, no matter how sought after on the job market, will be worthwhile if students can't pass the required courses. Another piece of good advice is to investigate what occupations people get into following graduation in a certain major. Students should interview people holding these jobs to see if they are pleased with their choice and to decide if this occupation will suit them as well. It all sounds like a great amount of effort, but the rewards of having chosen the right major are peace of mind and, perhaps, better grades.

MINI-LESSON 9: LEVELS OF USAGE

Effective writers suit their writing to their audience and purpose for writing, and this advice applies to the words writers choose as well as to sentence structure and proper grammar. You would feel foolish talking to your friends in the same language and tone as you would use to deliver a speech at a political rally or to address the members of your religious congregation. Similarly, different writing situations require different levels of usage. What follows is a discussion of *five* levels of usage:

1. *Formal.* Formal writing is used for many academic assignments, including research papers. The term does *not* mean writing that is very fancy with every long word that you possess in your vocabulary tumbled onto the page. Rather it means no contractions (*will not* instead of *won't, it is* instead of *it's*) and no words or expressions labeled informal or colloquial in a dictionary (such as "hide-out" for "hiding place" or "catch on" for understanding something—"Oh, I catch on now"). If you are in doubt, check a dictionary and if the word or phrase has "inf." or "colloq." before it, it is not formal usage.

2. *Informal or colloquial.* Words used in everyday conversation are usually a mixture of formal and informal use. Television announcers use some contractions in their speech as well as other words that are colloquial, such as reporting that a gangster's "hideout" was "stormed" by police. Such a mixture of formal and informal is often called Standard English. Language usage changes constantly, and some words, once considered colloquial, may now be fully accepted and words which began as slang (see below) are now perhaps considered informal use.

3. *Slang.* Originally the speech of criminals who needed to use words that no one else would understand, "slang" now applies to any words used by a small group of people but unknown to the general public *or* words considered to be outside standard usage. If adopted by enough people, such words become colloquial. The word "cop" for policeman is still considered slang by many dictionaries but may soon come to be considered colloquial. Slang is generally not acceptable in academic or business writing.

4. *Regional or dialectal.* Many of us live in parts of the country that have their own words or phrases which other people from other places would not recognize or use. If you say "chaw of terbaccer" for "chew of tabacco," you are using a regional pronunciation. If you say "the fence needs painting" instead of "the fence needs to be painted," you are using a regional expression. There are also many dialects of English which produce different grammatical structures and pronunciations. If you say "I be going" instead of "I am going," you are using a dialectal expression. There is nothing wrong with conversing in a regional or dialectal way as long as your audience can understand you, that is, as long as your purpose of being understood is met.

But if you are outside your region or are speaking to people who do not speak your dialect, you may not be understood and should therefore learn Standard English. Writing situations almost always demand the use of Standard English.

5. *Nonstandard.* This label is usually applied to an ungrammatical use of language, such as using "ain't" or "I don't know nothing."

A note about jargon: Jargon refers to those specialized words used by people in certain occupations or other special situations (such as hobbies) to communicate with each other. A doctor knows that a "myocardial infarction" is a heart attack and uses that term (or its abbreviation MI) with other doctors. A car hobbyist knows that a "Mopar" is a type of car, usually a Plymouth or Dodge. Problems occur only when jargon is used to communicate with an audience who doesn't know the meaning of the words.

Exercises

1. Classify the following italicized words as to their level of usage. If in doubt, check your dictionary.

   a. The *feds* conducted a successful *sting.*
   b. The *mob* frequently tries to *launder* their money.
   c. The class was *aggravated* by the professor's *sappy* jokes.
   d. His *old man* hit him *upside the head* for getting himself *busted.*
   e. I was really *bummed* out when I couldn't get any money *off* my brother.
   f. The *bottom line* was that *marginal utility* had been reached.
   g. She *should of brung* her book to class.
   h. We should *red up* the parlor before the folks *come a'callin.*
   i. The mother was heard to say to her young child, *"Come on! How come* you're so slow today?"
   j. We grow *too soon old* and *too late smart.*

2. What examples of slang can you think of that are current on your campus?
3. What regional or dialectal words or expressions are you familiar with?
4. What examples of jargon do you know from business, law, medicine, or other sources?

MINI-LESSON 10: BETTER SPELLING

Some experts think that the way you learned to read affected your ability to spell. Generally, people who learned to sound out words are better spellers than those who did not. But to improve your spelling, you can't begin all over again. You have to learn a few basic principles and *practice.*

1. Most errors occur in words that sound the same or close to the same. Read the following list and try to memorize what you don't already know. (*Hint:* Begin by reading each pair out loud. Some words may become clear just by careful pronunciation. In fact, pronouncing by syllables will help you spell many words.)

1. *accept:* I will accept your offer of the bicycle.
   except: He took everything except the rugs.
2. *advice:* Free advice is usually not worth much.
   advise: Dr. Mills said that she would advise me this term.
3. *affect:* His silly jokes don't affect me. (verb)
   effect: His humor has a bad effect on his boss. (noun)
4. *all ready:* They were all ready to go home.
   already: They had already left when we telephoned the house.
5. *cite:* She cited three good examples.
   site: The site of the new school has not been decided upon.
   sight: They were awed by the sight of the new skyscraper.
6. *coarse:* The coarse sand blew in my face.
   course: We discussed the course to take. Of course, he may come with us.
7. *complement:* Because of their different talents, the two workers complemented each other.
   compliment: It is easier to pay a compliment than a bill.
8. *council:* Jan was appointed to the executive council.
   counsel: I sought counsel from my friends. They counseled moderation. He employed counsel to defend him.
9. *desert:* Out in the lonely desert, he tried to desert from his regiment.
   dessert: We had apple pie for dessert.
10. *dining:* We eat dinner in our dining room.
    dinning: Stop dinning that song into my ears!
11. *formerly:* She was formerly a student at Carnegie-Mellon University.
    formally: You must address a presiding judge formally and respectfully.
12. *its:* Your plan has much in its favor. (possessive of *it*)
    it's: It's too late now for excuses. (contraction of *it is*)
13. *lose:* You must not lose your purse.
    loose: He has a loose button. The dog is loose again.
14. *past:* It is futile to try to relive the past.
    passed: She smiled as she passed me. She passed the test.
15. *peace:* He was picked up for disturbing the peace.
    piece: I'd like another piece of pie.
16. *personal:* Write her a personal letter.

personnel: The personnel here is a select group.
17. *presence:* We are honored by your presence.
    presents: The child demanded expensive presents.
18. *principal:* The principal of a school; the principal (chief) industry; the principal and the interest
    principle: He is a man of high principles.
19. *quiet:* You must keep quiet.
    quite: You have been quite good all day.
20. *stationary:* The stationary benches could not be moved.
    stationery: He wrote a letter on hotel stationery.
21. *than:* She sings better than I.
    then: He screamed; then he ran.
22. *their:* It wasn't their fault. (possessive pronoun)
    there: You won't find any gold there. (adverb of place)
    they're: They're sure to be disappointed. (contraction of *they are*)
23. *to:* Be sure to speak to them. (preposition)
    too: He is far too old for you. (adverb)
    two: The membership fee is only two dollars. (adjective)
24. *were:* Whom were you with last night?
    where: The man asked, "Where is the ticket office?"
25. *whose:* Whose book is this? (possessive pronoun)
    who's: I wonder who's with them now. (contraction of *who is*)

2. There *are some* logical rules in English spelling.

Rule 1: If a word ends in silent e and you add a suffix beginning with a vowel (a, e, i, o, u, y), drop the e:

> fame + ous = famous
> force + ible = forcible
> noise + y = noisy

If a word ends in silent e and you add a suffix beginning with a consonant (anything except a, e, i, o, u, y), keep the e:

> excite + ment = excitement
> hope + less = hopeless
> lone + ly = lonely
> force + ful = forceful

Exception: Words ending in ce or ge such as "notice" or "advantage" keep the e if you add able or ous:

noticeable   advantageous

(There are some other minor exceptions.)

Rule 2: i before e except after c:

belief		ceiling
niece	*but*	conceit
thief		perceive

Exceptions:

neither/either	weird
financier	leisure
seize	neighbor
species	weigh

Rule 3: Double a letter when you add a suffix (*key:* vc = vowel consonant; v = vowel; c = consonant):

drag + ed = dragged
vc   v

occur + ed = occurred
  vc   v

equip + ing = equipping
  vc   v

But there are some cases in which you should not double a letter (accent on the first syllable):

díffer + ent = different
  vc   v

ópen + ed = opened
  vc v

Also, don't double a letter if the suffix begins with a consonant:

equip + ment = equipment

Rule 4: Add a suffix to a word ending in y:

busy + ly = busily

buy + er = buyer

icy + er = icier

but   monkey + s = monkeys

try + ed = tried

enjoy + ing = enjoying

study + es = studies

Exceptions:
study + ing = studying
carrying + ing = carrying
lady + like = ladylike

3. Memory devices can help you remember problem words:

"Separate" has "a rat" in it.
"Principal" is your "pal."

Make up some of your own sentences to help you remember problem words.

4. *Really* use a dictionary.

5. Keep a list of your problem words in a notebook. Look at the list— spelled correctly—frequently, and test yourself from time to time.

See if the words you misspell are similar to each other in any way. For example, do you always or often forget to put the s on a verb in the third person singular, present tense (she walks), or do you drop the ed from verbs in the past tense? If you see a pattern, practice writing the correct forms of that pattern several times.

Exercises

Choose the correct form of each pair of words.

1. I will (accept, except) the invitation to the party unless you (advice, advise) me not to.
2. She thought that the others were out of (sight, site, cite) when she made the turn into the new building (sight, site, cite).
3. Ramona did not know what the (affect, effect) of her resignation would be from the town (council, counsel).
4. Marcus is more concerned about (who's, whose) going to clean up the mess in the living room (than, then) he is about who did it in the first place.
5. If my mouth is going to give me any (peace, piece), I had better get a dentist to look at my (loose, lose) tooth.
6. Jim played his first round on the golf (coarse, course) in April and found the sand trap to be full of (coarse, course) stones.
7. The little girl had been (quiet, quite) contented all day, playing with her new video game, which was one of her birthday (presence, presents).
8. Students will find that (their, they're, there) grades will go up if they learn the (principals, principles) of effective studying.
9. Some business people take such a (personal, personnel) interest in the success of their companies that the time they spend at work adversely (affects, effects) their relationships with others.
10. Some time in the (passed, past), the family moved away. However, whenever they returned for a visit, they (passed, past) their house.

Index